# THE MA GUIDEBOOK OF ESSENTIAL SUBJECTS

EVERY MARINE'S MANUAL OF
**VITAL SKILLS**, **HISTORY**,
AND **KNOWLEDGE**

POCKET/TRAVEL SIZE,
COMPLETE & UNABRIDGED

P1500.44A

United States Marine Corps

**The Marine Guidebook of Essential Subjects: Every Marine's Manual of Vital Skills, History, and Knowledge - Pocket/Travel Size, Complete & Unabridged (P1500.44A)**

**U.S. Marine Corps**

This edition first published 2019 by Carlile Military Library. "Carlile Military Library" and its associated logos and devices are trademarks. Carlile Military Library is an imprint of Carlile Media (a division of Creadyne Developments LLC). The appearance of U.S. Department of Defense (DoD) visual information does not imply or constitute DoD endorsement. This book is published for information purposes only.

**Published in the United States of America.**

ISBN-13: 978-1-7957-4566-6
ISBN-10: 1795745665

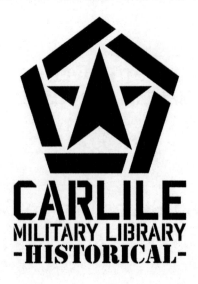

CARLILE
MILITARY LIBRARY
-HISTORICAL-

**UNITED STATES MARINE CORPS**
MARINE CORPS INSTITUTE
ARLINGTON, VA 22222-0001

MCIO P1500.44A
1 August 1986

# MARINE CORPS INSTITUTE ORDER P1500.44A

From:  Director
To:    Distribution List

Subj:  **The United States Marine - Essential Subjects**

1. **Purpose.** To publish the handbook, The United States Marine - Essential Subjects.

2. **Background.** The Commandant of the Marine Corps has directed that all Marines, regardless of grade, MOS, billet, or unit to which assigned, achieve and maintain proficiency in certain essential subjects. This proficiency is initially acquired in recruit training and is the hallmark of a Marine. It enables a Marine to sustain himself on the battlefield, to function effectively in garrison, and to practice those personal and professional traits characteristic of Marines. After recruit training, Marines are evaluated by their commanders to determine if essential subjects proficiency is being maintained.

3. **Training Resources.** This publication, The United States Marine - Essential Subjects, contains information on all the essential subjects and provides a condensed, readily available study aid to supplement more detailed information contained in Fleet Marine Force Manuals and other sources.

4. **Additional Copies.** Additional copies are available upon request. Requests should be made to the Director, Marine Corps Institute. All requests should include Reporting Unit Code (RUC) and Autovon/commercial phone number.

5. **Certification.** Reviewed and approved this date.

R. A. MALONEY
Deputy

DISTRIBUTION: SPECIAL

# CONTENTS

# Chapter 1. Code of Conduct, Military Justice, and The Law of War

## Section I. Code of Conduct, Rights and Obligations of POW's, Conduct in War

Objectives:

   *1. Provided with a list of the six articles of the Code of Conduct, explain the meaning of each article.*
   *2. Provided with a list of rights and obligations of a POW, explain the meaning of each right and obligation.*
   *3. Provided with a list of the nine principles of the Law of War, explain the meaning of each principle.*

### A. CODE OF CONDUCT ARTICLES

1.   ARTICLE I.   "I am an American fighting man. I serve in the forces which guard my country and our way of life. I am prepared to give my life in their defense."

INTERPRETATION: I am a Marine. I will fight and, if necessary, die for my country and our way of life.

EXAMPLE: Resistance can demand the ultimate sacrifice, YOUR LIFE. Lance Corporal Jimenez made that sacrifice while serving as a Fire Team Leader with Company K, Third Battalion, Seventh Marines, First Marine Division in operations against the enemy in the Republic of Vietnam on 28 August 1969. On that date, Lance Corporal Jimenez's unit came under heavy attack by North Vietnamese Army soldiers concealed in well-camouflaged emplacements. Lance Corporal Jimenez reacted by seizing the initiative and plunging forward toward the enemy position.

He personally destroyed several enemy personnel and silenced an antiaircraft weapon. Shouting encouragement to his companions, Lance Corporal Jimenez continued his aggressive forward movement. He slowly maneuvered to within ten feet of hostile soldiers who were firing automatic weapons from a trench and, in the face of vicious enemy fire, destroyed the position. Although he was by now the target of concentrated fire from hostile gunners intent upon halting his assault, Lance Corporal Jimenez continued to press forward. As he moved to attack another enemy soldier, he was mortally wounded. Because of his unconquerable courage, aggressive fighting spirit, and unfaltering devotion to duty, Lance Corporal Jimenez was awarded the Medal of Honor posthumously.

**2. ARTICLE II.** "I will never surrender of my own free will. If in command, I will never surrender my men while they still have the means to resist."

**INTERPRETATION:** I will never surrender as long as I can fight, nor will I surrender my men if they can fight. If they lose the means to fight, they will take all possible steps to evade capture.

**EXAMPLE:** During the Vietnam War, Captain Walsh, an aviator, ejected from his stricken aircraft and parachuted to the ground. He landed in the midst of a sizeable enemy unit. He immediately drew his service revolver and fired on the opposing force, inflicting a casualty. Taking cover, he continued to engage his adversaries until he ran out of ammunition, at which time he was captured. Placed in a boat en route to a POW camp, he attempted to escape, but was unsuccessful. Once formally imprisoned, Captain Walsh maintained his high degree of courage by resisting his steadfast policy of noncooperation with the enemy, he provided leadership by example for his fellow POW's. For his courage, resourcefulness, and devotion to duty, he was awarded the Bronze Star Medal.

**NOTE:** Suppose a man surrenders while he still has the means to fight back or can remain in hiding. What can he expect to gain in captivity? During the Korean War, four out of every ten Americans who became prisoners of the communists died. Untold numbers were coldly executed shortly after laying down their arms, and these were not included in the "prisoner" statistics. The odds are in favor of the man who "sticks by his guns." Since many deaths in a prison camp result from lack of will, the person who surrenders to the enemy is even less likely to survive.

**3. ARTICLE III.** "If I am captured, I will continue to resist by all means available. I will make every effort to escape and aid others to escape. I will accept neither parole nor special favors from the enemy."

INTERPRETATION: If I am captured, I will not take any favors or special treatment from the enemy, but I will resist and escape, if possible. If I can help others to escape, I will do so.

EXAMPLE: One prisoner who escaped against great odds was Lieutenant Charles F. Klusmann, a U.S. Navy pilot, shot down over Laos and captured by the communists in June 1964. Lieutenant Klusmann at once decided to escape, if possible. In August, after 2 months of solitary confinement, he was moved to another building where some Laotians were imprisoned. Here, he and two other prisoners cautiously mapped out

an escape plan. Their moment came in late August, and they succeeded in breaking out of the prison compound. Throughout the night, the three escapees traveled through rice paddies and along wooded trails. A communist patrol recaptured one of the Laotians the next day, but the other two escapees evaded the patrol by moving in the brush. After running for 2 hours, they slowed to a walk, keeping to animal trails. A chilling rain that night added to their misery. At dawn the following day, they were on their way again, heading toward friendly troops which they believed to be beyond a high mountain. Keeping a close watch for communist patrols, the two succeeded in crossing over the mountain by late afternoon. That night they risked a small fire to cook some squash they had found.

Early the next morning, after finishing the remains of the squash, they resumed their march. Since their escape, Lieutenant Klusmann and his companion had been bothered by painful leech bites which caused their legs to swell. Klusmann's right leg was in such bad shape that he could not lift it without using his hand to lever it along, but by midafternoon the two reached a friendly outpost. That evening a plane was called in to fly Lieutenant Klusmann to safety, capping his escape with a final triumph.

4. ARTICLE IV. "If I become a prisoner of war, I will keep faith with my fellow prisoners. I will give no information nor take part in any action which might be harmful to my comrades. If I am senior, I will take command. If not, I will obey the lawful orders of those appointed over me and will back them up in every way."

INTERPRETATION: If I am a prisoner, I will help my fellow prisoners and not sell them out for favors from the enemy. If senior, I will take charge; if not, I will follow the orders of the senior prisoner, regardless of his branch of service (U.S. or allied nation).

EXAMPLE: While interned as a prisoner of war by the Viet Cong in Vietnam from December 1964 to December 1967, Colonel (then Captain) Cook answered the call for leadership. Repeatedly assuming more than his share of manual labor so the other prisoners of war could improve the states of their health, Colonel Cook willingly and unselfishly put the interests of his comrades before that of his own well-being and, eventually, his life. Giving more needy men his medicine and drug allowance while constantly nursing them, he risked infections from contagious diseases while his health deteriorated rapidly. This unselfish and exemplary conduct, coupled with his refusal to stray even the slightest from the Code of Conduct, earned him the deepest respect from not only his fellow prisoners, but his captors as well. Rather than negotiate for his own release or better treatment, he steadfastly frustrated attempts by the Viet Cong to break his unconquerable spirit. He passed the same resolve on to the men with whose well-being he so closely associated himself. He knew his refusals would prevent his release prior to the end of the war. Also knowing his chances for prolonged survival would be small in the event of continued refusal, he chose nevertheless to adhere to a Code of Conduct far above that which could be expected. Colonel Cook was awarded the Medal of Honor posthumously.

5. **ARTICLE V.** "When questioned, should I become a prisoner of war, I am required to give name, rank, service number, and date of birth. I will evade answering further questions to the utmost of my ability. I will make no oral or written statements disloyal to my country and its allies or harmful to their cause."

INTERPRETATION: If a prisoner, I will give my service number (social security number), name, rank, and date of birth. I may fill out a Geneva Convention Capture Card, but I am not required to. I may also write letters home and talk with the enemy about matters of health and welfare. I will say or sign nothing that may hurt my fellow prisoners, my country, or its allies.

EXAMPLE: Shortly after his capture during the Vietnam War, Captain (then First Lieutenant) Dibernardo and a group of prisoners began a journey to a permanent installation.

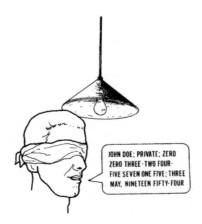

During this journey, he exerted positive leadership, by maintaining the military organization of the men at all times. In the first of the temporary camps the group occupied, he instructed his group to resist providing anything more than the most basic biographical information. Although subjected to routine cruelties for refusal to cooperate, Captain Dibernardo continued to provide leadership and guidance for his group.

6. **ARTICLE VI.** "I will never forget that I am an American fighting man, responsible for my actions, and dedicated to the principles which made my country free. I will trust in my God and in the United States of America."

INTERPRETATION: I am a Marine fighting for my country. I will be responsible for my conduct, and I will trust in my God and my country.

EXAMPLE: In 1966, Lieutenant (jg) Dieter Dengler, a U.S. Navy pilot, added another illustrious chapter to the traditions of U.S. fighting men. While on a mission over North Vietnam near the Laotian border on 1 February, his plane was crippled by ground fire and crashed. Unable to avoid capture, Lieutenant Dengler repeatedly refused to give his captors any military information or to sign a propaganda statement condemning the United States. He was severely mistreated for refusing to comply. Months later on 29 June, Lieutenant Dengler and another prisoner, U.S. Air Force First Lieutenant Duane Martin, a helicopter pilot, escaped. The two men, barefoot and weakened by malnutrition and illness, traveled by foot and raft toward safety. Lieutenant Martin was killed by a villager, but Lieutenant Dengler managed to signal a friendly plane and was rescued by helicopter on the 22d day of his trek to freedom.

## B. RIGHTS AND OBLIGATIONS OF A POW

There are two practical reasons why you, as a member of the Armed Forces, should know about the Geneva Convention.

First, in any combat situation you must be ready to capture and control enemy prisoners until they are sent to permanent prisoner of war camps. The Geneva Convention tells us how to treat prisoners.

The second reason is also related to duty, but in a more personal way. Under the Code of Conduct, a U.S. Armed Forces member cannot voluntarily choose to become a prisoner of war. But it is recognized that we sometimes may be captured against our wills because of the overwhelming enemy force and a lack of further means to resist. If you should ever become a prisoner of war, knowing your rights and obligations under the Geneva Convention could help you.

### 1. Rights of a POW

    a. Receive sanitary, protective housing and clothing.

    b. Receive enough food to stay in good health.

    c. Receive adequate medical care.

    d. Receive necessary facilities for proper hygiene.

    e. Practice religious faith.

    f. Keep personal property except weapons, military equipment, and military documents.

    g. Send and receive mail.

    h. Receive packages containing food, clothing, educational, religious, or recreational materials.

    i. Select a fellow POW to represent you.

    j. Receive humane treatment by your captors.

k. Have a copy of the Geneva Convention on Premises of War and its annexes, including any special agreements, posted where you can read them. They must be written in English. If they are posted where you cannot read them, you are entitled to a copy upon request.

l. Have a copy of all camp regulations, notices, orders, and publications about your conduct as a prisoner of war posted where you can read them. They must be written in English. If posted where you cannot read them, you are entitled to a copy upon request.

## 2. Obligations of a POW

a. Tell captors your name, rank, service number, and date of birth.

b. Obey all lawful rules established by your captors.

c. If required by captors, perform labor for pay that is nonmilitary and not humiliating, dangerous, or unhealthy.

d. Continue military discipline and courtesy in the POW camp. You are required to render appropriate honors to your captors who are officers.

# C. LAW OF WAR

## 1. Purposes of the Law of War

The conduct of armed hostilities on land is regulated by the law of land warfare which is both written and unwritten. It is inspired by the desire to diminish the evils of war by:

o    Protecting both combatants and noncombatants from unnecessary suffering.
o    Safeguarding certain fundamental human rights of persons who fall into the hands of the enemy, particularly prisoners of war, the wounded, the sick, and civilians.
o    Helping to bring peace.

## 2. Background

The Secretary of Defense has directed the Armed Forces of the United States to comply with the Law of War in the conduct of military operations and to establish programs to prevent violations of the Law of War as required by those international treaties which regulate armed conflicts.

3. Principles of the Law of War

Discipline in combat is essential. Disobedience to the Law of War dishonors the Nation, the Marine Corps, and the individual Marine; and far from weakening the enemy's will to fight, it strengthens it. The following principles require the Marine's adherence in the accomplishment of any mission:

o    Marines fight only enemy combatants.
o    Marines do not harm enemies who surrender. Disarm them and turn them over to your superior.
o    Marines do not kill or torture prisoners.
o    Marines collect and care for the wounded, whether friend of foe.
o    Marines do not attack medical personnel, facilities, or equipment.
o    Marines destroy no more than the mission requires.
o    Marines treat all civilians humanely.
o    Marines do not steal. Marines respect private property and possessions.
o    Marines should do their best to prevent violations of the Law of War. Report all violations of the Law of War to your superior.

Violations of these principles detract from the commander's ability to accomplish his mission, have an adverse impact on public opinion (both national and international), have on occasion served to prolong conflict by inciting an opponent to continue resistance, and in most cases constitute violations of the UCMJ. These principles are consistent with the principles of war, principles of leadership, and tactical considerations. Violations of these principles disregard these basic military tenets and prejudice the good order and discipline essential to success in combat.

4. Sources of the Law of War

The Law of War is derived from two principal sources:

o    Lawmaking treaties (or conventions)
o    Custom

Under the Constitution, treaties constitute part of the "Supreme Law of the Land" and have a force equal to laws enacted by Congress. Although some of the Law of War is not incorporated in any treaty or convention to which the United States is a party, this body of unwritten or customary law is firmly established by the custom of nations. It is also part of the law of the United States and is binding upon the United States, its citizens, and persons serving in the Armed Forces of this country.

---

For more information in this area, refer to:

1.  MCO 3300.2       Law of War Training in the Marine Corps

2.  NAVMC 2681       Code of the U.S. Fighting Man

3.  NAVMC 2628       POW, Your Rights and Obligations Under the Geneva Convention

4.  FM 27-10         Law of Land Warfare

# Section II.    Military Law/UCMJ


Objective:    *Provided with a list of the rights of the accused before judicial and nonjudicial proceedings, explain the meaning of each.*

## A. PURPOSE AND FUNCTION OF THE MILITARY JUSTICE SYSTEM

The purpose of the military justice system is to establish a means for ensuring good order and discipline within the military community. The system serves the same function as criminal statutes in a civilian community. Obedience to military law is the responsibility of each Marine.

## B. RIGHTS OF THE ACCUSED

An accused person has certain rights before a court-martial and also before any judicial or nonjudicial proceeding in which the accused is subject to charges or in which his conduct is subject to inquiry. Nowhere in any legal system is a person given more protection of his rights than he is under the Uniform Code of Military Justice (UCMJ). The Code is of great importance to you because it explains your legal responsibilities while protecting and guaranteeing your rights. Listed below are some of the rights to which every Marine is entitled.

1.    Judicial Rights

a. Innocent until proven guilty. The basic principle of law, both in and out of the service, is that an accused person is considered to be innocent until proven guilty beyond a reasonable doubt. The burden to prove guilt beyond a reasonable doubt is always on the prosecution. Unless at least two-thirds of the court (or the military judge who the accused elects for trial) are convinced beyond any reasonable doubt by the prosecution in court, then the accused is acquitted (set free), even though he may not have presented any evidence in his own defense.

b. Right to remain silent. This is a protection against self-incrimination. In other words, you cannot be forced to say anything that might be used to help convict you. The prosecution has to prove the case against you on its own. The right to remain silent about a crime applies to investigations as well as to a court-martial. Under the UCMJ, anyone who is investigating a crime is required to advise you of this right before he can ask you any questions about the crime. If you decide to answer the questions, you are warned that your answers can be used as evidence against you in a subsequent trial.

c. Right to be represented by a lawyer. You have the right to consult with a lawyer before being questioned about a crime in which you are suspect and to have your lawyer present during questioning. A military lawyer will be appointed to defend you at no expense, unless you wish to hire a civilian attorney at your own expense.

d. Protection against double jeopardy. Every Marine is protected against former jeopardy (double jeopardy). This means that once a person has been declared innocent of wrongdoing by a court-martial, he can never be tried again by a court-martial for the same crime.

e. Right to call witnesses. The accused has the right to compel witnesses to appear in court who can present evidence favorable to him. If the witness is a civilian, he can be issued a subpoena which is an order from the court-martial to appear. He must appear or be in violation of Federal law. If the witness is in the military, then his service will prepare orders sending him to testify.

f. Right to sentence review. Every Marine has the right to have a conviction and sentence reviewed by a higher authority. In the military, every case is reviewed automatically by higher authority. The sentence can never be increased, but may be decreased or left as is.

g. Right to speedy public trial. The accused has the right to a speedy and public trial.

h. Right to be informed of charges. A Marine has the right to be informed of charges preferred against him for any courts-martial. The immediate commander will inform him of the charges against him. Further, at the beginning of an investigation of charges that may result in trial by a general court-martial, the accused Marine must be informed of the offense charged against him, the name of the accuser, and the names of known witnesses against him.

i. Right to an interpreter. Any Marine who does not fully understand the English language has the right to have an interpreter present at any court-martial proceedings to translate all questions or statements.

j. Protection against illegal search or seizure. Evidence obtained through illegal search or seizure cannot be used against an accused.

k. Right to challenge members of the court. You may challenge for cause the right of any member of the court to sit in judgment of you.

l. Right to have enlisted representation on the court. When tried by a general or special court-martial, and no enlisted members have been appointed to the court, you may request in writing that enlisted members be so assigned. If enlisted membership is requested, at least one-third of the court membership must be enlisted.

m. Right to be tried by a military judge. If you are the accused in a general or special court-martial, you may request, in writing, to be tried by a military judge alone rather than by a court-martial.

n. Right to trial by court-martial. You have the right to refuse Article 15 punishment (office-hours) and demand trial by court-martial instead, unless embarked upon a vessel. You also have the right to object to trial by a summary court-martial. You may then be awarded a special or general court-martial by the appropriate convening authority.

2. Nonjudicial Rights
a. Right to appear before boards. You have the right to appear before an administrative discharge board.

**b. Right to appear before fact-finding bodies.** When you are a party before a fact-finding body, you have the right to be present during the proceedings of the body except when the investigation is cleared for deliberations. Your presence before the fact-finding body affords you specific rights of considerable importance. You have the right to:

o     Examine and object to the introduction of physical and documentary evidence and written statements.

o     Object to the testimony of witnesses and to cross-examine witnesses other than your own.

o     Introduce evidence in your own behalf.

o     Testify as a witness in your own behalf.

o     Make a voluntary statement for the official record.

---

For more information in this area, refer to:

1.   JAGINST 5800.7B    Manual of the Judge Advocate General

2.   MCO P1900.16B       Marine Corps Separation and Retirement Manual

# Section III.    Request Mast

Objective:  *On command without reference, explain the procedures required to request mast.*

## A. DEFINITION

Request mast is a procedure in which an individual can discuss any matter with commanding officers in the chain of command. The Marine Corps uses the chain of command to accomplish its mission and see to the morale, physical well-being, and general welfare of Marines.

## B. PURPOSE

1.  Request mast procedures are designed to provide timely and appropriate responses to petitions of individual Marines by commanding officers in the chain of command. These procedures are meant to create confidence in request mast as a way to solve problems. Compliance with the spirit and intent of these procedures will maintain this confidence and encourage the resolution of personal problems at the lowest possible level.

2.  Marines may not be prohibited from speaking with their commanding officers at a proper time and place. Persons who try to prevent access to the commanding officer may be subject to disciplinary action. However, a commanding officer can deny request mast if disciplinary action is pending concerning the matter and the request mast would improperly affect the pending reviewing action of the officer who began the disciplinary action.

3.  Every Marine also has the right to be granted request mast with commanders up to and including the immediate commanding general within the chain of command who is located at the same base or immediate geographic location. An individual may write to higher commanders including the Commandant of the Marine Corps and the Secretary of the Navy and ask for request mast, but does not have a right to personally meet with either.

## C. PROCEDURES

Marine Corps chains of command are clear; however, a few commands are dispersed over a wide area. This has caused some confusion concerning who should be the commanding general for the purpose of request mast. Also, it is not always possible for a Marine to request mast with the commanding general when the commanding general is in another geographic area. To identify the commanding general for purposes of request mast for areas where there is no general officer immediately assigned, you should refer to the current edition of MCO 1700.23, Request Mast.

1. Requesting Mast below the Commanding General Level

a. Requests will be submitted at the lowest echelon and forwarded via the chain of command to the commander before whom the requestor wishes to appear.

b. The requestor does not have to state the matter of concern, either orally or in writing, to anyone in the chain of command except to the officer with whom the Marine wishes to request mast.

c. There should be no more than a 24-hour delay at any level, whenever possible.

d. Marines may request mast without fear of prejudice to their interest.

e. Upon completion of request mast, the requestor must make a written statement regarding his degree of satisfaction with the outcome.

f. If a request mast petition with a higher commander is resolved by a lower commander, the requestor will make a witnessed, written statement in the record indicating his satisfaction with the action taken and his willingness to withdraw his request mast to the higher commander.

g. Request mast will be conducted at the earliest reasonable time and not later than 72 hours after submission of the request, whenever possible. Emergency cases will be heard as soon as possible, usually within 24 hours from preparation of the request mast.

## 2. Requesting Mast with a Commanding General

a. The requestor must prepare a complete written statement stating the reasons for the request mast. It must include a list of witnesses with a summary of the expected testimony of each.

b. If applicable, documents to support the request mast must be attached.

c. The written statement must also include a list of persons in the chain of command whom the requestor has seen at request mast and the action taken by these individuals.

---

For more information in this area, refer to:

1. MCO 1700.23A     Request Mast

# Chapter 2. Marine Corps History, Customs, and Courtesies

## Section I. Marine Corps History

Objectives:

*1. On command without reference, state the Marine Corps mission in your own words.*
*2. On command without reference, state four examples of the accomplishment of the Marine Corps' mission.*
*3. On command without reference, state the birthdate and birthplace of the U.S. Marine Corps.*
*4. On command without reference, explain what each of the three elements of the Marine Corps emblem represents.*
*5. On command without reference, state the motto of the Marine Corps and explain what it means.*

### A. MARINE CORPS MISSION

Historically, Marine Corps preparedness has generally been characterized by the phrase, "The First to Fight." Marines are trained, organized, and equipped for offensive amphibious employment and as a "force in readiness." Officially, the mission of the Marine Corps is set forth in the National Security Act of 1947 as amended (1952). The key parts of the act are listed below:

1. To seize or defend advanced naval bases and to conduct such land operations as may be essential to the prosecution of a naval campaign.

2. To provide detachments and organizations for service in armed vessels of the Navy or for protection of naval property on naval stations and bases.

3. To develop, with the other Armed Forces, the tactics, techniques, and equipment employed by landing forces in amphibious operations.

3.  To train and equip, as required, Marine forces for airborne operations.

5.  To develop, with the other Armed Forces, doctrine, procedures, and equipment of interest to the Marine Corps for airborne operations which are not provided for by the Army.

6.  To be able to expand from peacetime components to meet the needs of war in accordance with mobilization plans.

## B. MARINE CORPS PARTICIPATION IN WARS AND CONFLICTS

Our mission and readiness has caused us, throughout our history, to take part in many wars and conflicts in the defense of freedom. Some of the more prominent examples where the Marine Corps' mission has been accomplished are listed below:

1.  PRE-WORLD WAR II

    a. Revolutionary War
    b. Naval War with France
    c. War with Tripoli
    d. War of 1812
    e. Florida Indian War
    f. Mexican War
    g. Civil War
    h. Spanish-American War
    i. Philippine Insurrection
    j. Boxer Rebellion
    k. World War I
    l. Banana Wars in Haiti, Dominican Republic, and Nicaragua

2.  WORLD WAR II

    a. Wake
    b. Midway
    c. Solomon Islands
       (1) Guadalcanal
       (2) New Georgia
       (3) Bougainville
    d. Gilbert Islands, Tarawa
    e. Marshall Islands
       (1) Roi-Namur
       (2) Kwajalein
    f. Marianas Islands
       (1) Saipan
       (2) Tinian
       (3) Guam
    g. Palau Islands, Pelelieu
    h. Iwo Jima
    i. Okinawa

3.  POST-WORLD WAR II

    a. Korea
    b. Dominican Republic
    c. Republic of Vietnam
    d. Seizure of the Mayaguez
    e. Beirut, Lebanon
    f. Grenada

## C. BIRTHDAY/BIRTHPLACE

The birthday of the Marine Corps is 10 November 1775. The legendary birthplace of the Marine Corps was Tun Tavern, a favorite meeting place in 18th century Philadelphia, Pennsylvania.

## D. EMBLEM

The emblem of the Marine Corps consists of the eagle, globe, and anchor. The globe and anchor signify worldwide service and sea traditions. The spread eagle is a symbol of the Nation itself. The emblem was adopted by Brigadier General Jacob Zeitin, 7th Commandant, in 1968.

## E. MOTTO

The motto of the Corps is "Semper Fidelis" which is Latin for "always faithful."

---

For more information in this area, refer to:

1. Marine Corps Museum Historical Pamphlets

2. Marine Corps Manual

# Section II. Marine Corps Customs

Objectives:

*1. On command without reference, state the customs associated with the celebration of the Marine Corps birthday.*
*2. As appropriate, use sea service terminology.*

The Marine Corps is rich in customs and traditions. These are the things that make the Marine Corps what it is. You begin your knowledge of customs and traditions in recruit training and continue this education throughout your life as a Marine. Every Marine should know the following important facts.

## A. MARINE CORPS BIRTHDAY

All Marine Corps activities, if at all practical, shall provide for suitable observance of the Marine Corps birthday, 10 November. When 10 November falls on Sunday, the Marine Corps birthday will be celebrated on the preceding Saturday, 9 November. Such observances shall be appropriate to the size and mission of the activity concerned, in consonance with local conditions, and within the financial means of the personnel of the host activity.

Birthday observances should take the following general form:

1. Troop formations to include parades when practical and the reading of General John A. Lejeune's birthday message.

2. Social observances to include the traditional cake-cutting ceremony.

3. Recognition of oldest Marine present.

4. Recognition of youngest Marine present.

## B. SEA SERVICE TERMINOLOGY

This glossary is a compilation of terms traditionally used in the Naval Service. Use of these terms is inherent in Marine Corps tradition and history. The list is not meant to be all inclusive, but rather a starting point to familiarize all Marines with the proper use of traditional sea-going language.

| | |
|---|---|
| ADRIFT | Loose from towline or moorings; scattered about; not in proper stowage. |
| AFT | Referring to or toward the stern (rear) of a vessel. |
| ALL HANDS | All members of a command. |
| ASHORE | Any place outside of a naval or Marine Corps reservation. It does not matter if the barracks are miles from the sea; once the Marine steps outside the gate of a naval reservation, he is "ashore." |
| AS YOU WERE | Resume former activity. |
| AWEIGH | Said of the anchor. As soon as the anchor has broken from and is no longer fast to the bottom, it is said to be "aweigh." |
| AYE, AYE, SIR | Required official acknowledgment of an order meaning: "I have received, understand, and will carry out the order or instructions." |
| BELAY | To make fast or secure, as in "belay the line." To cancel or to disregard a statement just made. |
| BELOW | When a Marine goes downstairs, he goes BELOW. |
| BOONDOCKS | The "sticks"; a long way from the center of action. |
| BREAKOUT | Take out of stock or storage. To prepare for use. |
| BRIG | A place of confinement. A prison. |
| BROWN BAGGER | Slang for a married man. One who carries his lunch. |

| | |
|---|---|
| BOW | The front of a ship. |
| BRIDGE | That portion of a ship's structure from which the ship is controlled when underway. |
| BROW | A portable walkway from the pier or jetty to the ship's quarterdeck—usually fitted with wheels or rollers at one end. |
| BULKHEAD | A wall. |
| BUTTKIT | An ashtray. |
| CARRY ON | The order to resume previous activity. |
| CHIT | A receipt or authorization; a piece of paper. |
| C.P. | Command Post in the field. |
| DECK | The floor. Technically, when speaking of shipboard locations, horizontal platforms located below the main deck are referred to as decks; those above the main deck are called "levels." |
| FANTAIL | The main deck of a ship at the stern. |
| FIELD DAY | Barracks cleanup. |
| FIELD SCARF | Regulation Marine Corps uniform neck tie. |
| FORECASTLE | The upperdeck at the bow on which is located the ground tackle. (Pronounced "fo'csle.") |
| GALLEY | Shipboard kitchen; kitchen of a mess hall, mobile field mess. |
| GANGWAY | An opening in the rail or bulwarks giving access to the ship. A command or announcement to stand aside or to stand clear to let someone through or go ahead (usually a senior). |
| GATOR | An amphibious ship. One who serves in the amphibious Navy. |

| | |
|---|---|
| GEEDUNK | Candy, ice cream, soda, etc.; also called "pogie bait." The place aboard ship where these items can be purchased. |
| HATCH | Door or doorway. |
| HEAD | Latrine or toilet. |
| LADDER | Stairs. |
| LIBERTY | Absence from the ship or command for less than 96 hours for purposes of rest and recreation which is not charged as leave. Said only of enlisted personnel. Officers take "shore leave." |
| LINE | What civilians call a rope. In the Navy, line is never referred to as rope. |
| OVERHEAD | A ceiling. |
| PASSAGEWAY | A hallway. |
| PETTY OFFICER | A Navy NCO, E-4 through E-9. |
| POLICE | To straighten or tidy up. |
| PORT | Left. |
| QUARTERDECK | The ceremonial location on board ship when the ship is moored or at anchor. It is located very close to the brow or accommodation ladder and is the watch station for the Officer of the Deck. The quarterdeck location may change depending upon the arrangements for access to the ship. |
| RATE | A sailor's occupational specialty. |
| SCUTTLEBUTT | Gossip or unfounded rumor; also a drinking fountain. |
| SEABAG | The bag used by a sailor or Marine to stow his personal gear. Men who have all the articles or clothing required by the Uniform Regulations are said to have a "full seabag." |
| SECURE | Stop, finish, end. |

2-7

| | |
|---|---|
| SHIPPING OVER | Reenlisting. |
| SICK BAY | Hospital or dispensary. |
| SKIPPER | A term applied to a Marine or Navy captain who is in command (Commanding Officer). |
| SKYLARK | Goof off; loiter. |
| SMOKING LAMP | With regard to tobacco use when smoking is permitted; the smoking lamp is said to be "lighted." |
| SQUARE AWAY | To straighten, make ship-shape, or to get settled in a new job or home; also to inform or admonish someone in a abrupt or curt manner. |
| STARBOARD | Right. |
| STERN | The blunt end (rear) of a ship. |
| SQUARED AWAY | Used to describe a ship or a person. The highest compliment. Marine or seamanlike, efficient, and confident. Opposite of lubberly. |
| SWAB | A mop. |
| TOPSIDE | Upstairs. |
| TURN TO | Begin work, get started. |
| WARDROOM | On board ship, the officer's living room and dining area; also used to signify all of the officers serving in the ship. |

# Section III. Marine Corps Courtesies

Objectives:

*1. On command without reference, render all required military courtesies and honors.*
*2. On command without reference, demonstrate the procedures for reporting to a senior officer.*

## A. SALUTING OFFICERS

1. When meeting an officer who is either walking or riding, salute between 6-30 paces to give the officer time to return your salute before you are abreast of the officer. Hold the salute until it is returned, and accompany the salute with "Good morning, sir or ma'am;" or some other appropriatre greeting.

2. Render the salute only once if the senior remains in the immediate vicinity. If conversation takes place, however, again salute when the senior leaves, or when you depart.

3. When passing an officer who is going in the same direction as you, come abreast of the officer, salute and say, "By your leave sir or ma'am." He or she will return the salute and say "Carry On" or "Granted." You then finish your salute and pass ahead.

4. When armed with a rifle, the rifle salute is executed except when on guard duty, when Present Arms is rendered.

5. Do not salute if you are engaged in work or play unless spoken to directly.

6. Members of the naval service are required to render a salute to officers, regular and reserve, of the Navy, Army, Air Force, Marine Corps, Coast Guard, and to foreign military and naval officers whose governments are formally recognized by the Government of the United States.

7. Upon the approach of a superior officer, individuals or a group not in formation are called to attention by the first person noticing the officer, and all come smartly to attention and salute.

8. In general, one does not salute when: at work indoors (except when under arms), guarding prisoners, under battle conditions, or when a prisoner.

9. Individuals not armed with a rifle and in formations do not salute except at the command "Present Arms."

## B. REPORTING TO AN OFFICER

1. When ordered to report to an officer, either outdoors or indoors, if under arms, approach the officer at attention and halt about two paces from the officer. Render the appropriate salute and say "Sir or Ma'am, reporting as ordered," using your name and grade. For example: "Sir or Ma'am, Private Jones reporting as ordered." Hold the salute until it is acknowledged. When the business is completed, salute; and after the salute has been returned, take one step backward, execute about face, and depart at attention.

2. When reporting to an officer indoors when not under arms, follow the same procedure except remove your headgear before approaching the officer and do not salute.

## C. SALUTING WHILE STANDING GUARD AS A SENTRY

1. If you are walking a post, halt and salute by presenting arms when you carry a rifle with a parade sling. If you are otherwise armed, or if you are carrying your rifle at sling arms, give the hand salute. If you are touring a roving post, you do not halt unless spoken to, but you give the rifle salute when armed with a rifle and the hand salute when otherwise armed.

2. During the hours when you are required to challenge, salute an officer as soon as he or she is recognized. If your orders require you to come to the position of raise pistol while challenging, you will not salute.

3.   You salute an officer as he comes to your post. If the officer stops to hold a conversation with you, assume the position of port arms if armed with a rifle. If unarmed, assume the position of attention throughout the conversation. You salute again when the officer leaves.

4.   If you are in a conversation with an officer, do not interrupt the conversation to salute another officer. If the officer to whom you are talking salutes a senior, you also salute.

5.   When the flag is raised at morning colors or lowered at evening colors, you stand at attention at the first note of the National Anthem or "To the Colors" (Standard) and render the prescribed salute. If you are engaged in some duty which would be hampered, you need not salute. You usually face the flag while saluting, but if your duty requires it, you can face in another direction. When the music sounds "Carry On" you resume regular duties.

## D. RENDERING HONORS DURING COLORS AND PLAYING OF THE NATIONAL ANTHEM

1.   Whenever the National Anthem or "To the Colors" is played and you are not in formation and not in a vehicle, render the prescribed salute. Hold the salute until the last note of music is sounded.

2.   If no flag is near, face the music and salute.

3.   If in formation, salute only on the command "Present Arms."

4.   Vehicles in motion are brought to a halt. Troops riding in vehicles do not disembark. They and the driver remain seated at attention and do not salute. Drivers and passengers riding either in military or private vehicles remain seated at attention and do not salute.

5.   If outdoors and uncovered, stand at attention and face the direction of the flag or music. When the national Anthem is played indoors, officers and enlisted men will stand at attention and face the music or flag if one is present.

6.   When passing or being passed by an uncased color which is being paraded, presented, or is on formal display, salute at six paces distance and hold the salute until six paces beyond it or until it has passed you by six paces.

2-11

7. If uncovered, stand or march at attention when passing or being passed by an uncased color. The marks of respect shown above are also rendered to the National Anthem of any friendly country when played upon official occasions.

## E. RENDERING HONORS DURING THE PLAYING OF THE MARINE'S HYMN

An important part of Marine traditions is the Marine's Hymn. During the playing of this music, all Marines stand at attention whether in uniform or civilian attire. This tradition also applies to former Marines.

## F. PROCEDURES FOR ENTERING VEHICLES AND BOARDING VESSELS

1. When entering an automobile, small boat, or ship, the junior goes first and the others follow in inverse order of rank.

2. When boarding a naval ship, upon reaching the top of the gangway (brow), face aft and salute the National Ensign (see figure below). After completing this salute, salute the officer of the deck who will be standing on the quarterdeck at the head of the gangway (brow) and request permission to come aboard. When leaving the ship, render the salutes in reverse order. First, salute the officer of the deck and request permission to go ashore; then salute the National Ensign and leave the ship.

**BOARDING - - - 0800 TO SUNSET**

First, salute the National Ensign at top of gangway (brow).

Second, turn and salute OOD and request permission to come aboard.

### DEPARTING - - - 0800 TO SUNSET (reverse procedure)

1. First, salute OOD and request permission to go ashore.

2. Second, go to top of gangway (brow), turn, aft and salute the National Ensign.

### BOARDING AND DEPARTING --- SUNSET TO 0800

Follow the above procedure, but do not turn aft and salute the National Ensign.

---

For more information in this area, refer to:

1. NAVMC 2691          Drill and Ceremonies Manual

2.                              U.S. Navy Regulations

# Chapter 3.   Close Order Drill

Objectives:

*1.   On command without reference, state the purpose of close order drill.*

*2.   On command without reference, with and without arms, execute individual drill movements.*

*3.   On command without reference, with and without arms, participate in unit drill.*

*This text will not attempt to duplicate NAVMC 2691, but will present highlights or key points.*

## A. THE PURPOSE OF CLOSE ORDER DRILL

A unit leader uses drill to:

1.   Move a unit from one place to another in a standard, orderly manner.

2.   Provide simple formations from which combat formations may be readily assumed.

3.   Teach discipline by instilling habits of precision and automatic response to orders.

4.   Increase the confidence of subordinate leaders by allowing them to exercise command, give proper commands, and control drilling Marines.

5.   Give Marines an opportunity to handle individual weapons.

## B. HALTED DRILL MOVEMENTS WITHOUT ARMS

1. **ATTENTION**. When given the commands FALL IN or ATTENTION, assume the position of attention as shown in figure 3-1. The command ATTENTION is preceded by a preparatory command designating the size of the unit, such as SQUAD/PLATOON/COMPANY, ATTENTION.

Fig 3-1. Attention.

2. **RESTS**. There are four positions of rest for halted Marines. All are executed from the position of attention.

   a. **Parade Rest**. When you receive this command move your left foot smartly 12 inches to the left. At the same time join hands behind your back, right hand inside the left, palms to the rear just below the belt, right hand loosely holding left thumb, fingers extended and joined. Do not move. Do not talk.

   b. **At Ease**. When you receive this command keep your right foot in place. You may move about, but do not talk.

   c. **Rest**. When you receive this command you may move, adjust equipment, and talk; but you must keep your right foot in place.

   d. **Fall Out**. When you receive this command you may leave your position in ranks, but you must remain in the immediate area. When you receive the command FALL IN, assume your place in ranks at the position of attention.

3. EYES RIGHT (LEFT). When the command of execution is given, turn your head smartly to the right (left) at a 45° angle. At the command READY, FRONT, turn your head and eyes smartly back to the front. When a reviewing officer troops the line, the command READY, FRONT will not be given. As the reviewing officer passes your unit, follow him with your head and eyes until you are looking directly to the front.

4. HAND SALUTE. This movement will be executed when given the command HAND, SALUTE or PRESENT, ARMS. You will remain in this position (figure 3-2) until you receive the command READY, TWO or ORDER, ARMS.

Fig 3-2. Hand salute.

5. FACING MOVEMENTS. All facing movements are conducted at the position of ATTENTION and at quick time cadence. While facing, your arms should not swing out from your sides. The three facing movements are: Right face, Left face, and About face.

## C. MARCHING MOVEMENTS

With the exception of RIGHT STEP, all steps in marching which begin from the halt start with the left foot.

1. QUICK TIME. From the halt, the command is FORWARD, MARCH. The step is 30 inches long at a cadence of 120 steps per minute.

2. **DOUBLE TIME.** From the halt, mark time, or quick time, the command is DOUBLE TIME, MARCH. Take 180, 36-inch steps per minute. To resume quick time cadence, the command is QUICK TIME, MARCH.

3. **HALT.** The command SQUAD/PLATOON/COMPANY, HALT is given as either foot strikes the deck for all movements except side step (given when the heels are together). To execute the halt from all movements except double time, take one more step after the command HALT, then bring the heels together at the position of attention. From the double time, take one more double time step after the command HALT, take one step at quick time, then bring the heels together at the position of attention.

4. **MARK TIME.** This command may be given from the halt, while marching forward at quick time, at half step, or while double timing in place. The command is MARK TIME, MARCH. The ball of the foot is raised approximately two inches from the deck at a quick time cadence. To resume forward movement at quick time cadence, the command is FORWARD, MARCH.

5. **DOUBLE TIME IN PLACE.** The command IN PLACE, DOUBLE TIME, MARCH may be given while halted, marching at the double time, or marking time. The forearms are raised parallel to the deck, and alternating in place, feet are raised six inches above the deck at a double time cadence.

6. **HALF STEP.** To march forward with 15-inch steps at a quick time cadence, the command is HALF STEP, MARCH. To resume the 30-inch step, the command is FORWARD, MARCH.

7. **SIDE STEP.** The command for this movement is LEFT (RIGHT) STEP, MARCH. This command may only be given when halted. At the command of execution MARCH, move your left (right) foot 12 inches to the left (right), then place the opposite foot beside the left (right). Continue to march until the command SQUAD/PLATOON/COMPANY, HALT is given.

8. **BACK STEP.** The command BACKWARD, MARCH is given only from the halt. Take 15-inch steps to the rear until the command SQUAD/PLATOON/COMPANY, HALT is given.

9. **TO FACE IN MARCHING OR MARCH BY THE FLANK.** The command for this movement is BY THE RIGHT (LEFT) FLANK, MARCH. Except for instruction, this command is only given when marching. To resume marching to the original front, the opposite flanking movement is used.

3-4

10. **TO FACE ABOUT WHILE MARCHING.** The command TO THE REAR, MARCH is given when the right foot strikes the deck. When marching forward at quick time or at the halt, take one step with the left foot, turn about to the right on the balls of both feet, then immediately step off "to the rear" with your left foot. From the double time, take two more steps, then turn about to the right by taking four steps in place at the double time cadence. Resume the double time to the rear.

11. **TO CHANGE STEP.** The command CHANGE STEP, MARCH is given as the right foot strikes the deck and may be given at quick or double time, while marking time, or while double timing in place. At quick or double time, take one more step with your left foot. As your right foot comes forward on the next step, place the toe near the heel of your left foot, then step out again with the left foot. While marking time, lift the left foot twice in succession on the command MARCH, then continue marking time. While double timing in place, hop twice on the left foot on MARCH, then continue double timing in place.

12. **TO MARCH AT EASE.** The command is AT EASE, MARCH. Maintain distance and interval, but do not talk.

13. **TO MARCH AT ROUTE STEP.** The command is ROUTE STEP, MARCH. Maintain distance and interval. You may talk in a low voice.

14. **TO RESUME MARCHING AT QUICK TIME FROM ROUTE STEP OR AT EASE.** The command is SQUAD/PLATOON/COMPANY, ATTENTION. The unit leader will call cadence. Pick up step as soon as possible.

## D. MANUAL OF ARMS

Prior to commencement of the manual of arms, the magazine is removed from the rifle, and the sling is drawn tight and positioned on the left side of the weapon (parade sling).

1. **ORDER ARMS.** Order arms, as shown in figure 3-3, is the basic position from which a Marine may execute other drill movements. All facing movements, alignments, and short distance marching movements are executed from order arms.

2. **TRAIL ARMS.** When at order arms and a command is given to move a unit a short distance, face the unit, or align the unit, automatically execute trail arms on the command of execution for the movement. Automatically return the rifle to order arms on completion of the movement. For training purposes, the command TRAIL, ARMS may be given while halted at order arms (figure 3-4).

completion of the movement. For training purposes, the command TRAIL, ARMS may be given while halted at order arms (figure 3-4).

Fig 3-3. Order arms.          Fig 3-4. Trail arms.

**3. PARADE REST.** This command may only be given from order arms. The left foot is moved smartly 12 inches to the left. The left hand is moved behind the back, palm to the rear just below the belt. The right arm is moved straight ahead, grasping the muzzle of the barrel while keeping the butt of the weapon on the deck (figure 3-5.)

Fig 3-5. Parade rest.

3-6

**4. PRESENT ARMS.** This command is given in formations to render honors. It is also a proper salute given by an armed sentry.

    a.   Present arms from order arms  (figure 3-6).

Fig 3-6. Present arms from order arms.

    b.   Order arms from present arms  (figure 3-7).

Fig 3-7. Order arms from present arms.

5.  **PORT ARMS.** From port arms the Marine may execute order arms or continue to left (right) shoulder arms. It is basically an intermediate movement between order arms and shoulder movements.

a.  Order arms to port arms  (figure 3-8).

Fig 3-8. Order arms to port arms.

b.  Port arms to order arms  (figure 3-9).

Fig 3-9. Port arms to order arms.

c.   Port arms to right shoulder arms  (figure 3-10).

Fig 3-10. Port arms to right shoulder arms.

d.   Port arms to left shoulder arms  (figure 3-11).

Fig 3-11. Port arms to left shoulder arms.

## 6.  RETURN TO ORDER ARMS

a.  Right shoulder arms to order arms  (figure 3-12).

Fig 3-12. Right shoulder arms to order arms.

b.  Left shoulder arms to order arms  (figure 3-13).

Fig 3-13. Left shoulder arms to order arms.

3-10

## 7. RIFLE SALUTES

a. Rifle salute from right shoulder arms (figure 3-14).

Fig 3-14. Rifle salute from right shoulder arms.

b. Rifle salute from order arms (figure 3-15).

Fig 3-15. Rifle salute from order arms.

3-11

C.    Rifle salute from left shoulder arms (figure 3-16).

Fig 3-16. Rifle salute from left shoulder arms.

d.    Rifle salute from trail arms (figure 3-17).

Fig 3-17. Rifle salute from trail arms.

3-12

8. INSPECTION ARMS

    a. Order arms to inspection arms (figure 3-18).

Fig 3-18. Order arms to inspection arms.

b.   Inspection arms to port arms  (figure 3-19).

Fig 3-19. Inspection arms to port arms.

## E.  MARCHING MANUAL

1.   The manual of arms may be executed while on the march. In each case, the command of execution will be given on the same foot as the direction of movement of the rifle. For example, to move from right shoulder arms to left shoulder arms or port arms, the command of execution is given as the left foot strikes the deck. To move from left shoulder arms to right shoulder arms or port arms, the command of execution is given as the right foot strikes the deck.

2.   The rifle movements may be combined in any number of ways while on the march. The basic movements must be learned separately then combined during drill to ensure knowledge and proficiency of the unit.

3.   Marching manual is conducted in the quick time cadence.

## F.  EXECUTION OF SQUAD DRILL MOVEMENTS

When the squad is armed with the service rifle, the command RIGHT (LEFT) SHOULDER, ARMS, or SLING (PORT), ARMS is given before giving a command to move the squad. If the squad is only to be moved a short distance, it may be done at trail arms which will be assumed automatically at the command, MARCH. The squad will automatically come to order arms at the command, HALT.

1. **FORMATION**. The normal formation of a squad is a rank (line) or file (column) as shown in figures 3-20a and 3-20b. The squad marches in line for minor changes of position only.

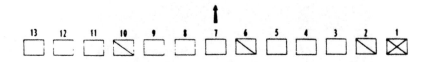

Fig 3-20a. Squad in rank (line).

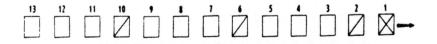

Fig 3-20b. Squad in file (column).

**NOTE:** Symbols used in the figures showing drill movements in this chapter are taken from the Marine Corps Drill and Ceremonies Manual.

## 2. TO FORM THE SQUAD

a. To form the squad at normal interval (figure 3-21) the command is FALL IN. As soon as each Marine has obtained his interval, he will assume the position of attention.

Fig 3-21. Normal interval.

b. To form the squad at close interval (figure 3-22) the command is AT CLOSE INTERVAL, FALL IN.

Fig 3-22. Close interval.

**NOTE:** If the squad is armed, the squad will fall in at order arms.

3-16

### 3. TO DISMISS THE SQUAD

a. The squad is dismissed from a line at the position of attention.

b. If armed, the troops are given the commands INSPECTION, ARMS; PORT, ARMS; DISMISSED.

c. Unarmed troops are given the command, DISMISSED.

### 4. COUNT OFF

a. On line, the command is COUNT, OFF. All Marines except the man on the right flank turn their heads and eyes smartly to the right. As the right flank man shouts ONE, the next Marine turns his head to the front and shouts TWO, the next THREE, and so on down the line. This movement is executed at quick time cadence.

b. In column, the command is FROM FRONT TO REAR, COUNT, OFF. Each Marine in succession, starting with the front man, turns his head to the right and shouts his number as his head returns to the front.

### 5. ALIGN THE SQUAD

a. To align the squad the command is DRESS RIGHT, DRESS. To align the squad at close interval the command is AT CLOSE INTERVAL, DRESS RIGHT, DRESS. Alignment and interval are obtained as in FALL IN (figures 3-21 and 3-22). At normal interval, all Marines except the right flank man position themselves by taking short side steps until their right shoulder touches the fingertips of the Marine to their right as in figure 3-21. At close interval, the right arm touches the elbow of the Marine on the right as in figure 3-22. The unit leader places himself on line with the squad, one pace from the right flank man, and faces down the line. He orders the men to move backward or forward as necessary.

b. When alignment is correct, the leader faces to the right as in marching, and moves three paces forward, halts, faces to the left and gives the command READY, FRONT.

c. In column, the command is COVER. Marines will move as necessary to place themselves directly behind the man to their immediate front, still maintaining a 40-inch distance from back to chest.

6. **TO OBTAIN CLOSE INTERVAL FROM NORMAL INTERVAL ON LINE.** The command is CLOSE, MARCH. All Marines except the right flank man face to the right as in marching, march forward until a four-inch interval has been obtained, halt, and face to the left. Then obtain the proper interval as in falling in at close interval.

7. **TO OBTAIN NORMAL INTERVAL FROM CLOSE INTERVAL ON LINE.** The command is EXTEND, MARCH. All Marines except the right flank man face to the left as in marching, march forward until the approximate normal interval is obtained, halt, and face to the right. Then obtain normal interval as in falling in.

8. **TO OBTAIN DOUBLE ARM INTERVAL ON LINE**

    a.   The command is TAKE INTERVAL TO THE LEFT, MARCH. Movement is as in extending except that both arms are raised (right flank man raises only his left arm, and the left flank man raises only his right arm).

    b.   To return to normal interval, the command is ASSEMBLE TO THE RIGHT, MARCH. Movement is as in closing except form at normal interval.

9. **MARCH TO THE FLANK WHILE ON LINE**

    a.   The commands are RIGHT (LEFT) FACE; FORWARD, MARCH.

    b.   Under arms, the commands are RIGHT (LEFT) FACE; RIGHT (LEFT) SHOULDER, ARMS or SLING (PORT), ARMS; FORWARD, MARCH.

10. **MARCH TO THE OBLIQUE**

    a.   The command is RIGHT (LEFT) OBLIQUE, MARCH. Each Marine faces half right (left) in marching and steps off at a 45° angle from the original direction of march.

    b.   To return to the original direction of march, the command is FORWARD, MARCH.

    c.   If marching in the oblique and you receive the command HALT, each Marine will take one more step in the oblique, face 45° in the original direction of march, and halt.

    d.   For a temporary halt in the oblique, the command is IN PLACE, HALT. The only command that you may receive while in this position is RESUME, MARCH.

**11. MARCH TO THE FLANK**. To move a column a short distance to the right or left while marching, the command is BY THE RIGHT (LEFT) FLANK, MARCH. Each Marine takes one more step and faces to the right (left) as in marching and steps out in the new direction of march. This command will not be given at the halt.

**12. TO CHANGE DIRECTION OF A COLUMN**

a.   The command is COLUMN RIGHT (LEFT) or COLUMN HALF RIGHT (LEFT), MARCH. The front Marine faces to the right (left) in marching and steps out with his right (left) foot in the new direction of march. Other Marines in the column continue to march to where the front Marine pivoted. At that point, they will successively face to the right (left) in marching and continue in the new direction.

b.   When halted, at the command MARCH, the front Marine faces to the new direction of march and steps out with his left foot. At the same time, all other Marines march forward and successively face in the new direction of march, pivoting in the same spot as the front Marine.

c.   For slight changes of direction, the command is INCLINE TO THE LEFT (RIGHT). At the command, the front Marine changes the direction of march; all other Marines do the same when they come to the pivot point used by the front man. This is not a precision movement. It is executed when marching around a curve in the road or to by-pass an obstacle such as a parked car.

## 13. TO FORM A COLUMN OF TWOS FROM A SINGLE FILE (figure 3-23).

a. When the squad is halted in column, the command is COLUMN OF TWOS TO THE LEFT (RIGHT), MARCH.

b. On MARCH, the front man stands fast. Even-numbered men (counting from the front to rear) face half right in marching, and move forward until next to and at normal interval from the odd-numbered men who were in front of them. Odd-numbered men, except the front man, march forward and halt as they reach normal distance from the odd-numbered men in front of them. All men required to move do so at the same time.

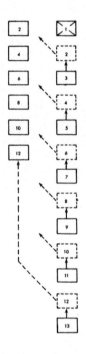

Fig 3-23. Forming column of twos from a single file.

3-20

## 14. TO FORM A SINGLE FILE FROM A COLUMN OF TWOS (figure 3-24).

a. When the squad is halted in column of twos, the command is COLUMN OF FILES FROM THE RIGHT (LEFT), MARCH.

b. At the command MARCH, number one man and number two man step off at the same time. Number one man moves forward and the number two man faces to the half right, moves two steps and faces half left in marching, and follows the number one man at normal distance. Remaining odd-numbered and even-numbered men step off in pairs, execute the same movements as one and two, and follow in file at normal distance.

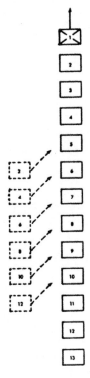

Fig 3-24. Forming single file from a column of twos.

## G. PLATOON DRILL

### 1. FORMATIONS

a. Column and line are the two formations for a platoon (figures 3-25 and 3-26).

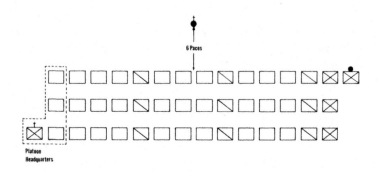

Fig 3-25. Platoon on line.

Fig 3-26. Platoon in column.

b. The platoon normally forms in line with the squad leaders on the right of their squads and the guide on the right of the first squad leader. The platoon marches in line for short distances only.

2. **TO FORM THE PLATOON.** The platoon is normally formed by the platoon sergeant with the command FALL IN. The guide takes his post and the platoon aligns on him using the same procedure as in squad drill.

3. **TO DISMISS THE PLATOON.** The platoon is dismissed only from a line with the Marines at attention. The procedure is the same as for squad drill except that the platoon sergeant normally dismisses the platoon.

4. **TO ALIGN THE PLATOON.** The procedure is the same as in squad drill except that the platoon commander will verify alignment of all three squads. Upon commanding READY, FRONT, he then commands, COVER.

5. **TO MARCH TO THE RIGHT OR LEFT.** With the platoon in line, to march to the right or left, the commands are RIGHT (LEFT), FACE; FORWARD, MARCH. The platoon will become inverted if faced to the left, so this command should only be done for short movements.

6. **TO CHANGE THE DIRECTION OF A COLUMN** The command is COLUMN RIGHT (LEFT), MARCH or COLUMN HALF RIGHT (LEFT), MARCH (figure 3-27).

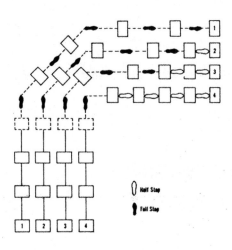

Fig 3-27. Column right (left).

7. **SUPPLEMENTARY COMMANDS.** When commands are given for movements in which all squads of the platoon do not move at the same time, the squad leaders give appropriate supplementary commands.

8. **TO FORM LINE FROM COLUMN.** The commands are PLATOON, HALT; LEFT, FACE.

9. **TO MARCH TOWARD A FLANK.** The command is BY THE RIGHT (LEFT) FLANK, MARCH.

10. **TO OPEN RANKS.** The commands are OPEN RANKS, MARCH; READY, FRONT. At the command MARCH, the front rank takes two paces forward, halts and executes dress right, dress. The second rank takes one pace forward, halts and executes dress right, dress. The third rank stands fast and executes dress right, dress. The platoon commander verifies alignment as for dress right, dress.

11. **TO CLOSE RANKS.** The command is CLOSE RANKS, MARCH. The front rank stands fast; the second rank takes one pace forward and halts; the third rank takes two paces forward and halts.

12. **TO FORM COLUMN OF TWOS OR SINGLE FILE AND REFORM.**

a.    Being in a column of threes at a halt, to form a column of twos, the command is COLUMN OF TWOS FROM THE RIGHT (LEFT), MARCH. The two right squads march forward; the left squad forms a column of twos to the left and then executes column half right and column half left so as to follow the leading squads in column as in figure 3-28.

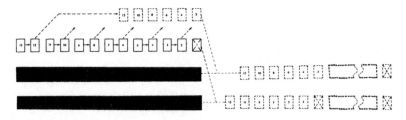

Fig 3-28. Column of twos from a column of threes and reform.

3-24

b. Being in a column of twos, to reform a column of threes, the command is COLUMN OF THREES TO THE LEFT (RIGHT), MARCH. The two leading squads stand fast. The rear squad forms a single file from the right (left), moving into its normal place next to the leading squads as shown in figure 3-29.

Fig 3-29. Column of threes from a column of twos.

c. Being in a column of twos or threes, to form a single file, the command is COLUMN OF FILES FROM THE RIGHT (LEFT), MARCH.

d. Being in single file, to reform a column of twos or threes, the command is COLUMN OF TWOS (THREES) TO THE LEFT (RIGHT), MARCH.

---

For more information in this area, refer to:

1. NAVMC 2691     Drill and Ceremonies Manual

3-25

# Chapter 4.  Military Security

## Section I.  Eleven General Orders, Reporting and Challenging A Post, and Deadly Force

Objectives:

*1.  On command without reference, state the eleven General Orders.*
*2.  On command without reference, when posted as a sentry, report a post properly.*
*3.  On command without reference, when posted as a sentry, challenge properly to include the use of the challenge and password.*
*4.  On command without reference, state the interior guard chain of command.*
*5.  On command without reference, define deadly force according to Marine Corps regulations.*
*6.  On command without reference, explain the occasions under which deadly force may be applied while posted as a sentry.*
*7.  On command without reference, state the procedures for applying deadly force.*

### A.  PURPOSE OF INTERIOR GUARD

The guard is detailed by a commander to preserve order, protect property, and enforce regulations within the jurisdiction of command.

## B. GENERAL ORDERS

1. **GENERAL ORDER 1.** "To take charge of this post and all government property in view."

a. TAKE CHARGE OF THIS POST—You are responsible for your post and everything that takes place on it.

b. ALL GOVERNMENT PROPERTY IN VIEW—Check your post thoroughly when posted, e.g., windows, doors, standing lights, everything. Watch for violations and unusual activity on and off your post during your tour.

2. **GENERAL ORDER 2.** "To walk my post in a military manner, keeping always on the alert and observing everything that takes place within sight or hearing."

a. TO WALK MY POST IN A MILITARY MANNER—Your attention to duty while posted as a sentry is reflected in your general appearance, carriage, and alert attitude.

b. KEEPING ALWAYS ON THE ALERT AND OBSERVING EVERYTHING THAT TAKES PLACE WITHIN SIGHT OR HEARING—Don't let boredom get the better of you. Find ways to stay alert, and DO observe everything that takes place on or near your post.

3. **GENERAL ORDER 3.** "To report all violations of orders I am instructed to enforce."

a. Your actions while on post will be guided by the 11 General Orders, the special orders for your post, and any additional instruction given by officers and noncommissioned officers of the guard.

b. REPORT ALL VIOLATIONS—You must report all violations pertaining to any of the orders that guide your actions while on post to the Corporal of the Guard.

**4. GENERAL ORDER 4.** "To repeat all calls from posts more distant from the guardhouse than my own."

a. TO REPEAT ALL CALLS—If you hear any call, you will pass it on to the guardhouse.

b. FROM POSTS MORE DISTANT FROM THE GUARDHOUSE THAN MY OWN—You will often find that your post is equipped with a radio or telephone. Sometimes the sentry on another post will not be able to get to his phone. If you hear his call, you will have to use your own judgment to determine if you should use your phone or simply repeat the call.

**5. GENERAL ORDER 5.** "To quit my post only when properly relieved."

a. TO QUIT MY POST ONLY WHEN PROPERLY RELIEVED—You may quit (leave) your post only if relieved by a member in the guard chain of command.

b. If you become sick or for some other reason need to be relieved, you must remain at your post until a proper relief arrives.

**6. GENERAL ORDER 6.** "To receive, obey, and pass on to the sentry who relieves me, all orders from the commanding officer, officer of the day, and officers and noncommissioned officers of the guard only.

a. As a sentry, you will receive orders pertaining to the conduct of your post only from members of the guard.

b. Upon being relieved, you must pass on all orders you were given prior to and during your tour on your post.

7. **GENERAL ORDER 7.** "To talk to no one except in the line of duty."

    a. TALK TO NO ONE—You may be tempted to talk to people who are on or near your post. DON'T! Keep your mind on your duties.

    b. EXCEPT IN THE LINE OF DUTY—Line of duty means government business pertaining to your job as sentry on your post. Conversations with all personnel will be short, concise, and official.

8. **GENERAL ORDER 8.** "To give the alarm in case of fire or disorder."

    TO GIVE THE ALARM—This is the key to your action. Sound the proper alarm immediately by the fastest and most effective means available.

9. **GENERAL ORDER 9.** "To call the Corporal of the Guard in any case not covered by instructions."

    a. TO CALL THE CORPORAL OF THE GUARD—As a sentry on post, you are to call the guardhouse for instructions or assistance when you are in doubt concerning the proper action to take.

CPL OF THE GUARD. POST No 9 REQUEST PERMISSION TO ADMIT A STAFF NCO WHO LEFT HIS KEYS IN HIS OFFICE.

    b. IN ANY CASE NOT COVERED BY INSTRUCTIONS—You will usually have special orders and instructions pertaining to the conduct of your post. When an incident not covered occurs, you must call the Corporal of the Guard.

10. **GENERAL ORDER 10.** "To salute all officers and all colors and standards not cased."

    a. TO SALUTE ALL OFFICERS—Which officers? All officers of the guard, U.S. Armed Forces, and U.S. Allies are to be saluted by you, as a sentry, on post.

b. ALL COLORS AND STANDARDS NOT CASED—You must remain alert to the military courtesy required of a sentry. You will salute uncased colors and standards.

11. GENERAL ORDER 11. "To be especially watchful at night and during the time for challenging, to challenge all persons on or near my post, and to allow no one to pass without proper authority."

a. BE ESPECIALLY WATCHFUL AT NIGHT—Be aware of the limits of your post and its problem areas and watch for intruders.

b. CHALLENGE PERSONS ON OR NEAR MY POST—Challenge and check all persons on or near your post to determine their business on your post.

c. ALLOW NO ONE TO PASS WITHOUT PROPER AUTHORITY—Detain anyone attempting to pass without authority. Allow no one to pass if you are in doubt about him.

## C. GENERAL ORDER MEMORY KEY

1. TO TAKE
2. TO WALK
3. TO REPORT
4. TO REPEAT
5. TO QUIT
6. TO RECEIVE
7. TO TALK
8. TO GIVE
9. TO CALL
10. TO SALUTE
11. TO BE

## D. REPORTING A SENTRY POST

1. A sentry reports his post to a superior by saying: "Sir, (rank and name) reports post number ( ) all secure" (or report anything that is out of the ordinary).

2. Following the above report, the sentry will add appropriate comments. Examples:

    a. "Nothing unusual has occurred during my tour."

    b. "There are several standing lights which are not working."

## E. CHALLENGING ONE PERSON

| ACTION OF THE MARINE SENTRY | ACTION OF THE PERSON CHALLENGED |
| --- | --- |
| To a person about to enter his post: | |
| "HALT WHO IS (GOES) THERE?" | Person halts immediately and answers:<br><br>"LT JONES, THE SUPPLY OFFICER." |
| Sentry will order person forward: | |
| "ADVANCE LT JONES TO BE RECOGNIZED." | Person will advance without replying. |
| When person is close enough to identify, the sentry commands: | |
| "HALT!" (LT JONES IS NOT RECOGNIZED.) | Person will halt on command and wait for further instructions. |
| Challenge—The sentry will challenge in a low voice: | |
| "The WATER in the river is low." | Person challenged will reply with the password in a low voice:<br><br>"It's always low in the SUMMER." |

When the sentry has
identified the person, he
will permit him to proceed:

"PASS SIR!"                           Person will proceed on his
                                      way when told to pass.

## F. CHALLENGING A GROUP

| ACTION OF THE MARINE SENTRY | ACTION OF THE GROUP CHALLENGED |
| --- | --- |
| To a group of persons about to enter his post:<br><br>"HALT, WHO IS (GOES) THERE?" | Group will immediately halt, and senior will answer.<br><br>"CORPORAL OF THE GUARD WITH THE RELIEF." |

Sentry will order the senior
(Cpl of the Guard) forward:

| | |
|---|---|
| "ADVANCE CORPORAL OF THE GUARD TO BE RECOGNIZED." | Person will advance without replying. |

When the Corporal of the
Guard is close enough to
identify, the sentry will
command:

| | |
|---|---|
| "HALT!" | Corporal of the Guard will halt. |

Upon recognizing the
Corporal of the Guard,
the sentry will command:

| | |
|---|---|
| "ADVANCE THE RELIEF TO BE RECOGNIZED." | The relief will come forward when directed to be identified by the Corporal of the Guard. |
| The sentry will halt, identify and/or control the relief as the situation demands. | Relief will be effected by the Corporal of the Guard. |

## G. CHALLENGING TWO PEOPLE COMING FROM DIFFERENT DIRECTIONS

You are a sentry on a challenging post. It is night and you observe two people approaching from different directions. After you have challenged both, you determine that one is the Sergeant of the Guard and the other is the Officer of the Day (OOD). Which one do you deal with first? The senior is dealt with first.

## H. THE CHAIN OF COMMAND FOR INTERIOR GUARD

1. **Commanding Officer.** Any officer authorized to establish and maintain a guard. It could be the commanding officer of a ship, commanding general, or commanding officer of a shore installation or unit based ashore.

2. **Field Officer of the Day.** The officer designated by and responsible to the commanding officer for the supervision of the entire interior guard and execution of all orders of the commanding officer relating to the security of the command.

3. **Officer of the Day.** The officer or noncommissioned officer directly responsible to the commanding officer (or the field officer of the day, when assigned) who supervises the guard, and who ensures that all orders of the commanding officer relating to security of the command are executed.

4. **Commander of the Guard.** The officer or noncommissioned officer who ensures proper instruction, discipline, and performance of duty of the main guard.

5. **Sergeant of the Guard.** The noncommissioned officer of the guard who assists the commander of the guard in ensuring proper instruction, discipline, and performance of duty of the guard.

6. **Corporal of the Guard.** An enlisted man assigned to take charge of a relief of the guard.

## I. DEADLY FORCE

Deadly force is defined as that force which a person uses with the purpose of causing—or which he knows or should reasonably know would create substantial risk of causing—death or serious bodily harm. Deadly force is justified under conditions of extreme necessity and only as a last resort when all lesser means have failed or cannot reasonably be employed. The firing of weapons at another person by a member of the guard is considered justified only under one or more of the circumstances listed below.

## J. APPLICATION OF DEADLY FORCE

1. **In Self-Defense.** When deadly force reasonably appears to be necessary to protect military law enforcement or security personnel who reasonably believe themselves to be in imminent danger of death or serious bodily harm.

2. **In Defense of Property Involving National Security.** When deadly force reasonably appears necessary:

a. To prevent the threatened theft of, damage to, or espionage aimed at property or information specifically designated by the commanding officer or other competent authority as vital to the national security.

b. To prevent the actual theft, or damage to, or espionage aimed at property or information which—though not vital to the national security—is of substantial importance to the national security.

3. **In Defense of Property Not Involving National Security, But Inherently Dangerous to Others.** When deadly force reasonably appears to be necessary to prevent the actual theft or sabotage of property, such as operable weapons or ammunition, which is inherently dangerous to others; i.e., presents a substantial potential danger of death or serious bodily harm to others.

4. **To Prevent Serious Offenses Against Persons.** When deadly force reasonably appears to be necessary to prevent the commission of a serious offense involving violence and threatening death or serious bodily harm to other persons, such as arson, armed robbery, aggravated assault, or rape.

5. **Apprehension and Escape**

a. When deadly force reasonably appears to be necessary to apprehend or prevent the escape of a person reasonably believed to have committed an offense of the nature specified in paragraphs 2a, 2b and 3 found above, or the offense having been personally observed by the sentry.

b. When deadly force reasonably appears to be necessary to apprehend or prevent the escape of an individual whose unauthorized presence in the vicinity of property or information vital to the national security, reasonably appears to present a threat of theft, damage, or espionage. Property shall be specifically designated as vital to the national security only when its loss, damage, or compromise would seriously prejudice the national security or jeopardize the fulfillment of an essential national defense mission.

c. When deadly force has been specifically authorized by competent authority and reasonably appears to be necessary to prevent the escape of a prisoner.

4-10

6. **Lawful Order.** When the application of deadly force has been directed by the lawful order of a superior authority.

## K. PROCEDURES FOR APPLYING DEADLY FORCE

If in any of the circumstances set forth above it becomes necessary to use a firearm, the following precautions will be observed. This is provided if it is possible to do so consistent with the prevention of death or serious bodily harm:

1. An order to halt shall be given and shots will not be fired unless it is reasonably apparent that the order is being disregarded.

2. Shots shall not be fired if they are likely to endanger the safety of innocent bystanders.

3. Shots shall be aimed to disable. However, if circumstances render it difficult to direct fire with sufficient precision to ensure that the person will be disabled rather than killed, such circumstances will not preclude the use of a firearm provided such use is authorized by competent authority.

**NOTE:** WARNING SHOTS SHALL NOT BE FIRED.

## L. ADDITIONAL INSTRUCTIONS INVOLVING FIREARMS

1. All military law enforcement and security personnel will be fully instructed in the use and safe handling of the weapons they are armed with in accordance with the provisions of appropriate manuals and orders pertaining to the variety of other weapons associated with military law enforcement and security duties.

2. In view of the dangers inherent in automatic pistols, personnel so armed will not insert a loaded magazine in the weapon until the weapon has been cleared, the slide released, the trigger pulled, and the pistol placed in the holster. The pistol will only be drawn from the holster when required in the performance of duty.

## M. SPECIFIC INSTRUCTIONS FOR ARMED SENTRIES

I am justified in using the weapon with which I am armed to apply deadly force only under conditions of absolute necessity and only as a last resort when all other means have failed or cannot be employed. If such is the case, I can use deadly force:

1. To protect myself, if I reasonably believe that I am in immediate danger of death or serious bodily harm.

2. To protect others, if I reasonably believe that they are in immediate danger of death or serious bodily harm.

3. To prevent acts which reasonably appear to threaten property or information designated by my commanding officer as vital to national security and to prevent the escape of someone who presents such a threat.

4. To prevent the actual theft or destruction of property designated by my commanding officer as having substantial importance to national security.

5. To prevent the actual theft or destruction of property that is, of itself, dangerous to others, e.g., explosives, weapons, ammunition, etc.

6. To affect the apprehension of someone I reasonably believe has committed a serious offense, such as murder, rape, aggravated assault, armed robbery, or arson.

7. To prevent the escape of a particular prisoner when specifically authorized on an individual basis by my commanding officer.

8. On any other occasion, when directed by the lawful order of a superior in my chain of command.

---

For more information in this area, refer to:

NAVMC 2691A      U.S. Marine Corps Interior Guard Manual

# Section II.   Terrorism

Objectives:

*1.   On command without reference, define terrorism.*
*2.   On command without reference, describe the types of terrorist attacks.*
*3.   On command without reference, describe measures to protect yourself against terrorists.*

## A. GENERAL

Terrorism involves a criminal act, often symbolic in nature, intended to influence an audience beyond the immediate victims. Terrorism is the calculated use of violence or the threat of violence to attain political, religious, or ideological goals by instilling fear or using intimidation or coercion.

## B. TYPES OF TERRORIST ATTACKS

The types of attacks used by terrorists normally center on the abilities of their organization.

1.   **Bombings.** Over one-half of all terrorist incidents in the last decade involved bombs. Bombs are cheap, reliable, easy to make; and the materials are readily available. Additionally, a mix of real bombs and hoaxes can tie up security forces and keep the public in a panic. They are often used in pairs and can be delivered by a wide variety of means. Terrorist bombs are becoming more powerful and destructive.

2.   **Arson.** Arson is a useful tactic against public utilities, hotels, houses of government, and industrial centers. Incendiary devices are cheap and easy to hide. An act of arson can also be used to draw a crowd to the killing zone of a bomb or other weapon.

3. Hijacking/Vehicle
Thefts. This is a popular
terrorist tactic to provide an
organization with the contents
of the vehicle hijacked or
stolen and to provide a means
of delivery. Hijackings and
the theft of certain vehicles
could indicate the intended
use of a vehicular bomb.

4. Skyjacking/Aircraft Thefts. This terrorist tactic provides the organization with hostages and/or the means for unique delivery of explosives to a target. Skyjacking and aircraft thefts could indicate the intended use of an aircraft for a "kamikaze" type terrorist attack.

5. **Ambushes** A well-planned ambush allows for assassination or kidnapping to occur at the place and time of the terrorist's choosing. Ambush is particularly easy to accomplish if the victim always follows the same routine.

6. **Kidnappings**
Kidnapping is a favorite method
of financing terrorist movements
or forcing governments to agree
to terrorist demands such as
prisoner release. Kidnapping
generally requires a "safe
house" in which to keep the
victim while bargaining.

4-14

7. **Hostage-Taking.** Hostage-taking is overt and is designed to attract and hold the media's attention. Because the hostages' lives are threatened, this can be used to force concessions from the government. The terrorist is bargaining with the lives of his hostages. His target is the audience, not the victim (hostage).

8. **Robberies and Expropriations.** In some environments these methods enhance other terrorist activities. However, these are not required when terrorists are functioning as surrogates of other nations and do not require a means of gaining their own funds or other resources.

9. **Psychological Terror.** This form of terrorism is designed to alter behavioral characteristics of an individual, group, or activity/organization through the application of sophisticated techniques.

10. **Biological and Chemical Attack.** The use of biological and chemical agents by terrorists cannot be dismissed. While there is no indication of such terrorist activity in the past, this form of warfare must be considered when planning to combat terrorism.

11. **Assassination.** Historically, terrorists have killed specifically targeted individuals for major psychological effect and can be expected to do so in the future.

## C. MEASURES TO PROTECT YOURSELF AGAINST TERRORISTS

As Marines we find ourselves in every "clime and place." Whether we are conducting operations or going on liberty, we are symbols of the United States of America. As representatives of our country, we become targets of terrorists who oppose the United States and its policies. The attitude "it will never happen to me" increases the potential of becoming a target. Three areas have proven themselves significant in reducing the chance of being selected as a target: keep a low profile, be unpredictable, and remain vigilant. An antiterrorism program is not effective unless all three are demonstrated.

1. **Keep a Low Profile.** Your dress, conduct, and mannerisms should not attract attention. Make an effort to blend into the local environment. Avoid publicity and don't go out in big groups. Stay away from civil disturbances and demonstrations.

2. **Be Unpredictable.** Vary your route and time that you leave and return home during your daily routine. Vary the way you dress. Don't exercise at the same time and place each day, and never alone or on deserted streets or country roads. Let people close to you know where you are going and what you'll be doing.

3. **Remain Vigilant.** Watch for anything suspicious or out of place. Don't give out personal information over the telephone. If you think you are being followed, go to a preselected secure area. Immediately report the incident to the Military Police and your command duty officer.

---

For more information in this area, refer to:

1. MCDEC OH 7-14          Terrorism Counteraction

2. MCDEC OH 7-14.1        Unit Terrorism Counteraction

3. MCI Course 02.10       Terrorism Counteraction for Marines

# Chapter 5.   First Aid

## Section I.    Basic Measures

Objectives:

*1.   Given a simulated casualty or dummy, demonstrate the applications of the four lifesaving steps in sequence.*
*2.   Given a simulated casualty or dummy, demonstrate the procedures for mouth-to-mouth/mouth-to-nose resuscitation.*
*3.   Given a simulated casualty or dummy, perform chest pressure arm-lift respiration.*
*4.   Given a dummy, demonstrate procedures for closed-chest heart massage.*
*5.   Given a simulated casualty, apply a pressure dressing.*
*6.   Using parts of uniform or equipment, apply a field expedient tourniquet to control bleeding.*
*7.   Given appropriate material and a simulated casualty, splint a closed fracture.*
*8.   Given appropriate material and a simulated casualty, splint an open fracture.*
*9.   Given a simulated casualty or dummy, demonstrate the procedure to treat a casualty for shock.*
*10.   Given the necessary equipment, improvise a stretcher and carry a casualty 20 feet.*
*11.   On command without reference, use a fireman's carry to transport a casualty 20 feet.*

Marines must know the principles of first aid and be prepared to give competent assistance to persons injured in battle or accidents. It is essential that first aid techniques be practiced until all hands are prepared to act with calmness and precision despite excitement, danger, and confusion which may be present.

## A. LIFESAVING STEPS

The four lifesaving steps (measures) for casualties are:

o   Restore the breathing
o   Stop the bleeding.
o   Protect the wound.
o   Treat for shock.

1.   All four steps are closely related and the relative importance of each depends on the situation. You should examine the casualty to determine the full extent of his injuries. Then you can determine which of the lifesaving measures are necessary for treating him. In some cases, not all of the measures will be required.

2.   When evaluating the casualty, follow these procedures:

a. STEP 1.   Check for responsiveness. If conscious, ask the casualty to identify the problem. If he has an airway obstruction, clear his airway. If he is unconscious, proceed to step 2.

b. STEP 2.   Check for breathing. If he is breathing, proceed to step 4. If he is not breathing, attempt to ventilate. If an airway obstruction is apparent, clear the obstruction, then ventilate. After successfully clearing the casualty's airway, proceed to step 3.

c. STEP 3.   Check for pulse. If pulse is present, and the casualty is breathing, proceed to step 4. If pulse is present, but the casualty is still not breathing, start artificial respiration. If the pulse is not present, start cardiopulmonary resuscitation.

d. STEP 4.   Check for bleeding. Also check for both entry and exit wounds. If the casualty is bleeding from an open wound, perform the needed first aid measures.

e. STEP 5.   Check for shock. If signs/symptoms of shock are present, begin treatment immediately.

f. STEP 6.   Check for fractures. Treat accordingly.

g. STEP 7.   Check for burns. Treat accordingly.

h. STEP 8.   Check for possible head injury. Treat accordingly.

## B. RESTORE BREATHING

All living things must have oxygen to live. Through the breathing process, the lungs draw oxygen from the air and put it into the blood. The heart then pumps the blood through the body to be used by the living cells which require a constant supply of oxygen. Some cells are more dependent on a constant supply of oxygen than others. Cells of the brain may die within 4 to 6 minutes without oxygen. Providing oxygen to these cells when there is an absence of breathing, or an absence of breathing and circulation (heartbeat) is accomplished by performing cardiopulmonary resuscitation (CPR). This basic lifesaving technique involves four steps in sequence: a preliminary assessment or evaluation phase, opening the airway, artificial respiration (rescue breathing), and chest compression (closed-chest heart massage).

1. **Assessment (Evaluation) Phase.** Begin by checking for responsiveness. Establish whether the casualty is conscious by gently shaking him and asking "Are you O. K.?" Call for assistance. Position the casualty so that he is lying on his back and on a firm surface. If the casualty is lying on his chest (prone position), *cautiously* roll the casualty as a unit so that the body does not twist and complicate a neck or spinal injury.

a. Straighten the casualty's legs. Take the arm that is nearest to you and move it so that it is straight and above his head. Repeat the procedure for the other arm.

b. Kneel beside the casualty with your knees near his shoulders (leave space to roll the body). Place one hand behind the head and neck for support. With the other hand, grasp the casualty under his far arm.

c. Roll the casualty toward you using a steady and even pull. The head and neck should stay in line with his back.

d. Return the arms to the casualty's side. Straighten the legs.

2. **Opening the Airway**

The tongue is the single most common cause of an airway obstruction, and in most cases, the airway can be cleared by simply extending the neck. This action pulls the tongue away from the air passage in the throat.

a. Call for help and then position the casualty. Move (roll) the casualty onto his back.

b. Perform either the head tilt-neck lift, the head tilt-chin lift, or the jaw thrust technique to open the airway. The head tilt is an important procedure in opening the airway; however, use extreme care when lifting the neck. Excess force in performing this maneuver may cause further spinal injury. In a casualty with a suspected neck injury, the safest approach is the jaw thrust technique because in most cases it can be accomplished without extending the neck.

(1) Head tilt-neck lift technique . Kneel beside the casualty's head and place one hand on his forehead. Place the other hand under his neck. Gently lift the hand under the neck and press down with the hand on the forehead (figure 5-1). Use extreme care when lifting the neck. Excess force or a quick snapping motion may cause spinal injury.

Fig 5-1. Head tilt-neck lift technique.

(2) Head tilt-chin lift technique. Kneel beside the casualty's head and place one hand on his forehead. Place the fingertips of the other hand under the chin. While pressing on the forehead, lift the chin forward to open the airway (figure 5-2). Be careful not to press against the soft tissues under the chin; doing so may obstruct the airway. The teeth should be brought close together, but the mouth should not be closed completely.

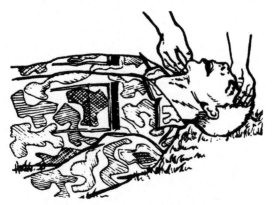

Fig 5-2.   Head tilt-chin lift technique.

(3)  Jaw thrust technique. Grasp the angles of the casualty's lower jaw and lift with both hands,   one on each side, displacing the jaw forward while tilting the head backwards (figure 5-3). Your elbows should rest on the same surface as the casualty. If the lips close, the lower lip can be retracted with the thumb. If mouth-to-mouth breathing is necessary, close the nostrils by placing your cheek tightly against them.

Fig 5-3.   Jaw thrust technique.

c. After establishing an open airway, it is important to maintain that airway in an open position. Often the act of just opening and maintaining the airway will allow the casualty to breathe properly. Once you use any of the techniques to open the airway, you should maintain that head position to keep the airway open. Failure to maintain the open airway will prevent the casualty from receiving an adequate supply of oxygen.

3. Artificial Respiration

If the casualty does not promptly resume breathing after the airway is open, artificial respiration (rescue breathing) must be started. Be calm! Think and act quickly! The sooner you begin rescue breathing, the more likely you are to restore the casualty's breathing. If you are not sure that the casualty is breathing, give artificial respiration, since it will do no harm to a person who is breathing.

There are several methods of administering artificial respiration. The mouth-to-mouth method is preferred; however, it cannot be used in all situations. If the casualty has a severe jaw injury, use the mouth-to-nose method. If mouth-to-mouth or mouth-to-nose methods cannot be used because the casualty has a crushed face, use the chest pressure arm-lift method.

#### Preliminary steps for all artificial respiration methods

o   Establish responsiveness. Call for help. Turn or position the casualty.

o   Open the airway.

o   Check for breathing. Place your ear over the casualty's mouth and nose and look toward his chest. Look for rise and fall of the casualty's chest while listening for sounds of breathing. Feel for breath on the side of your face. Allow 3 to 5 seconds to determine if the casualty is breathing.

If the casualty is not breathing, begin artificial respiration.

4. Methods of Artificial Respiration

a. Mouth-to-mouth method. In this method of rescue breathing, you inflate the casualty's lungs with air from your lungs by blowing air into the person's mouth (nose). The mouth-to-mouth rescue breathing method is performed as follows:

(1) If the casualty is not breathing, place your hand on his forehead, and pinch his nostrils together with the thumb and index finger of the same hand. Let this hand exert pressure on the forehead to maintain the backward head tilt and maintain an open airway. With the other hand, keep your fingertips on the chin (or your hand under the neck) to hold it upward (figure 5-4).

Fig 5-4.    Mouth-to-mouth method of artificial respiration.

(2) Take a deep breath and place your mouth (forming an airtight seal) around the casualty's mouth. (If the injured person is small, cover both the nose and mouth with your mouth, sealing your lips against the skin of his face.)

(3) Within 3 to 5 seconds, blow four quick full breaths into the casualty's mouth, taking a breath of fresh air each time before you blow. Watch out the corner of your eye for the casualty's chest to rise. Release the casualty's nose after the final breath. If the chest rises, sufficient air is getting into the casualty's lungs. Therefore, proceed as described in paragraph.

(4) If the chest does not rise, do the following and then attempt to ventilate again:

(a) Take corrective action immediately by reestablishing the airway. Make sure that air is not leaking from around your mouth or out of the casualty's pinched nose.

(b) Reattempt to ventilate.

5-7

(c) If the chest still does not rise, take the necessary actions to open an obstructed airway as described in paragraph (7).

(4) After giving four quick breaths which cause the chest to rise, attempt to locate a pulse on the casualty. Feel for the pulse on the side of the neck closest to you by placing the first two fingers of your hand on the groove beside the casualty's Adam's apple (figure 5-5). Maintain the open airway by keeping your other hand on the casualty's forehead. Allow 5 to 10 seconds to determine if there is a pulse.

(a) If a pulse is found and the casualty is breathing—STOP; allow the casualty to breathe on his own. If possible, keep him warm and comfortable

(b) If a pulse is found and the casualty is not breathing, continue artificial respiration.

(c) If a pulse is not found, perform cardiopulmonary resucitation (CPR). (See paragraph 6 for more detail.)

Fig 5-5. Checking for a pulse.

(5) If the casualty is not breathing, pinch his nostrils together with the thumb and index finger of the hand that is on his forehead. Let this same hand exert pressure on the forehead to maintain the backward head tilt.

(6) Take a deep breath and place your mouth (in an airtight seal) around the casualty's mouth.

5-8

(7) Blow a quick breath into the mouth forcefully to cause the casualty's chest to rise. If the chest rises, sufficient air is getting into the casualty's lungs.

(8) When the casualty's chest rises, remove your mouth from his and listen for the return of air from the lungs.

(9) Repeat this procedure (paragraphs (1) through (10) at a rate of one breath every 5 seconds to achieve 12 breaths per minute.

(10) Feel for a pulse after every 12th breath. If a pulse beat is not detected, cardiopulmonary resuscitation must be started immediately.

(11) Continue mouth-to-mouth resuscitation until the casualty breathes on his own, until you are relieved by another person, or until you are too tired to continue. As the casualty starts to breathe, adjust the timing of your efforts to assist him, ensuring at least 12 breaths per minute.

NOTE: After a period of resuscitation, the casualty's stomach may bulge from incoming air. Usually this is caused by having the individual's head tilted improperly. Reposition the head and continue. DO NOT attempt to push out air by pressing on the stomach.

b. Mouth - to - nose method. If you cannot perform mouth-to-mouth because the casualty has a severe jaw fracture or mouth wound, use this method. It is performed in the same way as the mouth-to-mouth method except that you blow into the nose while holding the lips closed with one hand. It may be necessary to separate the casualty's lips to allow the air to escape during exhalation.

c. Chest pressure arm - lift method. It is not always possible to use the mouth-to-mouth (nose) methods of artificial respiration. For example, a casualty may have severe facial injuries or be in an NBC environment. If you *must* use an alternate method, the chest pressure arm-lift method is preferred. This method is not recommended unless the mouth-to-mouth or mouth-to-nose method cannot be performed.

(1) Conduct the preliminary steps for all methods of artificial respiration.

5-9

(2) Position the casualty on his back with his face up and with a rolled blanket or a similar object under the casualty's shoulders to extend the neck.

**WARNING:** Do not place a blanket or other similar object under the shoulders if you suspect the casualty has a neck injury.

(3) Stand at the casualty's head and face his feet. Kneel on one knee and place your opposite foot on the other side of his head and against his shoulder to steady it. If you become uncomfortable after a period of time, quickly switch to the other knee.

(4) Grasp the casualty's hands and hold them over his lower ribs. Rock forward and exert steady, uniform pressure almost directly downward until you meet firm resistance (figure 5-6). This pressure forces air out of the lungs.

(5) Lift his arms vertically upward, then stretch the arms backward as far as possible. This process of lifting and stretching the arms increases the size of the chest and draws air into the lungs.

Fig 5-6.    Chest pressure arm-lift.

5-10

(6)   Replace his hands on his chest and repeat the cycle: PRESS, LIFT, STRETCH, and REPLACE. Give 10 to 12 cycles per minute at a steady, uniform rate. Give counts of equal length to the first three steps. Perform the fourth step as quickly as possible.

(7)   As the casualty attempts to breathe, adjust the timing of your efforts to assist him. Continue artificial respiration until the casualty starts to breathe on his own, or until you are relieved by another person.

(8)   If you become tired, have another Marine take your place without interrupting the rhythm of the cycle. Position your replacement next to you so he can grab the casualty's wrists during the stretch step and continue with the chest pressure arm-lift method as you move out of the way.

NOTE: If this procedure must be done in an NBC environment and the casualty is already wearing a protective mask, lift the mask only enough to perform the clearing of the airway, then return it to its proper position. If the casualty is not masked, mask him.

5.   External Chest Compression (Closed-Chest Heart Massage)

If a casualty's heart stops beating, you must immediately give him external chest compression (formerly called closed-chest heart massage). When a casualty's heart stops beating, he will almost immediately stop breathing and will require artificial respiration. To determine if the casualty's heart is beating, check his pulse by placing the tips of your fingers on his neck to the side of his windpipe (figure 5-5). If you do not detect a pulse immediately, don't waste time checking further; start external chest compression at once.

a. Principles. External chest compression provides artificial circulation to keep blood flowing until the heart begins to beat normally. The heart is located between the breastbone and the spine. Pressure on the breastbone pushes the heart against the spine, forcing blood out of the heart into the arteries. Release of pressure allows the heart to refill with blood.

b. **Procedure.** If another person is available to help, one of you should give external chest compression while the other gives artificial respiration. You should coordinate your efforts so that one is not blowing into the casualty's airway at the same time the other is pressing on his breastbone. If you must administer first aid alone, alternate between the two procedures.

(1) Prepare the casualty for mouth-to-mouth artificial respiration. The surface on which the casualty is placed must be solid. The casualty must be horizontal when external chest compression is performed. Elevate the legs about 6 inches while keeping the rest of the body horizontal.

(2) Position yourself close to the casualty's side and locate the site on his chest where compressions will be made. Locate the lower edge of the casualty's ribs with your fingers. Run the fingers up along the rib cage to the notch where the ribs meet the breastbone at the center of the lower chest (figure 5-7). Place the middle finger on the notch and the index finger next to the middle finger on the lower end of the breastbone. Place the heel of the other hand on the lower half of the breastbone next to the two fingers (figure 5-7).

Fig 5-7.   Fingers and hand on the lower breastbone.

(3) Remove the fingers from the notch and place that hand on top of the positioned hand, extending or interlacing the fingers (figure 5-8).

Fig 5-8. Positioning of the hands.

(4) With your hands in the correct position and your arms straight, lean forward to bring your shoulders directly above your hands; then press straight downward (figure 5-9). Apply enough pressure to push the breastbone down 1 1/2 to 2 inches. Too much pressure may fracture the casualty's ribs; therefore, do not push the breastbone down more than 2 inches.

Fig 5-9. Giving chest compressions.

5-13

(5) Release the pressure immediately. The heel of your hand should remain lightly in contact with the chest. However, pressure on the breastbone should be completely released so that it returns to its normal resting position between compressions. The time allowed for release should be equal to the time required for compression. Do not pause between compressions.

(6) If there are two Marines, one performing artificial respiration and the other administering external chest compression, the person administering external chest compression should compress the heart once every second (60 compressions per minute). He does not pause for breaths to be blown into the airway. The compressions must be uninterrupted, regular, and smooth.

(7) If you are alone, you will have to administer both mouth-to-mouth resuscitation and external chest compression. In this case, you should compress the chest 15 times and follow this by 2 quick but full lung inflations. To make up the time used for inflating the lungs, you must perform each series of 15 compressions at the faster rate of 80 compressions per minute.

6. **Clearing Airway Obstructions.** In order for air to flow to and from the lungs, the upper airway must be unobstructed.

a. Obstructions

(1) If the airway is partially obstructed, the casualty may still have an air exchange. A good air exchange means that the casualty can cough forcefully, though he may wheeze between coughs. You should not interfere, and you should encourage the casualty to cough up the object by himself.

(2) A poor air exchange may be indicated by a weak cough with a high pitched noise between coughs. Additionally, the casualty may display signs of shock. You should assist this casualty and treat him as though he had a complete obstruction.

5-14

(3) A complete airway obstruction (no air exchange) is indicated if a casualty cannot speak, breathe, or cough at all. He may be clutching his neck and moving erratically. In an unconscious casualty a complete obstruction is also indicated if after opening his airway you cannot ventilate him.

b. **Opening an obstructed airway (conscious casualty).** Clearing a conscious casualty's airway obstruction can be performed with the casualty either sitting or standing, and by following a relatively simple procedure.

(1) Check to see if the casualty indicates signs of choking. Ask him if he can speak. If he can, encourage him to attempt to cough. If he can speak or cough, do not interfere with his attempts to expel the obstruction.

(2) Listen for high pitched sounds when the casualty breathes or coughs (poor air exchange). If there is poor air exchange or no breathing, call for help and immediately initiate assistance by applying *back blows* using the procedure below:

o Position yourself to the side and slightly behind the casualty.

o Place your hand on his chest (breastbone) to support him.

o With the hand of the other arm, deliver four sharp blows in rapid succession to the casualty's back between the shoulder blades (figure 5-10).

Fig 5-10. Back blows.

(3) If successful (airway cleared), stop the procedure and monitor the casualty. If unsuccessful, apply the abdominal or chest thrust procedure (explained in the following paragraphs).

(4) Abdominal thrust. The abdominal thrust procedure should be used unless the casualty has an abdominal wound, is pregnant, or is so large that you cannot wrap your arms around the abdomen (stomach). Apply the abdominal thrust procedures as follows:

o Stand behind the casualty and wrap your arms around his waist.

o Make a fist with one hand and grasp it with the other (figure 5-11A). The thumb side of the fist should be against the casualty's abdomen, between the waist and rib cage (figure 5-11B).

o Give four quick, inward and upward thrusts (figure 5-11C).

o Repeat the back blows as described above and the abdominal thrusts (alternating) until the casualty can talk and breathe normally, or you are relieved, or the casualty becomes unconscious and requires a different procedure.

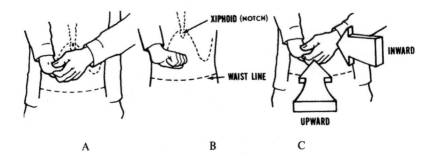

A                 B            C

Fig 5-11. Adominal thrusts.

(5) Chest thrusts. An alternate technique to the abdominal thrust is the chest thrust. This technique is useful when the casualty has an abdominal wound, when the casualty is pregnant, or when the casualty is so large that you cannot get your arms around the abdomen. To apply chest thrusts with the casualty sitting or standing:

o Stand behind the casualty and wrap your arms around his chest with your arms under his armpits.

o Make a fist with one hand and place the thumb side of the fist squarely on the breastbone (figure 5-12A).

o Grasp the fist with the other hand and exert four quick, inward and upward thrusts (figure 5-12B).

o Alternate the back blows and chest thrusts until the casualty can talk and breathe normally, or you are relieved, or the casualty becomes unconscious and requires a different procedure.

5-17

STERNUM

ARMPIT

QUICK
INWARD
THRUSTS

A                                    B

Fig 5-12.    Chest thrust.

    c.  **Opening an obstructed airway (casualty lying or unconscious).**
The following procedures are used to expel an airway obstruction in a
casualty who is lying down, who becomes unconscious, or who is found
unconscious (cause unknown). If the casualty is conscious and lying
down, perform the following steps:

    (1)    Roll the casualty onto his side, facing you, with his chest
            against your thigh.

    (2)    Deliver four sharp *blows* in rapid succession to the back
            between the shoulder blades (figure 5-13).

Fig 5-13.    Back blows on a victim who is lying or unconscious.

5-18

(3) Apply abdominal thrust.

    o  Position the casualty on his back.

    o  Perform the thrust either astride or along the side of the casualty. If you are along the side, your knees should be close to his hips.

    o  Straddle (in the astride position) the hips or one thigh of the casualty (figure 5-14).

Fig 5-14.  Abdominal thrust on unconscious casualty.

    o  Place the heel of one hand against the casualty's abdomen, between the waist and the rib cage. Put your second hand on top of the first one.

    o  Position and maintain your shoulders over the casualty's abdomen.

    o  Apply a quick, inward and upward abdominal thrust toward the casualty's head. Do this four times in rapid succession.

(4) Apply chest thrust. (Note that the chest thrust is an *alternate* technique that is used when the abdominal thrust cannot be applied.)

    o  Position the casualty on his back.

o   Kneel close to the side of the casualty's body and locate the lower edge of the rib cage with your fingers. Trace the rib cage to the notch where the ribs meet the breastbone in the center of the chest and position your hands (see figure 5-7).

o   With your hands in position, bring your shoulders directly over the casualty's breastbone. Keep your arms straight and press downward. Apply enough pressure to push the breastbone down 1 1/2 to 2 inches, and then release the pressure completely. Do this four times in rapid succession.

**NOTE:**  A foreign body or vomitus that is strongly suspected or can be seen should be removed with the fingers. If it cannot be seen, the combination of alternating back blows and manual thrusts may expel or dislodge it so that it is accessible for removal by the fingers.

(5)  Apply a finger sweep (if necessary). (Note that the finger sweep is done only on an *unconscious* casualty.)

o   Position the casualty's face up, open his mouth by grasping both his tongue and lower jaw between your thumb and fingers and pull up (tongue-jaw lift) (figure 5-15). If you are unable to open his mouth, cross your fingers and thumb (crossed-finger method) and push his teeth apart.

Fig 5-15.   Opening casualty's mouth (tongue-jaw lift).

o Insert the index finger of the other hand down along the inside of his cheek to the base of the tongue. Quickly sweep exposed foreign bodies or vomitus out of the mouth by using a hooking motion from the side of the mouth toward the center (figure 5-16). Be careful not to force the object deeper into the airway by pushing it with the finger.

o Attempt to ventilate.

(6) Repeat back blows, manual thrusts, finger sweeps, and attempts to ventilate. These steps should be repeated as often as necessary until the airway is cleared of the obstruction.

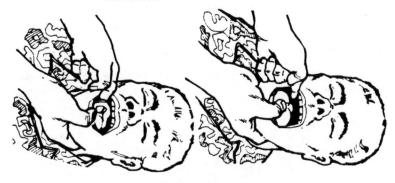

Fig 5-16.    Using finger to dislodge foreign body.

## C. STOP THE BLEEDING/PROTECT THE WOUND

Uncontrolled bleeding causes shock and, eventually, death. The use of a pressure dressing is the best method for the control of bleeding in an emergency situation. The application of a tourniquet is another method to control bleeding, but it should not be used unless the pressure dressing fails to stop the bleeding. Application of a sterile field dressing is the method used to protect most wounds.

1. **Application of a Field Dressing.** The application of a sterile dressing with pressure to a bleeding wound helps clots form, compresses the open blood vessels, and protects the wound from further invasion of germs. Before applying the dressing, examine the casualty to determine if there is more than one wound. The exit wound of a bullet or projectile is usually larger than the entrance wound. Apply the field dressing as follows:

a. Cut or tear away the clothing and carefully expose the entire area of the wound. Clothing stuck to the wound should be left in place. DO NOT touch the wound; keep it as clean as possible.

**CAUTION:** Do not remove protective clothing in a chemical environment. Apply the dressing over the protective clothing.

b. Use the casualty's field dressing. Remove it from the wrapper and grasp the tails of the dressing with both hands. DO NOT touch the white (sterile) side of the dressing and DO NOT allow the sterile side to come in contact with any surface other than the surface directly on the wound.

c. Hold the dressing directly over the wound with the white side down. Pull the dressing open and place it directly over the wound (figure 5-17).

Fig 5-17.   Placing the dressing directly over the wound.

d. Hold the dressing in place with one hand. Use the other hand to wrap one of the tails around the injured part, covering about half of the dressing. If the casualty is able, he may assist and hold the dressing in place.

e. Wrap the other tail in the opposite direction until the remainder of the dressing is covered. The tails should seal the sides of the dressing to keep foreign material from getting under it.

f. Tie the tails into a nonslip knot over the outer edge of the dressing. DO NOT TIE THE KNOT OVER THE WOUND. To allow the blood to flow to the rest of the injured limb, tie the dressing firmly enough to insert two fingers between the knot and the dressing (figure 5-18).

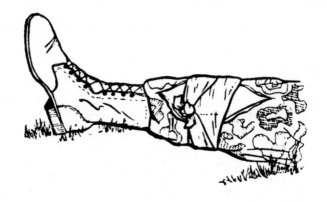

Fig 5-18.    Tails tied into a nonslip knot.

2.    Manual Pressure. If bleeding continues after applying the sterile field dressing, direct manual pressure may be used to help control the bleeding. Apply such pressure by placing the hand on the dressing and exerting firm pressure for 5 to 10 minutes. The casualty may be asked to do this for himself if he is conscious and can follow instructions. Elevate the injured limb 2 to 4 inches above the level of the heart to reduce the bleeding, but do not elevate a suspected fractured limb unless it has been properly splinted. If the bleeding stops, check, and treat for shock. If the bleeding continues, apply a pressure dressing.

3. **Application of a Pressure Dressing.** If additional pressure is required to stop the bleeding, apply a pressure dressing on top of the field dressing.

a. Place a wad of padding on top of the field dressing, directly over the wound.

b. Place an improvised dressing over the wad of padding. Wrap the ends tightly around the injured limb, covering the previously placed field dressing.

c. Tie the ends together in a nonslip knot, directly over the wound site (figure 5-19). The pressure dressing should be tight enough so that only the tip of one finger can be inserted between the dressing and the knot. DO NOT tie the dressing so tightly as to cause a tourniquet-like effect. Check and treat for shock when the bleeding stops. If bleeding continues and all other measures have failed, or if the limb is severed, apply a tourniquet and treat the casualty for shock.

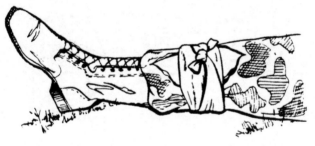

Fig 5-19.    Pressure dressing tied in a nonslip knot.

4. **Application of a Tourniquet.** A tourniquet is a constricting band placed around a limb to stop severe bleeding. The tourniquet should not be used unless a pressure dressing has failed to stop the bleeding, or an arm or leg has been severed. Once a tourniquet has been applied, inspect it and the dressing frequently to see if the tourniquet has slipped and if any sign of further bleeding is present. If necessary, tighten the tourniquet, but under no circumstances loosen it. It should only be loosened by medical personnel.

a. Improvising a tourniquet. In the absence of a specially designed tourniquet, a tourniquet may be made from a strong, pliable material, such as gauze or muslin bandage, clothing, web belts, or kerchiefs. An improvised tourniquet is used with a rigid stick-like object. To minimize skin damage, ensure that the improvised tourniquet is sufficiently wide (at least 2 inches) to remain at least 1 inch wide after tightening.

b. Placing the improvised tourniquet

    (1)   Place the tourniquet around the limb and between the wound and the heart. Place the tourniquet 2 to 4 inches above the wound. Never place it directly over a wound or fracture. For wounds just below a joint, place the tourniquet just above the joint.

    (2)   When possible, place the tourniquet over the smoothed sleeve or trouser leg to prevent skin from being pinched or twisted. Protection of the skin also reduces pain.

c. Applying the tourniquet

    (1)   Tie a half knot. Place a stick or similar rigid object on top of the half knot (figure 5-20).

Fig 5-20.   Rigid object on top of the half knot.

(2) Complete a full knot over the stick.

(3) Twist the stick (figure 5-21) until the tourniquet is tight around the limb and/or the bright red bleeding has stopped. In the case of amputation, dark oozing blood may continue for a short time. This is the blood trapped in the area between the wound and the tourniquet.

Fig 5-21.   Twisting the stick.

(4) Fasten the tourniquet to the limb by looping the free ends over the ends of the stick, bringing the ends around the limb to prevent the stick from loosening, and tying them together under the limb (figure 5-22).

Fig 5-22.   Free ends looped and tied.

(5)   DO NOT cover the tourniquet—leave it in full view. If the limb is missing (total amputation), apply a dressing to the stump.

(6)   Mark the casualty's forehead, if possible, with a "T" to indicate that a tourniquet has been applied. If necessary, use the casualty's blood to make this mark.

(7)   Check and treat for shock. Seek medical aid.

CAUTION: Do not loosen or release the tourniquet once it has been applied because it could enhance the probability of shock.

5.   Splinting Fractures. Fractures may be described as being either closed or open. A closed fracture is a broken bone that does not break the overlying skin. For splinting, dislocations and sprains should be treated as closed fractures. Open fractures are those in which the broken bone has pierced the overlying skin. The bone itself may break the skin, or a missile or shell fragment may go through the flesh and break the bone.

a. Immobilization.   A body part that contains a fracture must be immobilized to prevent the razor-sharp edges of the bone from moving and cutting tissue, muscles, blood vessels, and nerves. Immobilization is accomplished by splinting (figures 5-23 through 5-26).

b. Rules for splinting.   If the fracture is an open one, first stop the bleeding, apply a dressing, and bandage as you would for any other wound.

(1)   Apply the proven principle, "Splint them where they lie." This means to splint the fractured part before any movement of the casualty is attempted and without any change in the position of the fractured part. If a bone is in an unnatural position or a joint is bent, do not try to straighten it. If a joint is not bent, do not try to bend it. After a fractured part has been splinted, place the casualty on a litter before transporting him.

(2) If circumstances make it necessary to move a casualty with a fractured leg before a splint can be applied, use the uninjured leg as a splint by tying the fractured leg to the leg which serves as a splint. Then grasp the casualty beneath his armpits and pull him in a straight line, ensuring that the victim does not roll or move sideways.

(3) Apply splints so that the joint above the fracture and joint below the fracture are immobilized. Place a splint on each side of the wound.

(4) Use padding between the injured part and the splint to prevent undue pressure and further injury to tissue, muscles, blood vessels, and nerves. This is especially important at the crotch, in the armpit, and on places where the splints come in contact with bony parts, such as the elbow, wrist, knee, and ankle joint.

(5) Bind splints securely with bandages at several points above and below the fracture, but do not bind tightly enough to interfere with the flow of blood. Tie bandages with a nonslip knot and put the knot on the outer splint.

(6) Support a splinted arm which is bent at the elbow with a sling. A sling is also used to support a sprained arm or an arm with a painful wound.

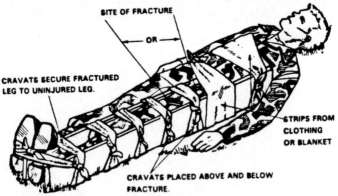

SITE OF FRACTURE

OR

CRAVATS SECURE FRACTURED LEG TO UNINJURED LEG.

STRIPS FROM CLOTHING OR BLANKET

CRAVATS PLACED ABOVE AND BELOW FRACTURE.

Fig 5-23.    Board splints applied to fractured hip or thigh.

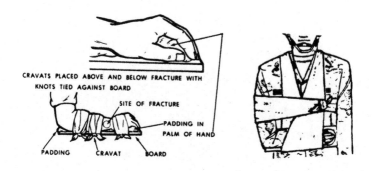

CRAVATS PLACED ABOVE AND BELOW FRACTURE WITH
KNOTS TIED AGAINST BOARD

SITE OF FRACTURE

PADDING IN
PALM OF HAND

PADDING    CRAVAT    BOARD

Fig 5-24.    Board splint of wrist and hand.

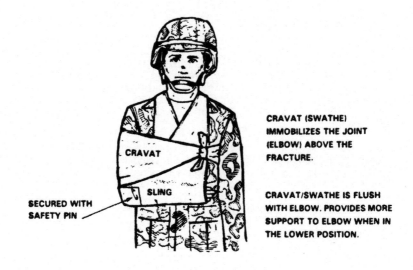

CRAVAT (SWATHE)
IMMOBILIZES THE JOINT
(ELBOW) ABOVE THE
FRACTURE.

CRAVAT

SLING

SECURED WITH
SAFETY PIN

CRAVAT/SWATHE IS FLUSH
WITH ELBOW. PROVIDES MORE
SUPPORT TO ELBOW WHEN IN
THE LOWER POSITION.

Fig 5-25.    Chest wall used as splint.

5-29

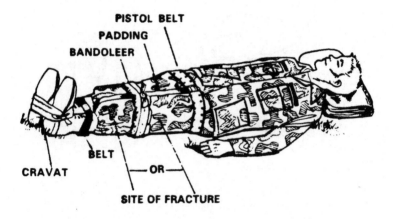

PISTOL BELT

PADDING

BANDOLEER

BELT

CRAVAT

— OR —

SITE OF FRACTURE

Fig 5-26.    Uninjured leg used as splint.

## D. TREAT FOR SHOCK

Shock may result from any type of injury. The more severe the injury, the more likely shock will develop. It is usually the result of significant loss of blood, heart failure, dehydration, severe and painful blows to the body, severe burns or wounds, or allergic reaction to drugs, food, or bites. Shock stuns and weakens the body. When the normal blood flow in the body is upset, death can result. Early identification and treatment may save a casualty's life.

1.    Signs/Symptoms. The early signs of shock are restlessness, thirst, paleness of the skin, and a rapid heartbeat. a casualty in shock may be excited, or he may be calm and appear very tired. He may be sweating even though his skin feels cool and clammy. As shock becomes worse, the casualty breathes in shallow, fast breaths or gasps even when his airway is clear. He may stare vacantly into space. His skin may have a blotchy or bluish appearance, especially around the mouth and lips. There may be nausea and/or vomiting.

2.    Treatment. In the field, the procedures to treat shock are identical to the procedures that would be performed to prevent shock. When treating a casualty, assume that shock is present or will occur shortly. By waiting until the actual signs/symptoms of shock are noticeable, you may jeopardize the casualty's life.

a. Position the casualty. Move the casualty to cover if it is available and the situation permits. The position in which the casualty should be placed varies, depending upon the type of wound or injury and whether the casualty is conscious or unconscious. Unless the casualty has an injury for which a special position is prescribed, gently place him on a blanket or another suitable protective item in one of the following positions:

(1) If the casualty is conscious, place him on his back on a level surface with his lower extremities elevated 6 to 8 inches to increase the flow of blood to his heart. This may be accomplished by placing his pack or another suitable object under his feet. Remember, however, do not move a casualty who has a fracture until it has been properly splinted.

(2) A casualty in shock after suffering a heart attack, chest wound, or breathing difficulty, may breathe easier in a sitting position. If this is the case, allow him to sit upright; but monitor carefully in case his condition worsens.

(3) If the casualty is unconscious, place him with his head turned to one side to prevent his choking on vomitus, blood, or other fluid.

b. Maintain adequate respiration. To maintain adequate respiration, you may need to do nothing more than clear the casualty's upper airway, position him to ensure adequate drainage of any fluid obstructing his airway, and observe him to ensure that his airway remains unobstructed. If you need to administer artificial respiration—do so.

c. Control bleeding. Control bleeding by application of pressure dressings, by elevation of specific limbs, and by use of pressure points as appropriate. Apply a tourniquet if necessary.

d. Loosen constrictive clothing. Loosen clothing at the neck and waist and at other areas which tend to bind the casualty. Loosen, but do not remove boots.

e. Reassure the casualty. Take charge. Show the casualty by your calm self-confidence and gentle yet firm manner that you know what you are doing. Initiate conversation and reassure him. Avoid talking to the casualty about his injuries. *Remember,* ill-timed or erroneous information can increase the casualty's anxiety.

f. Splint fractures. If the casualty has a fracture, apply a splint.

g. Keep the casualty comfortably warm without overheating. If possible, place a blanket, a poncho, a shelter half, or other suitable material under him. He may not need a blanket over him, depending upon the weather. Weather will dictate if the victim should be covered.

h. Do not give the casualty any food or drink.

## E. TRANSPORTATION OF SICK OR WOUNDED

Knowing how to transport a seriously injured person is one of the most important parts of first aid. Careless or rough handling may increase the seriousness of his injury and increase the likelihood of death. Unless there is good reason for transporting a casualty, do not do so until some means of medical evacuation is provided. In the event that no medical facilities are available, you will have to transport the casualty yourself. The casualty should receive appropriate first aid before he is moved. If he has a broken bone, do not transport him until you splint or immobilize the part. A litter should be used whenever possible. If the casualty has a fractured back or neck, special precautions must be taken prior to moving him with a litter.

1. Improvised Litters (Figures 5-27 through 5-29)

a. A litter can be improvised from many different things. Most flat-surface objects of suitable size can be used as litters. Such objects include boards, doors, cots, and poles tied together. If possible, these objects should be padded.

b. Satisfactory litters can also be made by securing poles inside such items as blankets, ponchos, shelter halves, jackets, or shirts. Poles can be improvised from strong branches, tent supports, skis, and other like items.

c. If no poles can be obtained, a large item such as a blanket can be rolled from both sides toward the center. The rolls then can be used to obtain a firm grip when carrying the casualty. If a poncho is used, make sure the hood is up and under the casualty and is not dragging on the ground.

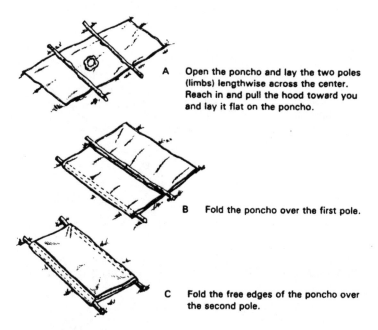

A   Open the poncho and lay the two poles (limbs) lengthwise across the center. Reach in and pull the hood toward you and lay it flat on the poncho.

B   Fold the poncho over the first pole.

C   Fold the free edges of the poncho over the second pole.

Fig 5-27.   Improvised litter with poncho and poles.

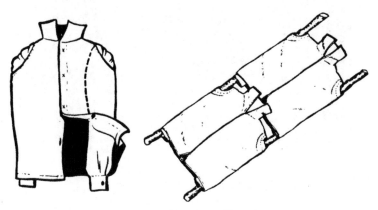

Fig 5-28.   Litter made with poles and jackets.

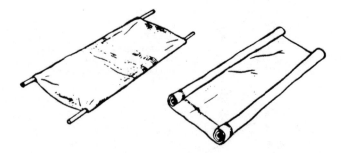

Fig 5-29.   Litters made with poles/sacks and by rolling blanket.

**2. Manual Carries.** Manual carries are accomplished by one or two bearers. Whenever possible, use a two-man carry, but be prepared to transport a casualty by yourself. Certain carries cannot be used if the casualty has a fractured arm, neck, back, hip, or leg. Figure 5-30 illustrates various one-man carries. Use the carry that is least likely to aggravate the injury.

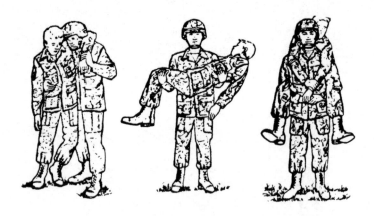

Fig 5-30.   One-man carries.

a. **Fireman's carry.** The fireman's carry is one of the easiest ways for one person to carry another. After an unconscious or disabled casualty has been properly positioned, he is raised from the ground. An alternate method for raising him from the ground is available, but it should only be used when you believe it to be safer for the casualty because of wound location. The steps for raising a casualty from the ground for the fireman's carry are also used in other one-man carries.

(1) Kneel at the casualty's uninjured side. Place one of your hands on the shoulder farthest from you and your other hand in the area of his hip or thigh.

(2) Roll him toward you onto his abdomen.

(3) After rolling the casualty onto his abdomen, straddle him; then extend your hands under his chest and lock them together (figure 5-31A).

(4) Lift the casualty to his knees as you move backward (figure 5-31B).

(5) Continue to move backward, thus straightening the casualty's legs and locking his knees (figure 5-31C).

(6) Walk forward, bringing the casualty to a standing position but tilted slightly backward to prevent his knees from buckling.

(7) As you maintain constant support of the casualty with your left arm, free your right arm, quickly grasp his right wrist, and raise his arm high. Instantly pass your head under his raised arm, releasing it as you pass under it (figure 5-31D).

(8) Move swiftly to face the casualty and secure your arms around his waist. Immediately place your right toe between his feet and spread them 6 to 8 inches apart.

(9) With your left arm, grasp the casualty's right wrist and raise his arm over your head (figure 5-31E).

(10) Bend at the waist and knees, then pull the casualty's arm over and down your left shoulder, thus bringing his body across your shoulders. At the same time, pass your right arm between his legs (figure 5-31F).

(11) Place the casualty's right wrist in your right hand and place your left hand on your left knee for support in rising (figure 5-31G).

(12) Rise with the casualty correctly positioned. Your left hand is free for use as needed (figure 5-31H).

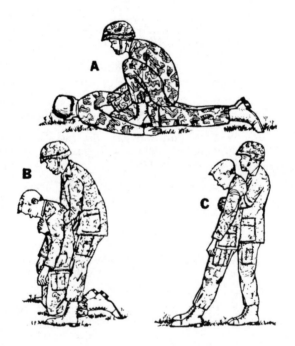

Fig 5-31. Fireman's carry.

Fig 5-31. Continued.

b. Alternate method of lifting for the fireman's carry.

(1) Kneel on one knee at the casualty's head, facing his feet, then extend your hands under his armpits, down his sides, and across his back (figure 5-32A).

(2) As you rise, lift the casualty to his knees; then secure a lower hold and raise him to a standing position with his knees locked (figure 5-32B).

(3) Secure your arms around the casualty's waist with his body tilted slightly backward to prevent his knees from buckling. Place your right toe between his feet and spread them 6 to 8 inches apart (figure 5-32C).

(4) Continue with the procedure for the fireman's carry as described above in subparagraph a(9).

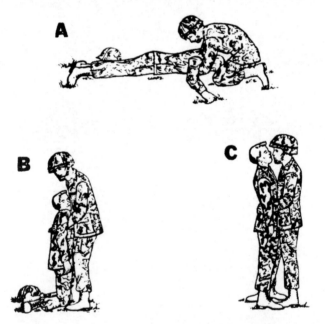

Fig 5-32.   Alternate method of lifting for the fireman's carry.

## Section II.   Special Injuries

Objectives:

*1.   Given a simulated casualty or dummy, demonstrate the procedures for treating a head injury.*
*2.   Given a simulated casualty or dummy, demonstrate the treatment of a sucking chest wound.*
*3.   Given a simulated casualty or dummy, demonstrate the treatment of an abdominal wound.*
*4.   Given a simulated casualty or dummy, demonstrate the treatment of burns.*
*5.   Given a simulated casualty or dummy, demonstrate the treatment for snake/insect/animal bites.*
*6.   Given a simulated casualty or dummy, demonstrate the prevention and treatment of foot injuries.*

## A. HEAD INJURIES

**1.   General.** A head injury may be isolated or it may contain multiple injuries. The damage can range from a minor cut on the scalp to a severe brain injury which rapidly causes death. Usually, serious skull fractures and brain injuries occur together; however, it is possible to receive a serious brain injury without a skull fracture. All severe head injuries are potentially life threatening. For recovery and return to normal function, casualties require proper first aid as a vital first step.

**2.   Symptoms.** A head injury may be open or closed. In open injuries, there is a visible wound and, at times, the brain may actually be seen. In closed injuries, no visible injury is seen; but the casualty may experience the same signs and symptoms. Either closed or open head injuries can be life threatening if the injury is severe enough. If you suspect a head injury, evaluate the casualty for the following:

a. Deformity of the head (abnormal pit or depression in the skull).

b. Blood or other fluid escaping from the scalp, ears, or nose.

c. Object penetrating or protruding from the head (e.g., glass, skull fragments, etc.) or exposed brain matter.

d. Nausea or vomiting, convulsions or twitches, confusion or slurred speech.

e. Current or recent unconsciousness (loss of consciousness).

3. **First Aid**. The casualty with a head injury (or suspected head injury) should be continually monitored for the development of conditions which may require the performance of basic lifesaving measures. For a head injury, apply the following measures:

a. Treat as a suspected neck/spinal injury until proven otherwise.

b. Place a dressing over the wound. DO NOT attempt to clean the wound.

c. Seek medical aid.

d. Keep the casualty warm.

e. DO NOT attempt to remove an impaled object from the head. In severe head injuries where brain tissue is protruding, leave the wound alone. Carefully place a first aid dressing over the tissue. DO NOT remove or disturb any foreign matter that may be in the wound. Position casualty so that his head is higher than his body.

f. DO NOT give the casualty anything to drink.

4. **Casualty Positioning**. The best position for a casualty with a simple head injury is with the head slightly elevated. DO NOT elevate the casualty's head if he is accumulating fluids in his throat. When there is bleeding from the mouth and throat, the casualty must be positioned on his side so that blood can drain out of the mouth and not down into the windpipe. If necessary, carefully position the casualty on his side opposite the site of injury to maintain an open airway (figure 5-33).

Fig 5-33.    Casualty on opposite side of injury.

**5. Convulsions.** Convulsions (seizures/involuntary jerking) may occur after a mild head injury. When the casualty is convulsing, protect him from hurting himself. Take the following measures:

a. Ease him to the ground and support his head and neck. Do not forcefully hold the arms and legs if they are jerking because this can lead to broken bones.

b. Maintain his airway and call for assistance. Do not force anything between the casualty's teeth—especially if they are tightly clenched because this may obstruct the casualty's airway.

c. Treat the casualty's wounds and evacuate him immediately.

**6. Dressings and Bandages.** When applying dressings, have the conscious casualty sit up unless other injuries are evident or he is unable to sit up under his own power. The casualty may also be positioned on his side with his face turned. In an unconscious casualty or one with a severe head injury, and where you strongly suspect a possible neck/spinal cord injury, immobilize the casualty and bandage in place. Figure 5-34 represents various methods of securing field dressings on casualties with head injuries.

Fig 5-34. Field dressings on head injuries.

## B. SUCKING CHEST WOUNDS

1. **General Symptoms.** Chest injuries may be caused by accidents, bullet or missile wounds, stab wounds, or falls. These injuries can be serious and may cause death quickly if proper treatment is not given. A sucking chest wound is caused by a puncture to the victim's chest wall. The sucking sound heard when he breathes is caused by air leading into his chest cavity. This particular type of wound is dangerous and will collapse the injured lung. Breathing becomes difficult for the casualty because the wound is open. A Marine's life may depend upon how quickly you make the wound airtight.

2. **First Aid**

      a.    Locate the open chest wound(s). Examine for both entry and exit wounds.

      b.    Expose the wound.

          (1)  If appropriate, cut or remove the casualty's clothing to expose the entire area of the wound.

(2) Do not remove clothing that is stuck to the wound because additional injury may result.

(3) Do not remove protective clothing in an NBC environment. Apply dressings over the protective clothing.

c. Open the casualty's field dressing plastic wrapper.

(1) Tear open one end of the plastic wrapper covering the field dressing and remove the inner packet (field dressing).

(2) Be careful not to destroy or touch the inside of the wrapper. The plastic wrapper will be used to create an airtight seal over the wound. Any airtight material may be used, such as cellophane wrappers or foil.

d. When the casualty exhales, place the inside surface of the plastic wrapper directly over the wound and hold it in place.

e. Apply the field dressing to the wound.

(1) Use your free hand and shake open the field dressing. Place the white side of the dressing directly over the plastic wrapper covering the open wound. Hold it securely in place to create an airtight dressing. If the casualty is able, he may assist. Use the casualty's field dressing, not your own.

(2) Have the casualty breath normally.

(3) Maintain pressure on the dressing while wrapping both tails around and under the body. Bring the tails around to the starting point (chest) where both can be grasped.

(4) While the casualty is exhaling, tie the tails into a nonslip knot over the center of the field dressing. The nonslip knot will create additional pressure on the wound, and also assist in creating an airtight seal (figure 5-35).

Fig 5-35. Nonslip knot over center of dressing.

       f.   Position the casualty in the prone position with his injured side toward the ground, or in a sitting position, whichever makes breathing easier.

       g.   Seek medical aid.

## C.  ABDOMINAL WOUND

   1.  General Symptoms. The most serious stomach wound is one in which an object penetrates the stomach wall and pierces internal organs or large blood vessels. In these instances, bleeding may be severe and death can occur rapidly.

   2.  First Aid

       a.   Position the casualty on his back with his knees up to prevent further exposure of the bowel/intestines. The knees-up position helps relieve pain and assists in the treatment of shock.

       b.   Expose the wound.

          (1)  Remove the casualty's loose clothing to expose the wound. However, do not attempt to remove clothing that is stuck to the wound; it may cause further injury.

(2) Do not remove protective clothing in a chemical environment. Apply the dressings over the protective clothing.

(3) Pick up any organs which may be on the ground. Do this with a clean, dry dressing or with the cleanest available material. Place the organs on top of the casualty's stomach (figure 5-36).

    o    Do not probe, clean, or try to remove any foreign object from the stomach.

    o    Do not touch any exposed organs with your bare hands.

    o    Do not push organs back inside the body.

Fig 5-36. Protruding organs placed near wound.

    c. Apply the field dressing. Use the casualty's field dressing, not your own. Improvised dressings may be made from clothing, blankets, or other available material because the field dressing may not be large enough for the entire wound. If this is the case, use the cleanest improvised dressing material available.

(1) Grasp the tails in both hands.

(2) Hold the dressing with the white side down directly over the wound.

(3) Place the dressing directly over the wound. If the casualty is able, he may hold the dressing in place.

(4) Hold the dressing in place with one hand and use the other hand to wrap one of the tails around the body.

(5) Wrap the other tail in the opposite direction until the dressing is completely covered.

(6) Tie the tails with a nonslip knot at the casualty's side.

(7) Tie the dressing firmly yet loosely enough to insert two fingers between the tie and the dressing.

(8) Field dressings should be covered with improvised reinforcement material (cravat, strips of torn T-shirt, or other cloth), if available, for support and additional protection. Tie the improvised bandage on the opposite side of the dressing ties. Keep the casualty in the knees-up position and evacuate him as soon as possible.

**NOTE:** Casualties with stomach wounds should not be given food or water (moistening the lips is allowed).

d. Seek medical aid.

## D. BURNS

1. General. Burns often cause extreme pain, scarring, or even death. Proper treatment will minimize further injury of the burned area. The four types of burns are thermal burns, which are caused by fire, hot objects, hot liquids, and gases of a nuclear blast or fire ball; electrical burns, which are caused by electrical wires, current, or lightning; chemical burns, which are caused by contact with wet or dry chemicals or white phosphorous (WP) from marking rounds and grenades; and laser burns.

2. First Aid

a. Remove the casualty from the source of the burn.

(1) Thermal burns. Remove the casualty quickly and cover the thermal burn with a field jacket or any large nonsynthetic material. Roll the casualty on the ground to smother the flames. If necessary, seek medical aid.

5-46

CAUTION: Synthetic materials will melt and cause further injury.

    (2) **Electrical burns.** Remove the casualty from the electrical source by using any nonconductive material. Do this by wrapping dry clothing or a dry rope around his back and shoulders. DO NOT make body-to-body contact with the casualty or touch any wires because you could also become a casualty. Turn off the electrical current, if the switch is nearby, but do not waste time looking for it. Seek medical aid as soon as possible.

    (3) **Chemical burns.** Remove the chemical from the burned casualty. Remove liquid chemicals by flushing with as much water as possible. Remove dry chemicals by brushing off loose particles (do not use the bare surface of your hand because you could become a casualty) and then flush with large amounts of water, if available. When burning phosphorous strikes the skin, smother the flame with water, a wet cloth, or wet mud. Seek medical aid as soon as possible.

    (4) **Laser burn.** Remove the laser burn casualty from the source. Seek medical aid as soon as possible.

    b. **Evaluate the casualty.** The casualty should be evaluated for conditions requiring basic lifesaving measures: clearing the airway, rescue breathing, CPR, shock, and/or bleeding.

    c. **Treat the burns.**

    (1) Expose the burn. Cut and gently lift away any clothing covering the burned area, without pulling clothing over the burns. Leave in place any clothing that is stuck to the burns.

    (2) Do not lift or cut away clothing if in a chemical environment. Remember, blisters are burns. Do not attempt to decontaminate skin where blisters have formed.

d. Apply a field dressing.

   (1) Grasp the tails of the casualty's dressing in both hands.

   (2) Hold the dressing directly over the wound with the white (sterile) side down, pull the dressing open, and place it directly over the wound. If the casualty is able, he may hold the dressing in place.

   (3) Hold the dressing in place with one hand and use the other hand to wrap one of the tails around the body.

   (4) Wrap the other tail in the opposite direction until the dressing is completely covered.

   (5) Tie the tails into a knot over the outer edge of the dressing. The dressing should be tied firmly yet loosely enough to insert two fingers between the tie and the dressing.

**NOTE:** Use the cleanest improvised dressing material available if a field dressing is not available.

e, Take the following precautions:

   (1) DO NOT place a dressing over the face or genital area.

   (2) DO NOT break the blisters.

   (3) DO NOT apply grease or ointments to the burns.

   (4) For electrical burns, check for both an entry and exit burn from the passage of electricity through the body. Exit burns may appear on any area of the body despite location of entry burn.

   (5) If the casualty is conscious and not nauseated, give him small amounts of water.

f. Treat for shock.

g. Seek medical aid.

## E. SNAKEBITES

1. **General.** If a Marine should accidentally step on or otherwise disturb a snake, it will attempt to strike. If an individual is bitten by a snake, a basic rule is—**TREAT ALL SNAKEBITES AS POISONOUS.** A probability exists that all snakes may be potential carriers of tetanus (lockjaw). If you are bitten by any snake, whether poisonous or nonpoisonous, you should seek medical attention immediately. Poisonous snakes do not always inject venom when they bite or strike a person. If you are bitten, identify and/or kill the snake and take it along to the corpsman for inspection/identification. This information is valuable to medical personnel when treating snakebites.

2. **Types of Snakes**

    a. **Nonpoisonous snakes.** There are approximately 130 different varieties of nonpoisonous snakes in the United States; they have oval-shaped heads and round pupils. See characteristics of a nonpoisonous snakebite (figure 5-37).

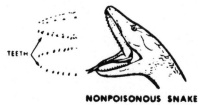

**NONPOISONOUS SNAKE**

Fig 5-37. Characteristics of nonpoisonous snakebites.

    b. **Poisonous snakes.** Poisonous snakes are found throughout the world, primarily in the tropical to moderate climates. Within the United States, there are four kinds: rattlesnakes, copperheads, water moccasins, and coral snakes. Poisonous snakes in other parts of the world include: the fer-de-lance, the bushmaster, and the tropical rattlesnake in tropical Central America; the Malayan pit viper in the tropical Far East; the cobra in Africa and Asia; the mamba (or black mamba) in Central and Southern Africa; and the krait in India and Southeast Asia.

(1)  Poison is injected from the venom sacs through grooved or hollow fangs. Depending on the species, these fangs can be either long or short. The pit viper, bushmaster, copperhead, fer-de-lance, moccasin, and rattlesnake all have long hollow fangs. These fangs are folded against the roof of the mouth and extend when striking. This allows them to strike quickly and then withdraw. Short, grooved fangs are found in the cobra, coral snake, krait, mamba, and sea snakes. These snakes are less effective in their attempts to bite, since they must chew after striking to inject enough venom (poison) to be effective. See characteristics of a poisonous snake bite (figure 5-38).

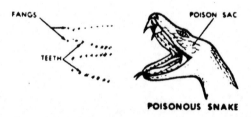

Fig 5-38. Characteristics of poisonous snakebites.

(2)  The venoms of different snakes cause different effects. Pit viper venoms (hemotoxins) destroy the tissues into which they are injected and also destroy blood cells. The cobra, rattler, and coral snakes inject powerful venoms (neurotoxins) which affect the central nervous system causing respiratory paralysis. Water moccasins and sea snakes have venom that is both hemotoxic and neurotoxic.

5-50

(3) Identifying poisonous snakes is very important because medical treatment will be different for each type of venom. Unless it can be positively identified, the snake should be killed and saved. If you can't kill the snake, then you must remember what it looks like so you can identify it. Be careful with your identification! Many venomous snakes resemble harmless varieties. When dealing with snakebites in foreign countries, seek advice, professional or otherwise, which may be useful in identifying species existing in that particular area of operations.

## 3. First Aid

a. The casualty should reach a medical treatment facility as soon as possible and with minimum movement.

b. Until evacuation or treatment is possible, the casualty should lie quietly and not move any more than necessary. If the casualty has been bitten on an extremity, do not elevate the limb; keep the extremity level with the body. Keep him comfortable and reassure him. (If the casualty is alone when bitten, it is better if he goes to the medical facility himself rather than wait for someone to find him.) Unless the snake has been positively identified, kill it and bring it with the casualty. Be sure that retrieving the snake does not endanger anyone or delay transporting the victim. All suspected snakebite victims should be evacuated to a medical facility.

c. If the bite is on an extremity, place a constricting band (narrow cravat (swathe) or narrow gauze bandage) above and below the bite (figure 5-39). If the bite is on the hand or foot, a single band is placed 1 to 2 inches above the wrist or foot. The band should be tight enough to stop the flow of blood near the skin, but not tight enough to stop the circulation. If no swelling is seen, place the bands about 1 inch from either side of the bite. If swelling is present, put the bands on the unswollen part at the edge of the swelling. If the swelling extends beyond the band, move the band to the new edge of the swelling. (If possible, leave the old band on, place a new one at the new edge of the swelling, and then remove and save the old one in case the process has to be repeated). If possible, place an ice bag on the area of the bite. DO NOT wrap the limb in ice or put ice directly on the skin. Cool the bite area—do not freeze it. Do not stop to look for ice, since it will delay evacuation and medical treatment.

d.     If the bite is located on an extremity, immobilize it at a level below the heart. DO NOT elevate an extremity even with or above the level of the heart.

**CAUTION:**     If a splint is used to immobilize the extremity, EXTREME care must be taken to insure that the splinting is done properly and does not bind. It will have to be watched closely and adjusted if any changes in swelling occur.

e.     When possible, clean the area of the bite with soap and water. DO NOT use ointments of any kind.

f.     NEVER give the victim food, alcohol, stimulants (coffee or tea), drugs, or tobacco.

g.     Remove rings, watches, or other jewelry from the affected limb.

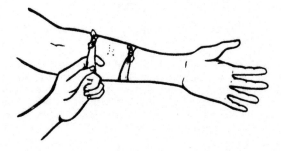

Fig 5-39. Constricting bands.

**NOTE:** DO NOT attempt to cut open the bite or suck out venom. If venom should seep through any damaged or lacerated tissues in the mouth, it could cause immediate unconsciousness and/or death.

## F. HUMAN AND OTHER ANIMAL BITES

Wounds may also be caused by human or other land animal bites. Such wounds are often torn, lacerated, or bruised. In addition to tissue damage, human or animal bites, whether domestic (dogs, cats) or wild (bats, raccoons, rats), always present the possibility of infection.

1. **Human Bites.** Human bites that break the skin may become seriously infected since the mouth is heavily contaminated with bacteria. All human bites MUST be treated by medical personnel.

2. **Animal Bites.** Land animal bites can result in both infection and disease. Tetanus, rabies, and various types of fevers can follow an untreated animal bite. Because of these possible complications, the animal causing the bite should, if possible, be captured or killed (without damaging the head). The animal will be observed and tested by competent authorities to determine if diseases were being carried.

3. Treatment

   a. Cleanse the wound thoroughly with soap or a detergent solution.

   b. Flush it well with water.

   c. Cover with a sterile dressing.

   d. Immobilize an injured extremity.

   e. Transport the victim to a medical treatment facility immediately.

   f. If unable to capture or kill the animal, provide medical personnel with any information possible that will help identify it. This will aid in appropriate treatment.

## G. INSECT BITES/STINGS

An insect bite or sting can cause great pain, disease, and inflammation. If not treated correctly, some bites/stings may cause serious illness or even death. When an allergic reaction is NOT involved, first aid is a simple process. In any case, medical personnel should examine the victim at the earliest possible time. It is important to properly identify the spider, bee, or other creature that caused the bite/sting, especially in cases of allergic reaction when death is a possibility.

5-53

1. **Types of Insects.** The insects found throughout the world that can produce a bite or sting are too numerous to mention in detail. The most commonly encountered insects are the brown recluse spider, black widow spider, tarantula, scorpion, urticating caterpillars, bees, wasps, centipedes, conenose beetles (kissing bug), ants, and wheel bugs. Upon being reassigned, especially to overseas areas, take the time to become acquainted with the types of insects that should be avoided in that area.

2. **Symptoms.** The following paragraphs discuss the most common effects of insect bites/stings. They can occur alone or in combination with the others.

   a. **Less serious.** Commonly seen signs/symptoms are pain, irritation, swelling, heat, redness, and itching. Hives or wheals (raised areas of the skin that itch) may occur. These are the least severe of the allergic reactions that commonly occur from insect bites/stings and usually are dangerous only if they affect the air passages which could interfere with breathing. The bites/stings of bees, wasps, ants, mosquitos, fleas, and ticks are usually not serious and normally produce mild and localized symptoms. A tarantula's bite is usually no worse than a bee sting. Scorpions are rare and their stings are painful but usually not dangerous.

   b. **Serious.** Emergency allergic or hypersensitive reactions sometimes result from the stings of bees, wasps, and ants. Many people are allergic to the venom of these particular insects. The bites/stings of these insects may produce more serious reactions, to include generalized itching and hives, weakness, anxiety, headache, breathing difficulties, nausea, vomiting, and diarrhea. Very serious allergic reactions (called anaphylactic shock) can lead to complete collapse, shock, and even death. Spider bites can also be very serious. The venom from the black widow spider affects the nervous system and can cause cramps, a rigid, nontender abdomen, breathing difficulties, sweating, nausea, and vomiting.

3. **Treatment.** There are certain principles that apply regardless of what caused the bite/sting.

   a. Wash area of bite/sting with soap and water. If only water is available, rinse off, but do not scrub.

b. Avoid scratching (except to remove the stinger), rubbing, or in any way irritating the area. In the process of rubbing or scratching, you may spread the toxin or introduce infection.

c. Watch for signs of allergic reaction and be prepared to perform CPR and treat for shock. In more serious reactions (severe and rapid swelling, allergic symptoms, and so forth) treat the bite/sting like you would treat a snakebite; that is, apply constricting bands above and below the site.

d. If the reaction is serious, attempt to capture the insect for positive identification, being careful not to become a victim yourself.

e. Keep the victim as calm and reassured as possible.

f. Since many of these injuries cause swelling, remove jewelry before the area swells. Ice, if available, may be used to reduce swelling, ease the pain, and slow the absorption of venom.

g. In extreme cases, transport the victim to the nearest medical treatment facility.

## H. FOOT CARE

1. General. Special attention should be paid by each Marine to the proper care of his feet. Foot problems can take you out of action almost as effectively as a bullet. Blisters, immersion foot, and fungal infection (athlete's foot) will be discussed in the following paragraphs.

2. Blisters. Blisters are caused by ill-fitting footwear, heat, moisture, and friction. Rubbing of the foot against the shoe over a period of time may result in this condition.

a. Symptoms

(1) Redness and soreness of the skin

(2) Puffiness in the sore area

(3) Fluid buildup under the skin

(4) Broken skin

5-55

b. **First Aid.** If blisters develop and medical personnel are not available, you should follow the steps listed below:

    (1)   Wash the blister area.

    (2)   Blisters should be dressed with an antiseptic, gauze pad, and tape. Puncturing blisters is discouraged since infection can easily become a very real and disabling factor.

c. **Preventive measures**

    (1)   Wear properly fitting boots and shoes.

    (2)   Wear properly fitting, clean socks.

    (3)   Keep feet clean and dry.

    (4)   Use foot powder.

3. **Immersion Foot.** Immersion foot and trench foot are injuries that result from fairly long exposure of the feet to wet conditions at temperatures from approximately $50^{o}$ to $32^{o}$F. Inactive feet in damp or wet socks and boots, or tightly laced boots impair circulation and are even more susceptible to injury. This injury can be very serious; it can lead to loss of toes or parts of the feet.

a. **Symptoms.** At first, the parts of the affected foot are cold and painless, the pulse is weak, and numbness may be present. Second, the parts feel hot, and burning and shooting pains begin as the parts are warmed. In the advanced stages (24 to 48 hours), the skin is pale with a bluish cast and the pulse decreases. Other signs/symptoms that may follow are blistering, swelling, redness, heat, bleeding, and gangrene.

b. **First aid**

    (1)   Gradually rewarm the injured part by exposure to air.

    (2)   DO NOT massage or moisten the skin.

    (3)   Protect the affected parts from trauma and secondary infection.

    (4)   Dry feet thoroughly; avoid walking.

    (5)   Seek medical treatment.

c. Preventive measures

(1) Socks and boots should be cleaned and dried at every opportunity.

(2) The feet should be dried as soon as possible after getting them wet. They may be warmed with the hands. Foot powder should be applied and dry socks put on.

(3) If it becomes necessary to wear wet boots and socks, the feet should be exercised continually by wiggling the toes and bending the ankles. Tight boots should never be worn.

4. Fungal Infection (athlete's foot). Fungal infection usually occurs between the toes and on the soles of the feet.

a. Symptoms

(1) Itchy feet

(2) Cracks in the skin between the toes

(3) Flaky patches of skin

b. First aid

(1) Apply foot powder daily.

(2) Apply fungicidal ointment.

(3) Seek medical aid if (1) and (2) fail to clear up the infection.

c. Preventive measures

(1) Clean and dry feet daily.

(2) Apply foot powder daily.

(3) Wear clean socks.

## Section III.    Climatic Injuries

Objectives:

*1.   Given a simulated casualty or dummy, demonstrate identification, treatment, and prevention of heat injuries.*
*2.   Given a simulated casualty or dummy, demonstrate identification, treatment, and prevention of cold injuries.*

### A. HEAT INJURIES

1.   **Heat Cramps.** Heat cramps are caused by not having enough available salt in the body.

      a. **Symptoms.** This condition causes muscle cramps in the arms and legs and/or stomach after prolonged exertion in hot weather. The casualty may have wet skin and extreme thirst.

      b.  Treatment

          (1)   Move the casualty to a shaded area or improvise shade.

          (2)   Loosen his clothing.

          (3)   Have him slowly drink at least one canteen full of water.

          (4)   Seek medical aid if cramps continue.

2.   **Heat Exhaustion.**   Heat exhaustion is caused by a loss of water through sweating without adequate fluid replacement.

a. **Symptoms.** The casualty experiences weakness or faintness; dizziness or drowsiness; cool, pale (or gray), moist (sweaty) skin; headaches; and loss of appetite. He may also sometimes experience heat cramps, nausea (urge to vomit) with or without vomiting, urge to defecate, chills (gooseflesh), rapid breathing (shortness of breath), confusion, or tingling of hands or feet.

b. **Treatment**

    (1)  Move the casualty to a shady area or improvise shade and have him lie down.

    (2)  Loosen or remove his clothing and boots unless in a chemical environment. Pour water on him and fan him if it is a very hot day.

    (3)  Elevate his legs.

    (4)  Have him slowly drink at least one canteen full of water.

    (5)  If possible, the casualty should not participate in strenuous activity for the remainder of the day.

    (6)  Monitor the casualty until the symptoms are gone, or if the symptoms persist, seek medical aid.

**3. Heatstroke.** This is a medical emergency and can be fatal if not treated promptly and correctly. It is caused by a failure of the body's cooling mechanisms. Inadequate sweating is a factor.

a. **Symptoms.** The casualty's skin is flushed, hot, and dry. He may experience dizziness, confusion, headaches, seizures, nausea, and his respiration and pulse may be rapid and weak. Unconsciousness and collapse may occur suddenly.

b. **Treatment.** Cool the casualty immediately by

    (1)  moving him into a shaded area.

    (2)  removing outer garments and/or protective clothing if the situation permits.

(3)  pouring water over him or immersing him in water and fanning him to permit a coolant effect of evaporation.

(4)  massaging his skin.

(5)  elevating his legs.

(6)  having him slowly drink water.

(7)  seeking medical aid because the casualty should be transported to a medical treatment facility as soon as possible.

CAUTION:  DO NOT delay evacuation in order to start cooling measures. The cooling measures should be done en route.

4. **Preventive Measures.** Prevention depends on availability and consumption of adequate amounts of water. The ideal fluid replacement is water. The availability of sufficient water during work or training in hot weather is very important as the body can lose more than one quart per hour through sweat. During these conditions, you should try to drink at least one full canteen of water each hour. Prevention also depends on proper clothing and appropriate activity levels. Acclimatization and protection from undue heat exposure are also very important. Instruction on living and working in hot climates also contributes toward prevention. Other conditions which may increase heat stress and cause heat injury include: infections, fever, recent illness or injury, overweight, dehydration, exertion, fatigue, heavy meals, and alcohol. Salt tablets *should not* be used as a preventive measure.

## B. COLD INJURIES

Cold injuries are most likely to occur when an unprepared individual is exposed to winter temperatures; however, they also can occur even with the proper planning. Cold injuries can usually be prevented. Marines must know the importance of personal hygiene, exercise, care of the feet and hands, and the use of protective clothing.

1. **General.** Once a Marine becomes familiar with the factors that contribute to cold injury, he must learn to recognize cold injury signs/symptoms.

a. Many Marines suffer cold injury without realizing what is happening to them. They may be cold and generally uncomfortable. These Marines often do not notice the injured part because it is already numb from the cold.

b. Superficial cold injury usually can be detected by numbness, tingling, or "pins and needles" sensations. These signs can often be relieved simply by loosening boots or other clothing and by exercising to improve circulation. In more serious cases involving deep cold injury, the Marine is often not aware that there is a problem until the affected part feels like a stump or block of wood.

c. Outward signs of cold injury include discoloration of the skin at the site if the injury. In light-skinned persons, the skin usually reddens, then becomes pale or waxy white. In dark-skinned persons, grayness in the skin is usually evident. An injured hand or foot feels cold to the touch. Swelling may be an indication of deep injury. Marines should work in pairs (buddy system) to check each other for signs/symptoms.

d. First aid for cold injuries depends upon whether they are superficial or deep. Cases of superficial cold injury can be treated adequately by warming the affected part using body heat. Deep cold injury (frostbite) is very serious and requires more aggressive first aid to avoid or minimize the loss of parts of the fingers, toes, hands, or feet.

2. Snow Blindness. Snow blindness is caused by glare on unprotected eyes from an ice field or a snowfield. It is more dangerous on cloudy or hazy days when Marines are less wary. Once you have had snow blindness you are more susceptible to further attacks.

a. Symptoms. Symptoms of snow blindness are a sensation of grit in the eyes with pain in and over the eyes, made worse by eyeball movement. Other signs/symptoms are watering, redness, headache, and increased pain on exposure to light. The same condition that causes snow blindness can cause sunburn of the skin, lips, and eyelids. If a snowburn is neglected, the result is the same as sunburn.

b. First aid. Cover the victim's eyes with a dark cloth to shut out all light. The victim should then be taken to a medical treatment facility.

c. Preventive measures

(1) Wear sunglasses when conditions warrant.

(2) Carry an extra pair of sunglasses in case of damage.

(3) Improvise eye coverings by cutting narrow slits in a small piece of cardboard, wood, leather, or cloth and tying it over the eyes.

**3. Frostbite.** Frostbite is the injury of tissue caused from exposure to freezing temperature. Frostbite can cause the loss of limbs or other serious, permanent injury. It is the most common cold injury. Frostbite may involve only the skin (superficial), or it may extend to a depth below the skin (deep).

**CAUTION:** If a frostbitten area of the body is thawed and then refrozen, the effects are more severe.

a. Symptoms. Frostbite starts with a sudden discoloration of the skin of the nose, ears, cheeks, fingers, or toes. This is followed by a tingling sensation for a short time. When the face, hands, or feet STOP hurting, look for signs of frostbite.

(1) Superficial frostbite primarily involves the skin and the tissue just beneath the skin. Some of the first signs of superficial frostbite are redness of skin in light-skinned individuals and grayish coloring of skin in dark-skinned individuals. This may be followed by blistering 24 to 36 hours after exposure and sloughing (casting off) of the superficial skin.

(2) Deep frostbite (freezing) is always preceded by superficial frostbite and involves freezing of the tissue below the skin, and possibly even muscle and bone. Unthawed, the skin is painless, pale-yellowish, and waxy looking. The frozen tissue may become swollen or wooden to the touch. Blisters appear within 12 to 36 hours after exposure unless rewarming is rapid and correctly done. Without proper treatment gangrene can occur.

b. First aid

(1)  Get the casualty into a heated shelter if possible. Seek shelter from the wind. Remove all items which constrict circulation without causing further injury to the frostbitten area.

(2)  The only safe way to warm a frostbite victim in the field is by body heat. Place frostbitten hands in the casualty's armpits and frostbitten feet on the stomach or between the thighs of another person. Warm frostbitten ears and face with bare hands.

(3)  A casualty with frostbitten feet should be treated as a litter case and should avoid walking if possible.

(4)  Reassure the casualty. Protect the affected area from further injury by covering it lightly with a blanket or any dry clothing.

(5)  Never rub or massage a frostbitten area. This may tear the frozen skin tissues and cause infection or gangrene.

(6)  Never rub any part of the body with ice or snow. Do not apply cold water to the affected part.

(7)  Never forcibly remove frozen shoes, mittens, or clothing. Thaw them first.

(8)  Never rewarm the frostbitten area by exposure to an open fire. Overheating can cause additional pain or injury.

(9)  Be prepared for pain when thawing occurs.

c. Preventive measures

(1)  Dress to protect yourself; wear sufficient clothing for protection against cold and wind. In high winds, take special precautions to protect your face.

(2)   Make every effort to keep your clothing and body dry. Avoid overdressing which causes excessive perspiration. Change your socks whenever your feet become moist either from perspiration or other sources.

(3)   In extremely low temperatures, be careful not to touch metal with your bare skin.

(4)   Exercise exposed parts of your body frequently. Exercise your fingers and toes from time to time to keep them warm and to detect numb or hard areas. Warm your face and ears from time to time with your hands for the same purpose.

(5)   Always use the buddy system. Watch your buddy's face to see if any frozen spots show, and have him watch yours. Thaw any frozen spots immediately, using bare hands or other sources of body heat.

(6)   Any interference with the circulation of your blood reduces the amount of heat delivered to your extremities. Wear properly fitted clothing and equipment. Tight-fitting socks, boots, and gloves are especially dangerous in very cold climates.

4. Hypothermia (severe chilling). Hypothermia is an unanticipated and deceiving injury resulting in a dangerous lowering of the entire body temperature. Hypothermia occurs when the individual loses body heat at a rate faster than it is produced.

a. Symptoms. As the body cools, there are several stages of progressive discomfort and impairment. A sign/symptom noticed immediately is shivering (the body's attempt to generate heat). The pulse is faint or difficult to detect. People with temperatures around 90° F may be drowsy, mentally slow, stiff, and uncoordinated, but they may be able to function minimally. As the body temperature drops further, shock becomes evident as the person's eyes assume a glassy state, breathing becomes slow and shallow, and the pulse becomes weaker or absent. The person becomes stiff and uncoordinated, and unconsciousness may follow quickly. As the body temperature drops even lower, the extremities freeze, and a core body temperature (below 85°F) increases the risk of irregular heart action.

b. **First aid.** Except in the most severe cases, the treatment of hypothermia is directed at rewarming the body evenly and without delay. Provide heat by using a hot water bottle, campfire, or other person's body heat.

(1)  Send for help as soon as possible.

(2)  Protect the casualty immediately with dry clothing or a sleeping bag, then move him to a warm place.

(3)  Warm liquids may be given gradually but must not be forced on an unconscious or semiconscious person.

(4)  The casualty should be transported on a litter because the exertion of walking may aggravate circulation problems.

(5)  Be alert for signs of shock and be prepared to start basic life support measures.

(6)  Seek medical treatment immediately.

(7)  Severe hypothermia. Treatment of a case of severe hypothermia is based upon the following principles:

o  Stabilize the temperature.
o  Attempt to avoid further heat loss.
o  Handle the casualty gently.
o  Evacuate as soon as possible.

c. **Preventive measures.** Prevention of hypothermia consists of all actions that will avoid rapid and uncontrollable loss of body heat. Marines should be properly equipped and properly dressed (as appropriate for conditions and exposure). Proper diet, sufficient rest, and general principles apply.

# Section IV.   Field Sanitation

Objectives:

*1.   On command without reference, state the measures for maintaining personal hygiene in a field environment.*
*2.   Given iodine tablets or calcium hypochlorite ampules, demonstrate the purification of water.*

## A. INDIVIDUAL WATER TREATMENT

When safe water is not available, each Marine must produce his own potable (drinkable) water by using his canteen and iodine purification tablets or calcium hypochlorite ampules.

1. **Iodine Tablets.** Drinking water should be drawn upstream from other activities as shown in figure 5-40. Iodine tablets should be used to purify water in a canteen as follows:

   a. Remove the cap from your canteen and fill the canteen with the cleanest water available.

   b. Put one tablet in clear water, or two tablets in very cold or cloudy water. Double the amounts if using a two-quart canteen.

   c. Replace the cap, wait 5 minutes, then shake the canteen. Loosen the cap and tip the canteen over to allow leakage around the canteen threads. Tighten the cap and wait an additional 25 minutes before drinking.

Fig 5-40.    Drawing water.

2.  Calcium Hypochlorite. The following procedure is used to purify water in a one-quart canteen with calcium hypochlorite ampules.

a. Fill the canteen with the cleanest, clearest water available, leaving airspace of an inch or more below the neck of the canteen.

b. Fill a canteen cup half full of water and add the calcium hypochlorite from one ampule, stirring with a clean stick until the powder is dissolved.

c. Fill the cap of a plastic canteen half full of the solution in the cup and add it to the water in the canteen, then place the cap on the canteen and shake it thoroughly.

d. Loosen the cap slightly and invert the canteen, letting the treated water leak onto the threads around the neck of the canteen.

e. Tighten the cap on the canteen and wait at least 30 minutes before using the water for drinking or cooking.

**3. Boiling of Water** This method is used when purification compounds are not available. It is a good method for killing disease producing organisms. However, it has several disadvantages: fuel is needed; it takes a long time for the water to boil and then cool; there is no residual protection against recontamination. Water must be held at a rolling boil for at least 15 seconds to make it safe for drinking.

## B. CLEANING INDIVIDUAL MESS GEAR

In the field, each Marine cares for his own mess gear. Proper washing is important; otherwise, food particles will create a breeding ground for germs.

**1. Equipment Required.** Four corrugated cans or other similar containers placed in a row are required for washing mess gear (figure 5-41). The first can is a scrap can used to dispose of waste products NOT eaten during the meal; the second can contains hot soapy water (150°F) with a long-handled brush; and the third and fourth cans contain clear water which is kept boiling (rolling boil) throughout the work period. Additional cans may be used for garbage and waste.

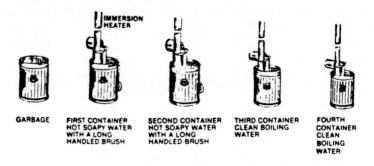

Fig 5-41.   Cleaning eating utensils.

## 2.  Procedures for Cleaning Mess Gear

a. Scrape the food particles from eating utensils into a garbage can.

b. Using the long-handled brush provided, wash the eating utensils in the first container of hot soapy water.

c. Immerse the eating utensils in the first container of clear boiling water for approximately 30 seconds.

d. Immerse the eating utensils in the second container of clear boiling water for approximately 30 seconds.

e. Shake the eating utensils to remove excess water. Check to ensure that the eating utensils are clean. If not, repeat the washing cycle above.

f. Allow to air-dry.

## C. WASTE DISPOSAL

The devices for disposing of human wastes in the field vary with the situation.

1.  Cat Hole. When Marines are on the march, each person uses a "cat hole" latrine during short halts (figure 5-42). It is dug approximately 1-foot deep and is completely covered and packed down after use.

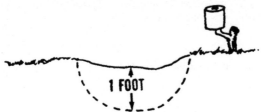

Fig 5-42.    Cat hole.

2. **Straddle Trench.** In a temporary bivouac of 1 to 3 days, the straddle trench is most likely to be used unless more permanent facilities are provided for a unit (figure 5-43). A straddle trench is dug 1 foot wide, 2-1/2 feet deep, and 4 feet long. The straddle trench should be located on the leeward (downwind) side of the camp, well away from the galley, and 50 to 100 yards away from the bivouac area. The number of trenches prepared should be sufficient to serve at least 8 percent of the unit strength at one time. The earth removed in digging is piled at the end of the trench along with a can or shovel so that each man can cover his waste after using the trench. This is continued until the unit leaves or the straddle trenches are filled to within 1 foot of the surface. Before breaking camp, all straddle trenches must be filled, mounded over, and marked with the date they were closed.

Fig 5-43. Straddle trench.

3. **Garbage and Rubbish Disposal.** Dispose of all garbage and rubbish in a temporary bivouac by burial.

---

For more information in this area, refer to:

1. FM 21-20                    Military Sanitation

2. FM 21-10                    Field Hygiene and Sanitation

3. FM 21-11                    First Aid for Soldiers

4. TEC Lesson Series 300       First Aid

# Chapter 6.   Uniform Clothing and Equipment

## Section I.  Marking and Displaying Clothing and Equipment

Objectives:

*1.  Given a list of uniform clothing, state where each article of uniform clothing is marked.*
*2.  Pass uniform clothing and equipment inspection.*

### A.  MARKING PROCEDURES

1.   **General.** Every article of uniform clothing in the possession of an enlisted Marine is required to be marked plainly and indelibly with the owner's name. When marking your uniforms, use name tapes or stamps, as appropriate. Use block letters not more than one-half inch in size. Size and location must be appropriate to the article of clothing and the space available for marking. Using sewn-on name tapes or embroidered name tags on the outside of the utility coat is prohibited. Mark your name in black letters on light colored material and in white letters on dark colored material. Make sure that the marks do not show when the uniform is worn. All items of organizational clothing must have name tags sewn in garmets. To standardize marking procedures and prevent variation, no elaboration of the following guide is authorized. Also, no greater precision in location may be prescribed.

If you obtain a uniform article that was previously owned by another Marine, block out the old owner's name and remark the article with your own, in accordance with these instructions. An appropriate entry must be made in your record book showing that you possess an article of clothing that has been remarked.

2. Location of Name of Articles (enlisted personnel).

a. Bag, duffel. On the outside of the bottom of the bag.

b. Belts (except trouser belts). On the underside, near the buckle end.

c. Belts, web, trouser. On one side only, as near the buckle end as possible.

d. Caps. Inside on the sweatband.

e. Coats. Inside the neckband.

f. Cover, cap. Inside the band.

g. Drawers. Immediately below the waistband, near the front.

h. Gloves. Inside at the wrist.

i. Handbag. On the space provided.

j. Havelock, plastic. On the underside of the sweatband.

k. Neckties. On the inside of the neckloop.

l. Necktabs. On the underside, near left end.

m. Shirts. Inside the neckband.

n. Trousers/skirts/slacks. Inside the waistband.

o. Shoes and boots. Inside near the top.

p. Scarf. Parallel to the width, near one end.

q. Socks. On the top of the foot.

r. Sweater. On the label, or on nametape sewn with olive green thread, inside back below neckband.

s. Undershirts. Inside the back near the neckband.

t. Liner, all-weather coat. Centered near the top.

## B. CLOTHING AND EQUIPMENT DISPLAYS

Clothing and equipment displays are the usual method of inspecting the number, marking, and condition of required items. Depending on the location of the unit and the types of facilities available, the commanding officer may have to prescribe displays that will vary from the suggested displays that follow. To promote uniformity throughout the Marine Corps, however, these illustrations should be used as the model displays whenever possible. A commander may require any combination of bunk and wall locker/wardrobe displays that is necessary to achieve his inspection purposes. (See figures 6-1 through 6-14.)

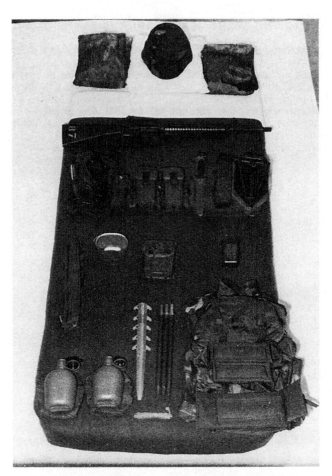

Fig 6-1. Field equipment and service rifle-bunk display.
(See footnotes 1 and 2 on page 6-18 and
11, 12, 13, and 14 on page 6-19.)

Fig 6-2. Field equipment and pistol-bunk display.
(See footnote 1 on page 6-18 and
11, 12, 13, and 14 on page 6-19.)

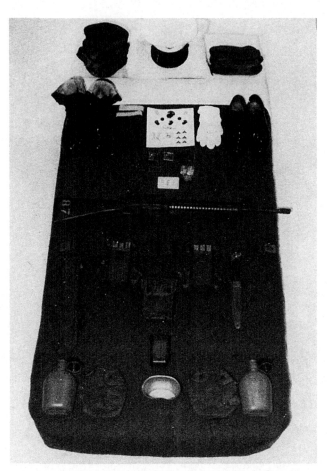

Fig 6-3. Garrison equipment and service rifle-bunk display.
(See footnotes 1, 2, 3, 4, and 5 on page 6-18.)

6-6

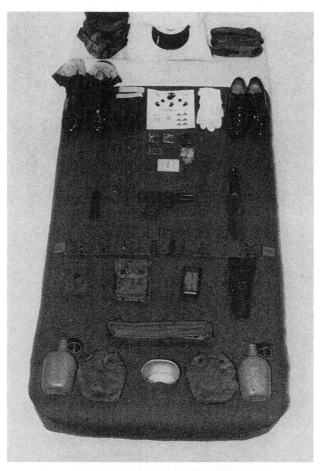

Fig 6-4.  Garrison equipment and pistol-bunk display.
(See footnotes 1, 2, 3, 4, and 5 on page 6-18.)

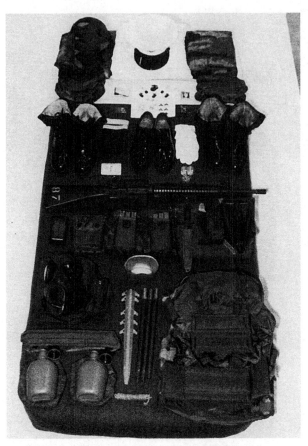

Fig 6-5. Field equipment, partial uniform clothing,
and service rifle-bunk display. (See footnotes
1, 2, 3, 4, and 5 on page 6-18 and
11, 12, 13, and 14 on page 6-19.)

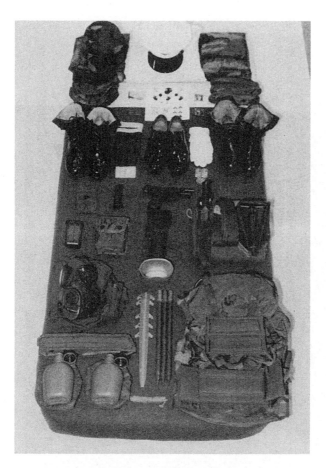

Fig 6-6. Field equipment, partial uniform clothing,
and pistol-bunk display. (See footnotes
1, 2, 3, 4, and 5 on page 6-18 and
11, 12, 13, and 14 on page 6-19.)

Fig 6-7. Uniform clothing-BEQ wardrobe display.
(See footnotes 3 and 6 on page 6-18.)

6-10

Fig 6-8. Field equipment and service rifle-field display.
(See footnotes 1, 2, and 8 on page 6-18
and 11, 15, and 16 on page 6-19.)

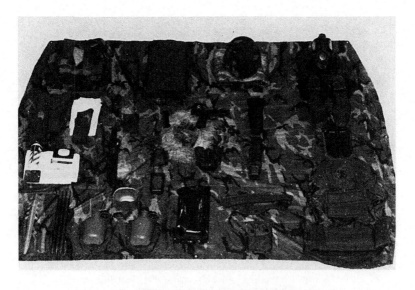

Fig 6-9. Field equipment and pistol-field display.
(See footnotes 1 and 8 on page 6-18 and
11, 15, and 16 on page 6-19.)

Fig 6-10.  Garrison equipment and service rifle-bunk display.
(See footnotes 1, 2, 3, 4, and 5 on page 6-18.)

6-13

Fig 6-11. Garrison equipment and pistol-bunk display.
(See footnotes 1, 2, 3, 4, and 5 on page 6-18.)

6-14

Fig 6-12. Field equipment, partial uniform clothing, and service rifle-bunk display. (See footnotes 1, 2, 3, 4, and 5 on page 6-18 and 11, 12, 13, and 14 on page 6-19.)

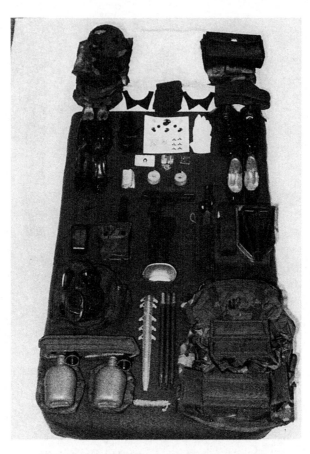

Fig 6-13. Field equipment, partial uniform clothing,
and pistol-bunk display. (See footnotes
1, 2, 3, 4, and 5 on page 6-18 and
11, 12, 13, and 14 on page 6-19.)

Fig 6-14. Uniform clothing-BEQ wardrobe display.
(See footnotes 3 and 10 on page 6-18.)

## FOOTNOTES

1.  Substitute or older items of equipment/clothing will be displayed in the approximate position of similar items shown.

2.  When extra rifle magazines are issued, they will be placed between magazine pouches, and the distance between pouches will be adjusted accordingly.

3.  All articles of uniform clothing possessed by an individual will be displayed regardless of current allowances. Items not displayed will be those worn by the individual at the time of the inspection and those accounted for by an itemized laundry, dry cleaning, tailor, or cobbler slip. Marking of uniform clothing is to be accomplished in accordance with the current edition of MCO P1020.34 (see section I of this chapter).

4.  Individuals required to wear a Medical Warning tag in accordance with the current edition of NAVMED instruction 6150.2 will display this tag next to their identification tags.

5.  This display is normally used with the display in figure 6-7.

6.  Trousers will be positioned together in the same right-to-left sequence as matching coats and shirts (e.g., all blue trousers, then all green service trousers, etc., right to left as the viewer faces the wall locker or wardrobe).

7.  The contents of the pack which are displayed are representative only. Commanders will designate specific contents and vary display accordingly.

8.  Organizational equipment such as those representative items shown (compass and binoculars) are to be positioned in the center of the display.

9.  This display is normally used with the display in figure 6-14.

10.  Skirts/slacks will be positioned immediately to the right of matching coats, e.g., all green service coats, then all green service skirts, etc., left to right as the viewer faces the wardrobe.

6-18

11. Camouflage flak jacket is located under the ALICE pack.

12. Poncho liner is located on top left corner of bunk.

13. Poncho is located on top right corner of bunk.

14. Shelter half is located under E-tool and cartridge belt.

15. Poncho liner is located under helmet.

16. Shelter half is located to left of helmet.

# Section II. Maintaining Uniforms and Equipment

Objective: *On command without reference, state procedures for maintenance of clothing and equipment.*

## A. MAINTAINING YOUR UNIFORM

1. General. After six months in the Marine Corps, you will accrue a clothing replacement allowance which is paid annually. It is to be used to replace unserviceable uniform clothing and to purchase newly adopted uniform clothing.

a. Proper care of your uniforms is important for maximum usage and proper appearance. When not using your uniforms, they should be hung neatly on appropriate hangers to preserve their shapes. Avoid crowding the articles together when hanging the uniforms on hangers. Wooden hangers are ideal for maintaining your uniform. If you store uniforms in a seabag or trunk, fold them carefully to preserve their shape. Also, note paragraph 7 below ("PREVENTING MOTH DAMAGE") when storing uniforms for a long time.

b. When wearing your uniform, avoid carrying long, bulky objects (e.g., key rings, wallets) in your pockets. Wear the appropriate uniform for the job or task that you are to perform.

2. Service Uniforms

a. The service uniform generally shows more wear at creased areas. This may be partially offset by periodically pressing out old creases and reforming them slightly to either side of the previous crease. Sleeve cuffs, trousers, slacks, and skirt hems should be examined periodically and turned if material permits.

b. Drycleaning preserves the original appearance and finish of wool and wool/polyester garments and is recommended over hand laundering. However, when drycleaning facilities are not available, and only as a last resort, wool and wool/polyester uniforms may be hand laundered using a neutral soap and fresh lukewarm water, $70^o$ to $80^o$. Thick suds are necessary for best results. To preserve the finish, rubbing should be held to a minimum. Thorough rinsing is necessary to remove all traces of the soap. After washing the garment, squeeze gently to remove water, shape garment by hand, and dry in open air. Colored garments should not be hung in the sun to dry. If this is unavoidable, turn the garments inside out. Never use chlorine bleaches on wool and wool/polyester materials.

3. Buttons and Insignia

a. Gold buttons should be cleaned with a weak solution of household ammonia and water. Do not use abrasives or polishing cloths containing chemicals. Gold-plated buttons that have had the plating removed are likely to turn green due to exposure to moist air. This can be removed by rubbing gently with acetic acid or any substance containing this acid, such as vinegar, followed by a thorough rinsing in fresh water and drying.

b. The gold filler parts and the sterling silver rhodium finish parts of metal insignia are cleaned by washing with soap and water. Avoid using silver polish or abrasive. Service insignia will not be polished. If continued use causes loss of the desired finish, the insignia will either be replaced or refinished with USMC approved liquid, black protective coating as sold through the Marine Corps exchange. The use of paints or other coloring agents are prohibited.

4. Footwear

a. Leather. Leather shoes and boots must be properly cared for to ensure optimum wear and to protect the feet. When shoes are not in use, the shape should be maintained by shoe trees. Footpowder should be sprinkled liberally inside shoes to absorb moisture. Shoes should be kept clean of sand, dirt, grit, and other substances that could produce a deteriorating action on shoe threads and shoe leather. Clean shoes perodically with saddle soap.

b. Synthetic leather shoes. For normal care, just wipe with a damp cloth or sponge. Regular shoe polish may be used to increase the shine. To cover abrasions or scuff marks, use a paste wax shoe polish. Stains should be wiped off as quickly as possible and then the shoes should be cleaned. For stubborn stains, try lighter fluid.

Do not use acetone, nail polish removers, chlorinated dry cleaning solvent, or alcohol. When in doubt about a cleaner or polish, try a little on the instep near the sole.

5. Laundering Web Belts. When belts are laundered, shrinkage is normal. To compensate for this, the belts are manufactured longer than the waist size. Belts should be washed at least three times before cutting to normal waist size. To prevent excessive shrinkage after laundering, hand stretch the belt while wet.

6. Repairing Cuts in Cloth. A tailor can repair a clean cut in a uniform by weaving the material.

7. Preventing Moth Damage. Frequent brushing and exposure to sunshine and fresh air will effectively prevent moths. If uniforms are to be put away for a long time and left undisturbed, they should be thoroughly cleaned and packed in an airtight plastic bag, or protected with camphor balls, cedar wood, or other commercial preparations.

8. Laundering of the Camouflage Utility Uniform. Washing instructions, to preclude a possible shrinkage problem of the camouflage pattern utility uniform, are as follows: During the washing, drying, and finishing cycle, use the lowest possible temperature setting so that at no time will the garment be exposed to temperatures greater than 130 degrees. Wear-life of the utility uniform is adversely affected by starch. Therefore, starching, "sizing," or otherwise artificially stiffening the utility uniform other than pressing is prohibited. Bleach will not be used on the utility uniform or on the green undershirt.

9. All-Weather Coat. The all-weather coat must be drycleaned only. A water repellency treatment should be applied after four or five drycleanings.

## B. MAINTAINING INDIVIDUAL EQUIPMENT

1. **General.** When equipment is entrusted to your custody by your unit, not only are you expected to account for each item, but you are responsible for properly maintaining each item. Proper maintenance of your equipment will prolong its wear and serviceability. The proper care of your equipment not only determines the success of the unit's mission, but also you and your fellow Marine's survival in combat.

2. **Canvas Equipment.** The following are representative items of canvas type equipment:

- o Bag, waterproof clothing
- o Cover, canteen
- o Cover, helmet
- o Pack, ALICE
- o Carrier, entrenching tool
- o Pouch, ammunition
- o Case, sleeping bag
- o Shelterhalf, tent
- o Vest, armor (armor, upper torso)
- o Carrier, protective mask

Clean canvas type items by dipping them vigorously in a pail of warm water containing a mild soap or detergent. This prolongs the life of the item and prevents discoloration.

If soiled spots remain after washing, scrub the spots with a white or colorfast cloth, using warm, soapy water or detergent solution. Do not use chlorine bleaches, wet stiff brushes, cleaning fluids, or dyes which will discolor the item. Dry canvas type items in a shaded area or indoors. Do not dry them in the sun because direct sunlight will discolor them.

> **NOTE:** Certain canvas type items, may be provided with fiberboard or plastic stiffeners. If so, clean these cases with a damp, soft brush and cool water only.

3. **Web Equipment.** The following are representative items of web equipment:

- o Belt, cartridge or pistol
- o Straps for helmet, helmet liner, pack, lanyards, suspenders, etc.

Clean web equipment the same way you clean canvas equipment. Do not use chlorine, cleaning fluids, or dyes. Rinse all soap carefully from web equipment after washing, and stretch the item back to its original shape while it dries. Dry equipment in a shaded area or indoors. Never use direct sunlight for drying. Do not launder or dry webbing in automatic laundry equipment.

4. **Coated Items.** The following are representative coated items:
   o Poncho
   o Pneumatic mattress
   o Protective mask

Wipe soiled, coated items with a clean cloth. Shampoo by hand with a soft-bristle brush using warm water and mild soap or synthetic detergent, and rinse thoroughly. Air dry the items. Do not machine wash, machine dry, or hot press iron coated items.

5. **Plastic Canteen and Metal Cup.** Your plastic (polyethylene) water canteen holds 1 quart. Wash the canteen and cup with warm, soapy water and rinse thoroughly. Keep them drained and dry when not in use. When required, replace the cap with the M-1 drinking device. This device allows you to drink water from the canteen while you are wearing a protective mask. Do not put the plastic canteen near an open flame or burner plate. The metal canteen cup should be scrubbed as soon as possible after use over an open flame or a hot plate to avoid discoloration of the metal.

6. **Kevlar Helmet.** The new Kevlar helmet, when combined with the camouflaged body armor, comprises the Personal Armor System; Ground Troops (PAS-GT). Kevlar is a tightly woven fiber material which offers increased ballistics protection over the steel helmet. It is a rigid, one-piece unit with a small visor that covers the front of the head and the temple region. It extends lower around the back to protect the ears and back of the head. The helmet contains a cradle suspension system with a buckle to adjust the headband and a velcro pull tab to make the drawstring height adjustment.

The chinstrap is a two-point suspension with an open chin cup having two adjustable buckles and a single pull-the-dot snap fastener on the left side. The helmet comes in four sizes, with four different weights: XS, 48oz; S, 49oz; M, 51oz; and L, 55oz. (The old steel helmet weighs 54oz). The camouflage cover comes in two sizes: Small, which fits XS and S helmets; and Large, which fits M and L helmets. Do not use the helmet as a shovel or hammer. Also, do not use it to heat water for cooking or hygiene purposes.

6-24

**NOTE:** It may require use of a small screwdriver and pliers to install the headband into the helmet.

7. **Sleeping Bag.** The sleeping bag requires special attention in cleaning. Do not dryclean the sleeping bag because the cleaning fluids will cause toxic fumes to linger within the bag. Consult your unit supply department for professional cleaning.

8. **Blankets, Field Jacket and Liner, Poncho Liner.** Wash frequently with lukewarm water and mild soap. Do not use hot or boiling water. Drying these items in intense heat will reduce the water repellent quality. Stretch each item back into shape while it is drying.

9. **All-Purpose Lightweight Individual Carrying Equipment (ALICE) Pack..** As a load carrying system the ALICE pack consists of a water-resistant, lightweight nylon material for quick drying, wide padded shoulder straps, and a lightweight metal pack frame. There are three easy access pockets on the outside of the pack for gear that is needed more frequently. Inside the pack is a pocket that will carry and conceal the field radio. The pack also has quick release straps that enable it to be separated from the normal fighting load which is suspended from the belt. The pack may be worn with or without the pack frame.

## C. MINIMUM REQUIREMENTS LIST-ISSUE

Each enlisted Marine receives a basic issue of uniform clothing under the "Clothing Monetary Allowance System." This system provides the initial issue made to you and a clothing replacement allowance. You are required to maintain, at a minimum, each article contained in your minimum requirements list; properly altered, serviceable, and ready for inspection at all times.

To properly maintain your clothing ready for inspection, make necessary repairs, and purchase replacement articles. You must know each item and its quantity contained in your minimum requirements list. Tables 6-1 and 6-2 list those items and quantities contained in the minimum requirements list from MCBul 10120.

Table 6-1. Minimum requirements list, men's.

| Quantity | Article |
|---|---|
| 1 | BAG, DUFFEL: w/carrying strap |
| 2 | BELT, TROUSERS: web, khaki |
| 2 | BUCKLE: f/belt, web, khaki |
| 1 | BUCKLE: f/belt (coat) |
| 1 | CAP, GARRISON: wool, serge, green |
| 2 | CAP, GARRISON: polyester/wool, green |
| 3 1/ | CAP, COMBAT: woodland camouflage pattern |
| 1 | CLASP, NECKTIE |
| 1 2/ | COAT, MAN'S: all-weather |
| 1 | COAT, MAN'S: wool, serge, green, w/belt |
| 1 | COAT, MAN'S: polyester/wool, green, w/belt |
| 4 1/ | COAT, COMBAT: woodland camouflage pattern, w/"USMC" insignia |
| 6 | DRAWERS, MAN'S: cotton, white, pair |
| 1 | GLOVES, LEATHER: black, pair |
| 1 | INSIGNIA, BRANCH OF SERVICE: collar, black, pair |
| 1 | INSIGNIA, BRANCH OF SERVICE: collar, black, left |
| 2 | NECKTIE: khaki |
| 1 | SCARF, NECKWEAR: wool, green |
| 3 | SHIRT, MAN'S: polyester/cotton, khaki, long-sleeve |
| 3 | SHIRT, MAN'S: polyester/cotton, khaki, quarter-length sleeve |
| 3 3/ | SHOE, DRESS/BOOT, COMBAT: leather, black, pair |
| 4 | SOCKS, MAN'S: black, pair |
| 4 | SOCKS, MAN'S: green, w/cushion sole, pair |
| 1 4/ | SWEATER: pull-over, olive green |
| 2 | TROUSERS, MAN'S: wool, serge, green, pair |
| 2 | TROUSERS, MAN'S: polyester/wool, green, pair |
| 4 1/ | TROUSERS, COMBAT: woodland camouflage pattern, pair |
| 3 | /UNDERSHIRT, MAN'S: cotton, white, V-neck |
| 3 | UNDERSHIRT: cotton, olive green, crew neck |

1/      The poplin camouflage cap, coat, and trousers may be used to satisfy the requirements for these items until replacement is required.

2/      The overcoat, man's, wool, green; and raincoat, man's, nylon, rubber-coated, may be used to satisfy the requirement for this item until replacement is required or 1 December 1986, whichever is earlier.

3/ Personnel assigned to the following categories of units are required to have in their possession footwear as indicated, except that personnel who are transferred between categories of units will be permitted to wear the footwear in their possession at the time of reporting until replacement is required. During this period, the types of footwear in the individual's possession will be considered as acceptable substitutes for those required for the category of the unit joined. At such time as an individual is required to purchase replacement footwear, it will be of the type appropriate to the category of the unit in which the individual is serving or to which the individual will be transferred. A further exception is that, after the expiration of 4 months from the date of reporting to a Fleet Marine Force (FMF) ground unit, activity commanders will require personnel to have in their possession footwear as indicated for the FMF ground units.

    a. FMF Ground Units

        2  BOOT, COMBAT: leather, black, pair
        1  SHOE, DRESS: black, pair

    b. Aviation Units (FMF and Non-FMF)

        2  BOOT, COMBAT: leather, black, pair
        1  SHOE, DRESS: black, pair

    c. Non-FMF Ground Units

        1  BOOT, COMBAT: leather, black, pair
        1  SHOE, DRESS: black, pair

AND

    d. Inspector-Instructor (I-I) Staff Personnel

        1  BOOT, COMBAT: leather, black, pair
        2  SHOE, DRESS: black, pair

4/ The mandatory possession date for this item is 1 October 1986.

Table 6-2. Minimum requirements list, women's.

| Quantity | Article |
|---|---|
| 1 | BAG, DUFFEL: w/carrying strap |
| 2 | BELT, TROUSERS: web, khaki |
| 1 | BOOT, COMBAT: leather, black, pair |
| 1 | BUCKLE: f/belt, web |
| 1 | CAP, GARRISON, WOMAN'S: polyester/wool, green |
| 1 | CAP, GARRISON, WOMAN'S: wool, serge, green |
| 1 | CAP, SERVICE: wool, serge, green |
| 2 1/ | CAP, COMBAT: woodland camouflage pattern |
| 3 1/ | COAT, COMBAT: woodland camouflage pattern, w/"USMC" insignia |
| 1 2/ | COAT, WOMAN'S: all-weather |
| 1 | COAT, WOMAN'S: polyester/wool, green |
| 1 | COAT, WOMAN'S: wool, serge, green |
| 1 3/ | GLOVES, LEATHER: black, pair |
| 1 | HANDBAG, WOMAN'S: black |
| 1 | HAVELOCK: plastic |
| 1 | INSIGNIA, BRANCH OF SERVICE: collar, black, left |
| 1 | INSIGNIA, BRANCH OF SERVICE: black (cap, screwpost) |
| 1 | INSIGNIA, BRANCH OF SERVICE: collar, black, pair |
| 2 | NECK TAB: green |
| 1 | SCARF, NECKWEAR: wool, green |
| 3 | SHIRT, WOMAN'S: polyester/cotton, khaki, long-sleeve |
| 3 | SHIRT, WOMAN'S: polyester/cotton, khaki, short-sleeve |
| 1 | SHOE, DRESS: oxford, black, pair |
| 1 | SHOE, DRESS: pump, black, pair |
| 2 | SKIRT, WOMAN'S: polyester/wool, green |
| 2 | SKIRT, WOMAN'S: wool, serge, green |
| 1 | SLACKS, WOMAN'S: polyester/wool, green |
| 1 | SLACKS, WOMAN'S: wool, serge, green |
| 4 | SOCKS: green, w/cushion sole, pair |
| 1 4/ | SWEATER: pull-over, olive green |
| 3 1/ | TROUSERS, COMBAT: woodland camouflage pattern, pair |
| 3 | UNDERSHIRT: cotton, olive green, crew neck |

1/ The poplin camouflage cap, coat, and trousers may be used to satisfy the requirements for these items until replacement is required.

6-28

2/    The overcoat, woman's, wool, serge, green; and raincoat, woman's, green, may be used to satisfy the requirement for this item until replacement is required or 1 December 1986, whichever is earlier.

3/    The black cloth gloves may be used to satisfy the requirement for this item until replacement is required.

4/    The mandatory possession date for this item is 1 October 1986.

Additional information and updates on minimum requirements list can be found in MCBul 10120.

# Section III. Wearing Uniforms and Equipment

Objective:   *Wear uniform as per current regulations.*

## A. WEARING THE UNIFORM (MEN)

1.   **Long-Sleeve Shirt Cuff.** The long sleeve shirt shall cover the wrist bone and extend to a point 2 inches above the second joint from the end of the thumb. A tolerance of 1/2 inch, plus or minus is acceptable.

2.   **Trouser Length and Hem.** The trousers will be long enough to break slightly over the shoe in front and to reach the junction of the welt of the shoe in the rear. A variation of 1/4 inch above or below the top of the heel is acceptable. Trousers should be finished with a hem from 2 inches to 3 inches.

3.   **Trouser Fit.** Trousers shall be of sufficient looseness around the hips and buttocks to prevent gapping of the pockets and visible horizontal wrinkles across the fly front or coat flap. The fly of the trousers shall hang in a vertical line without gapping when unzipped. The proper position for fitting of all trousers is by placing the bottom of the waistband atop the hipbone, plus or minus 1/2 inch in the direction that the individual would normally wear his trouser.

> **NOTE:** The tip end of the web belt will pass through the buckle to the wearer's left and will extend from 2 to 4 inches beyond the buckle. The right edge of the buckle is on line with the edge of the fly front.

4.   **Green Service Coat.** The left side of the front closure should overlap the right side between 3 and 4 inches. The coat sleeve will extend to a point 1-inch above the second joint from the end of the thumb, plus or minus 1/4 inch and cover the shirt cuff. The tip end of the green belt will extend from 2 3/4 inches to 3 3/4 inches past the buckle.

5.   Green Service Sweater.

a. The sweater may be worn with the service uniform with either the long- or quarter-length sleeve shirt (whichever is prescribed/authorized as the seasonal uniform shirt). When the sweater is worn, the shirt collar will be worn outside the sweater, without the necktie, and the collar button will be unbuttoned. The sleeves of the sweater may be turned up; however, the sleeves should cover the shirt cuff. The waistband of the sweater may be turned up; however, it should cover the belt.

b. When the sweater is worn with the camouflage utility uniform, it will be worn underneath the camouflage utility coat.

c. The sweater is authorized for wear with civilian clothing.

6.   Service Stripes. Each service stripe represents 4 years of honorable service, creditable for retirement. The stripes are worn on the dress and service coats.

7.   Garrison Cap. Garrison caps will be worn centered squarely, or slightly tilted to the right, with the top unbroken, and the base of the sweatband about 1 inch above the eyebrows.

8.   Service/Dress Cap. The service/dress cap will fit snugly and comfortably around the largest part of the head. The lower band of the frame will rest high enough on the head to preclude the top of the head forcing the cover above its natural tautness. The service/dress caps are worn centered and straight with the tip of the visor in line with the eyebrows.

## B.   WEARING THE UNIFORM (WOMEN)

1.   Slacks, Service. The slacks will be long enough to break slightly over the shoe in front and reach the junction of the welt of the shoe in the rear. A variation of 1/2 inch above the welt is acceptable. The hem on the slacks will be from 2 inches to 3 inches.

2.   Service/Dress Cap. Service and dress caps will be centered and worn straight with the tip of the visor in line with the eyebrows.

3. **Skirt Hems.** Skirts will have a hem or facing from 2 inches to 3 inches. Skirts will be knee length (not more than 1 inch above the top of the kneecap or more than 1 inch below the bottom of the kneecap).

4. **Service Coat.** The coat should fit easily through the waist, extending to a smooth flare over the hips, allowing for a 2-inch overlap in the center to hang evenly.

5. **Khaki Shirts.** The khaki shirt will not be tucked in, but will be worn outside the skirt at all times, except by those women who are required to wear a duty belt. The short-sleeve shirt may be worn with the service coat; however, the neck tab must be worn.

6. **Maternity Uniform.** The maternity uniform is currently available for issue and purchase by pregnant women. This uniform is required for wear by pregnant women Marines who do not elect to be separated when they can no longer wear the service uniform. Civilian clothes are not authorized for wear in lieu of the maternity uniform. Additional information on requisitioning and wearing the maternity uniform is contained in *MCBul 10120*.

7. **Green Service Sweater**

a. The sweater may be worn with the service uniform with either the long- or quarter-length sleeve shirt (whichever is prescribed/authorized as the seasonal uniform shirt). When the sweater is worn, the shirt collar will be worn outside the sweater, without the necktab, and the collar button will be unbuttoned. The sleeves of the sweater may be turned up; however, the sleeves should cover the shirt cuff. The waistband of the sweater may be turned up; however, it should cover the belt.

b. When the sweater is worn with the camouflage utility uniform, it will be worn underneath the camouflage utility coat.

c. The sweater is authorized for wear with civilian clothing.

## C. DESIGNATION OF UNIFORM

Authorized uniforms for enlisted personnel are designated as blue dress "A," blue dress "B," blue dress "C," blue dress "D," blue-white dress "A," blue-white dress "B," (blue-whites are authorized only for military ceremonies as directed by commanders) service "A," service "B," service "C," and utility.

## D. WEARING RIBBONS AND BADGES

Ribbons may be worn on a bar or bars, and pinned to the coat or shirt. If ribbons are worn on a bar, no portion of the bar or pin shall be visible. Ribbon bars are normally worn in rows of three; however, rows of four may be worn when displaying a large number of awards. If required, women may wear 2-ribbon rows to properly display the ribbons. When more than one row of ribbon bars is worn, all rows except the uppermost will contain the same number of ribbons (except as authorized below).

When the number of rows is so great as to cause ribbons to be concealed by the service coat lapel (one-third or more of a ribbon concealed), ribbon bars shall be placed in successively decreasing rows; e.g., 4-ribbon rows, 3-ribbon rows, 2-ribbon rows, single ribbon. The left edge of all decreasing rows will be in a line vertically; except that, when the uppermost row presents an unsatisfactory appearance when so aligned, it will be placed in the position presenting the neatest appearance (usually centered over the row immediately below it).

All authorized ribbons to which the Marine is entitled will be worn on coats and may be prescribed for wear on shirts by the local commander, except as follows:

    o  Ribbons shall NOT be worn on the sweater, utility coat, or all-weather coat.

    o  When shirts are worn as outer garments, ribbons are not required unless prescribed by the commander. If the Marine wears ribbons, he/she has two options:

    o  All authorized ribbons may be worn, or

    o  Only personal U.S. decorations along with U.S. unit awards and the Good Conduct Medal may be worn.

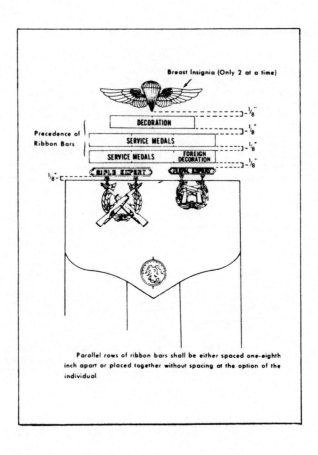

Breast Insignia (Only 2 at a time)

DECORATION

Precedence of
Ribbon Bars

SERVICE MEDALS

SERVICE MEDALS    FOREIGN DECORATION

RIFLE EXPERT    PISTOL EXPERT

1/8"

1/8"
1/8"
1/8"
1/8"

Parallel rows of ribbon bars shall be either spaced one-eighth inch apart or placed together without spacing at the option of the individual.

Fig 6-15.  Proper wearing of ribbons and badges.
(male Marines)

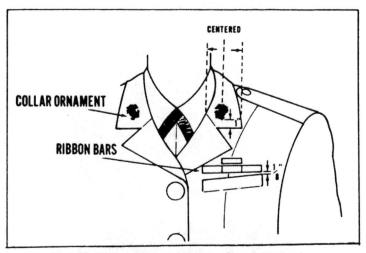

CENTERED

COLLAR ORNAMENT

RIBBON BARS

1"

Fig 6-16. Proper wearing of ribbons. (female Marines)

Legend for figure 6-15 and 6-16

1.  Bottom edge of rifle bar will be 1/8 inch above the edge of the pocket.

2.  Top of the pistol bar is even with the top of the rifle bar; therefore, the bottom of the pistol bar will be more than 1/8 inch above top edge of the pocket.

3.  The first row of ribbons will be 1/8 inch above the top edge of the shooting badges. The second and succeeding row(s) of ribbons will either be worn 1/8 inch apart or flush.

4.  Whether or not ribbons are worn, badges will be spaced so that outboard ends would be even with the ends of a 3-ribbon bar, which is 4-1/8 inches long. The center of this ribbon bar (whether real or imaginary) should coincide with the center of the pocket as shown.

5.  Ribbons must be worn in proper order of seniority.

6.  Stars will be worn with single ray up.

7.  Ribbons must be clean and not faded or frayed.

## E. PLACEMENT OF USMC DECAL

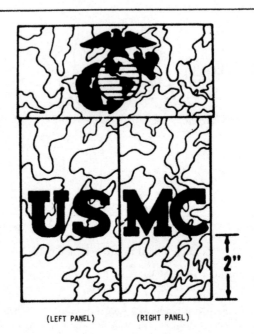

(LEFT PANEL)          (RIGHT PANEL)

A Marine gets one chance to properly place the iron-on USMC decal on his utility shirt left breast pocket. It must be done right.
The Eagle, Globe, and Anchor is placed on the pocket flap centered right to left, top to bottom.

The "USMC" portion is seperated into two parts. "US" and "MC". The "US" is placed on the left panel of the pocket. Centered left to right, 2 inches from the bottom. The "MC" is placed on the right panel of the pocket, centered left to right, 2 inches from the bottom edge.

Fig 6-17. Placement of USMC decal on camouflage utilities.
(with split pocket)

On the newer camouflage utilities, the pocket is not divided into panels. The Marine Corps emblem and the "USMC" decals are placed as shown in figure 6-18.

Fig 6-18.  Placement of USMC decal on camouflage utilities.
(w/out split pockets)

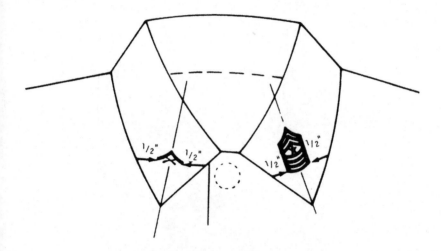

Fig 6-19. Insignia grade on collar.

## E. INSIGNIA OF GRADE

1. Grade insignia will be worn on the long sleeve shirt, service coat, and dress coat 4 inches down from the shoulder seam and centered on the sleeve.

2. Grade insignia will be centered on the sleeve of the quarter-length shirt for male Marines. For female Marines, grade insignia will be worn centered on the outer half of each sleeve, midway between the shoulder seam and the peak of the cuff.

3. Insignia of grade shall be worn on each side of the collar, placed vertically with the single point up and center of the insignia on a line bisecting the angle of the point of the collar, the lower outside edge being equally spaced one-half-inch from either side of the collar (figure 6-19).

# Section IV. Grooming Standards

Objective:  *Maintain grooming standards as per current regulations.*

## A. GROOMING (MALES)

1.  The face will be clean shaven, except that a mustache may be worn. When worn, a mustache will be neatly and closely trimmed and must be contained within the lines of B, and the margin area of the upper lip as shown in figures 6-19 and 6-20. The length of a mustache hair fully extended must not exceed 1/2 inch.

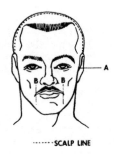

······SCALP LINE

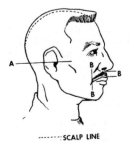

······:SCALP LINE

Fig 6-19. Frontal view of hair
and mustache limits.

Fig 6-20. Side view of
hair and view of hair and mustache
limits.

2.  Hair will be neat and closely trimmed. It may be clipped at the edges of the side and back and will be evenly graduated from zero length at the hairline on the lower portion of the head up to a maximum of 3 inches on the top of the head. Hair will be worn in such a manner so as not to interfere with the proper wearing of uniform headgear.

3.  Sideburns will not extend below the top of the orifice of the ear, as indicated by line A in figures 6-20 and 6-21. The length of hair on the sideburn will not exceed 1/8 inch when fully extended.

## B. GROOMING (FEMALES)

1.  The hair shall be neatly shaped and arranged in an attractive style. Elaborate hairstyles that do not allow for the proper wearing of the cap are prohibited. Hair may touch the collar but may not fall below the collar's lower edge. Conspicuous barrettes, pins, and combs shall not be worn in the hair when the uniform is worn. Hairnets shall not be worn unless authorized for a specific type of duty. If dyes, tints, or bleaches are used on the hair, the artificial color must harmonize with the complexion tone and eye color. Conspicuous artificial color changes are prohibited. Wigs, if worn in uniform, must look natural and conform to all of the above listed regulations.

2.  Cosmetics shall be applied conservatively. Exaggerated or faddish cosmetic styles are inappropriate with the uniform and shall not be worn. Lipstick, if worn with the green service or dress blue uniforms, shall harmonize with the scarlet trim of these uniforms. When the utility uniform is worn, red or pink shades of lipstick may be worn. Extreme shades of lipstick, such as lavender, purple, white or flesh color shall not be worn. Nail polish, if used, shall either harmonize with the lipstick or be colorless.

## C. GROOMING (ALL)

1.  Articles that are not authorized for wear as part of a regulation uniform will not be worn with, or exposed upon, the uniform unless otherwise authorized by the Commandant of the Marine Corps or higher authority. Examples of such articles include but are not limited to: pencils, pens, watch chains, fobs, pins, jewelry, handkerchiefs, combs, cigarettes, pipes, barrettes, hair ribbons/ornaments, flowers (corsages/boutonnieres, etc.), or similar items.

2. Articles that may be worn while in uniform include: inconspicuous wristwatches, watchbands, and rings. Sunglasses may be worn on leave, liberty, and in garrison; but not in formation with troops unless the need to wear sunglasses has been certified by medical authorities. When authorized for wear, sunglass lenses will be of a standard green/dark green/grey shade or may be the type commonly referred to as "photosensitive." When worn, eyeglasses/sunglasses will be conservative in appearance. Eccentric or conspicuous eyepieces are prohibited. Chains or ribbons will not be attached to eyeglasses, however, eyeglass restraints are authorized for safety purposes.

## D. WEIGHT

1. **General.** Any Marine who exceeds the weight standards or displays poor military appearance due to improper weight distribution will be placed in the unit's weight/personal appearance program. Weigh-ins will be used to monitor individual progress. If you do not satisfactorily lose excess body fat and/or improve your personal appearance, you may be discharged from the Marine Corps due to unsuitability.

2. **Male Weight Standards.** Weight standards for male Marines, regardless of age, are shown in table 6-3 below.

Table 6-3. Male weight standards.

| HEIGHT (inches) | 64 | 65 | 66 | 67 | 68 | 69 | 70 | 71 |
|---|---|---|---|---|---|---|---|---|
| **WEIGHT (pounds)** | | | | | | | | |
| Minimum | 105 | 106 | 107 | 111 | 115 | 119 | 123 | 127 |
| Maximum | 160 | 165 | 170 | 175 | 181 | 186 | 192 | 197 |

| HEIGHT (inches) | 72 | 73 | 74 | 75 | 76 | 77 | 78 |
|---|---|---|---|---|---|---|---|
| **WEIGHT (pounds)** | | | | | | | |
| Minimum | 131 | 135 | 139 | 143 | 147 | 151 | 153 |
| Maximum | 203 | 209 | 214 | 219 | 225 | 230 | 235 |

**3. Female Weight Standards.** Weight standards for women Marines, regardless of age, are shown in table 6-4 below:

Table 6-4. Female weight standards.

| HEIGHT (inches) | 58 | 59 | 60 | 61 | 62 | 63 | 64 | 65 |
|---|---|---|---|---|---|---|---|---|
| WEIGHT (pounds) | | | | | | | | |
| Minimum | 90 | 92 | 94 | 96 | 98 | 100 | 102 | 104 |
| Maximum | 121 | 123 | 125 | 127 | 130 | 134 | 138 | 142 |
| HEIGHT (inches) | 66 | 67 | 68 | 69 | 70 | 71 | 72 | 73 |
| WEIGHT (pounds) | | | | | | | | |
| Minimum | 106 | 109 | 112 | 115 | 118 | 122 | 125 | 128 |
| Maximum | 147 | 151 | 156 | 160 | 165 | 170 | 175 | 180 |

**4. Alternative Maximum Weight Limits for Male Marines.** The Marine Corps has established 18 percent and below as maximum allowable percent of body fat for the alternative weight limits for male Marines.

**5. Alternative Maximum Weight Limits for Female Marines.** The maximum allowable percent of body fat for the establishment of an alternate weight standard for female Marines is established at 26 percent and below.

# Section V. Civilian Attire

Objective: *Define proper civilian attire as per current directives.*

## APPROPRIATE CIVILIAN ATTIRE

The Commandant of the Marine Corps has extended the privilege of wearing civilian clothing to enlisted personnel of the Marine Corps within set limitations. When conditions require or permit the wearing of civilian clothing, only appropriate civilian attire will be worn.

Appropriate civilian attire is that type of clothing which, when worn by the individual Marine, presents a conservative personal appearance and is commensurate with the high standards traditionally associated with Marine Corps personnel. When civilian attire is authorized for wear in lieu of a uniform in a duty status, the appropriate civilian attire will be that which is comparable to the degree of formality as the uniform prescribed for such duty. No eccentricities of dress will be permitted at any time.

When civilian clothing is worn on base, Marine Corps personnel will ensure that their dress and personal appearance meet the same high standards established for personnel in uniform. No part of a prescribed uniform, except those items which are not exclusively military in character, will be worn with civilian clothing.

Men may wear gold cuff links, studs, and tie bar, mourning band, footwear, socks, gloves, underwear, black bow ties, service sweater, scarf, and the all-weather coat without insignia of grade with civilian clothes.

Women may wear the white shirt without insignia of grade, footwear, gloves, handbag, mourning band, maternity uniform, service sweater, scarf, and all-weather coat without insignia of grade with civilian clothes.

---

For more information in this area, refer to:

1. MCO 1020.34      Marine Corps Uniform Regulations

2. MCO 6100.10      Weight Control and Military Appearance

# Chapter 7.  Physical Fitness

Objective:  *When directed, pass the physical fitness test.*

## A. GENERAL

It is essential to the combat readiness of the Marine Corps that every Marine be physically fit. Implementation of the Commandant's policy on physical fitness requires that every Marine, regardless of age, grade, or duty assignment, engage in an effective physical conditioning program on a continuing and progressive basis.

The responsibility for maintaining a satisfactory level of physical fitness is shared by each Marine and his commanding officer. The habits of self-discipline required to gain and maintain a high level of physical fitness is inherent in the Marine Corps way of life and must be part of the character of all Marines. A program of regular, vigorous, and progressive physical fitness training results in an increase in work efficiency, self-confidence, and personal as well as unit pride. A Marine who is not physically fit is a detriment to the readiness and combat efficiency of his unit and detracts from the professionalism of the Marine Corps.

## B. DEFINITIONS

1.  Physical Fitness. To Marines, the term physical fitness means a healthy body and the endurance to withstand the stresses of prolonged activity and adverse environment.  It includes the capacity to endure the discomforts that accompany fatigue and the ability to maintain combat effectiveness.

2.  Stamina. A combination of muscular and cardiovascular endurance, stamina is the most important aspect of fitness for Marines. Cardiovascular fitness should be the basis for all physical training because of its contribution to overall health and long life. Muscular endurance is closely associated with cardiovascular endurance. It is the physical characteristic that will allow prolonged activity of a moderate tempo. For Marines, this represents the ability to march long distances with heavy loads, or to work long hours and still maintain the reserve to carry on in an emergency.

this represents the ability to march long distances with heavy loads, or to work long hours and still maintain the reserve to carry on in an emergency.

3. **Strength.** This is the ability to manipulate weight or, for a Marine, his own body weight. A certain amount of strength is also necessary for appearance, confidence, and load-carrying ability. It is essential that a Marine be able to handle his own body weight; if he cannot, he is either too heavy or too weak.

## C. PHYSICAL FITNESS TEST (PFT)

The Marine Corps physical fitness test measures acceptable levels of physical fitness for all Marines under 46 years of age. These Marines must maintain the ability to pass the test at any time, and each is tested at least semiannually. Those who fail the test are placed on a supervised program of physical conditioning until they attain the minimum acceptable level of fitness for their age group.

1. **Conduct.** The test will be conducted in a single session of one morning or afternoon. Movement from one event to another should provide adequate rest between events. Events may be conducted in any sequence prescribed by the unit commander. Marines may wear appropriate gym attire or a seasonally modified utility uniform. Gym shoes are recommended.

2. **Test Events and Standards**

a. **Physical fitness test for men.** The test consists of three events: pullups/chinups, bent-knee situps, and a 3-mile run. These events are designed to test the strength and stamina of the upper body (shoulder girdle), the midsection, and the lower body. Additionally, the run measures the efficiency of the cardiovascular system. To successfully pass the test, a Marine must complete the minimum requirement for each event, plus earn the required additional points for his age group. Failure to meet the required minimum in any event constitutes failure of the entire test, regardless of total number of points earned. Minimum acceptable performance standards and required minimum scores are listed in figure 7-1. The point system is shown in the performance chart in figure 7-3.

| Age | Pullups | Situps | 3-Mile Run minutes | Subtotal Points | Required Additional Points | Passing Score |
|-----|---------|--------|--------------------|-----------------|--------------------------|---------------|
| 17-26 | 3 | 40 | 28 | 95 | 40 | 135 |
| 27-39 | 3 | 35 | 29 | 84 | 26 | 110 |
| 40-45 | 3 | 35 | 30 | 78 | 7 | 85 |

Required minimum acceptable performance:

Required minimum scores:

| Age | Unsatisfactory | 3d Class | 2d Class | 1st Class |
|-----|----------------|----------|----------|-----------|
| 17-26 | 0-134 | 135 | 175 | 225 |
| 27-39 | 0-109 | 110 | 150 | 200 |
| 40-45 | 0- 84 | 85 | 125 | 175 |

Fig 7-1. Minimum Acceptable Performance (Men).

b. **Physical fitness test for women.** The test consists of three events: the flexed arm hang, bent-knee situps, and the 1 1/2-mile run. These events are designed to test the strength and stamina of the upper body (shoulder girdle), midsection, and lower body. Additionally, the run measures the efficiency of the cardiovascular system. To successfully pass the test, personnel must complete the minimum repetitions or time listed for each of the three events. Minimum acceptable performance standards are listed in figure 7-2. The point system is shown in the performance chart in figure 7-4.

| Age | Flexed Arm Hang (seconds) | Situps (repetitions) | 1½-Mile Run (minutes) | Total Points |
|-----|---------------------------|----------------------|----------------------|--------------|
| 17-26 | 16 | 22 | 15 | 100 |
| 27-39 | 13 | 19 | 16:30 | 73 |
| 40-45 | 10 | 18 | 18 | 56 |

Required Minimum scores:

| Age | Unsatisfactory | 3d Class | 2d Class | 1st Class |
|-----|----------------|----------|----------|-----------|
| 17-26 | 0-99 | 100 | 150 | 200 |
| 27-39 | 0-72 | 73 | 123 | 173 |
| 40-45 | 0-55 | 56 | 106 | 156 |

Fig 7-2. Minimum Acceptable Performance (Women).

7-3

Point system. The table below will be used to assign a point value to each of the three events. Maximum attainable score for any one event is 100 points, while 300 points represents a perfect score.

Example:  6 pullups  =  30 points
          40 situps  =  40 points
          23.50 run  =  65 points
          ───────────────────────
          Total score    135 points

| Points | Pullups | Situps | 3-mile run | Points | Pullups | Situps | 3-mile run | Points | Pullups | Situps | 3-mile run | Points | Pullups | Situps | 3-mile run |
|---|---|---|---|---|---|---|---|---|---|---|---|---|---|---|---|
| 100 | 20 | 80 | 18:00 | 75 | 15 |    | 22:10 | 50 | 10 | 50 | 26:20 | 25 | 5 | 25 | 30:30 |
| 99 |   |    | 18:10 | 74 |   | 67 | 22:20 | 49 |   | 49 | 26:30 | 24 |   | 24 | 30:40 |
| 98 |   | 79 | 18:20 | 73 |   |    | 22:30 | 48 |   | 48 | 26:40 | 23 |   | 23 | 30:50 |
| 97 |   |    | 18:30 | 72 |   | 66 | 22:40 | 47 |   | 47 | 26:50 | 22 |   | 22 | 31:00 |
| 96 |   | 78 | 18:40 | 71 |   |    | 22:50 | 46 |   | 46 | 27:00 | 21 |   | 21 | 31:10 |
| 95 | 19 |    | 18:50 | 70 | 14 | 65 | 23:00 | 45 | 9 | 45 | 27:10 | 20 | 4 | 20 | 31:20 |
| 94 |   | 77 | 19:00 | 69 |   |    | 23:10 | 44 |   | 44 | 27:20 | 19 |   | 19 | 31:30 |
| 93 |   |    | 19:10 | 68 |   | 64 | 23:20 | 43 |   | 43 | 27:30 | 18 |   | 18 | 31:40 |
| 92 |   | 76 | 19:20 | 67 |   |    | 23:30 | 42 |   | 42 | 27:40 | 17 |   | 17 | 31:50 |
| 91 |   |    | 19:30 | 66 |   | 63 | 23:40 | 41 |   | 41 | 27:50 | 16 |   | 16 | 32:00 |
| 90 | 18 | 75 | 19:40 | 65 | 13 |    | 23:50 | 40 | 8 | 40 | 28:00 | 15 | 3 | 15 | 32:10 |
| 89 |   |    | 19:50 | 64 |   | 62 | 24:00 | 39 |   | 39 | 28:10 | 14 |   | 14 | 32:20 |
| 88 |   | 74 | 20:00 | 63 |   |    | 24:10 | 38 |   | 38 | 28:20 | 13 |   | 13 | 32:30 |
| 87 |   |    | 20:10 | 62 |   | 61 | 24:20 | 37 |   | 37 | 28:30 | 12 |   | 12 | 32:40 |
| 86 |   | 73 | 20:20 | 61 |   |    | 24:30 | 36 |   | 36 | 28:40 | 11 |   | 11 | 32:50 |
| 85 | 17 |    | 20:30 | 60 | 12 | 60 | 24:40 | 35 | 7 | 35 | 28:50 | 10 | 2 | 10 | 33:00 |
| 84 |   | 72 | 20:40 | 59 |   | 59 | 24:50 | 34 |   | 34 | 29:00 | 9 |   | 9 | 33:10 |
| 83 |   |    | 20:50 | 58 |   | 58 | 25:00 | 33 |   | 33 | 29:10 | 8 |   | 8 | 33:20 |
| 82 |   | 71 | 21:00 | 57 |   | 57 | 25:10 | 32 |   | 32 | 29:20 | 7 |   | 7 | 33:30 |
| 81 |   |    | 21:10 | 56 |   | 56 | 25:20 | 31 |   | 31 | 29:30 | 6 |   | 6 | 33:40 |
| 80 | 16 | 70 | 21:20 | 55 | 11 | 55 | 25:30 | 30 | 6 | 30 | 29:40 | 5 | 1 | 5 | 33:50 |
| 79 |   |    | 21:30 | 54 |   | 54 | 25:40 | 29 |   | 29 | 29:50 | 4 |   | 4 | 34:00 |
| 78 |   | 69 | 21:40 | 53 |   | 53 | 25:50 | 28 |   | 28 | 30:00 | 3 |   | 3 | 34:30 |
| 77 |   |    | 21:50 | 52 |   | 52 | 26:00 | 27 |   | 27 | 30:10 | 2 |   | 2 | 35:00 |
| 76 |   | 68 | 22:00 | 51 |   | 51 | 26:10 | 26 |   | 26 | 30:20 | 1 |   | 1 | 36:00 |

Fig 7-3. Performance chart (men).

Maximum attainable score for any one event is 100 points, while 300 points represents a perfect score.

Example: Flexed Arm Hang   45 seconds  =   50 points
                            30 situps   =   60 points
                            13:50 run   =   54 points

                            Total score     164 points

| Points | Flexed Arm Hang | Situps | 1½-Mile Run | Points | Flexed Arm Hang | Situps | 1½-Mile Run | Points | Flexed Arm Hang | Situps | 1½-Mile Run | Points | Flexed Arm Hang | Situps | 1½-Mile Run |
|---|---|---|---|---|---|---|---|---|---|---|---|---|---|---|---|
| 100 | 70 | 50 | 10:00 | 75 | | | 12:05 | 50 | 45 | 25 | 14:10 | 25 | 25 | | 16:15 |
| 99 | | | :05 | 74 | 57 | 37 | :10 | 49 | | | :15 | 24 | 24 | 12 | :20 |
| 98 | 69 | 49 | :10 | 73 | | | :15 | 48 | 44 | 24 | :20 | 23 | 23 | | :25 |
| 97 | | | :15 | 72 | 56 | 36 | :20 | 47 | | | :25 | 22 | 22 | 11 | :30 |
| 96 | 68 | 48 | :20 | 71 | | | :25 | 46 | 43 | 23 | :30 | 21 | 21 | | :35 |
| 95 | | | :25 | 70 | 55 | 35 | :30 | 45 | | | :35 | 20 | 20 | 10 | :40 |
| 94 | 67 | 47 | :30 | 69 | | | :35 | 44 | 42 | 22 | :40 | 19 | 19 | | :45 |
| 93 | | | :35 | 68 | 54 | 34 | :40 | 43 | | | :45 | 18 | 18 | 9 | :50 |
| 92 | 66 | 46 | :40 | 67 | | | :45 | 42 | 41 | 21 | :50 | 17 | 17 | | 16:55 |
| 91 | | | :45 | 66 | 53 | 33 | :50 | 41 | | | 14:55 | 16 | 16 | 8 | 17:00 |
| 90 | 65 | 45 | :50 | 65 | | | 12:55 | 40 | 40 | 20 | 15:00 | 15 | 15 | | :10 |
| 89 | | | 10:55 | 64 | 52 | 32 | 13:00 | 39 | 39 | | :05 | 14 | 14 | 7 | :20 |
| 88 | 64 | 44 | 11:00 | 63 | | | :05 | 38 | 38 | 19 | :10 | 13 | 13 | | :30 |
| 87 | | | :05 | 62 | 51 | 31 | :10 | 37 | 37 | | :15 | 12 | 12 | 6 | :40 |
| 86 | 63 | 43 | :10 | 61 | | | :15 | 36 | 36 | 18 | :20 | 11 | 11 | | 17:50 |
| 85 | | | :15 | 60 | 50 | 30 | :20 | 35 | 35 | | :25 | 10 | 10 | 5 | 18:00 |
| 84 | 62 | 42 | :20 | 59 | | | :25 | 34 | 34 | 17 | :30 | 9 | 9 | | :10 |
| 83 | | | :25 | 58 | 49 | 29 | :30 | 33 | 33 | | :35 | 8 | 8 | 4 | :20 |
| 82 | 61 | 41 | :30 | 57 | | | :35 | 32 | 32 | 16 | :40 | 7 | 7 | | :30 |
| 81 | | | :35 | 56 | 48 | 28 | :40 | 31 | 31 | | :45 | 6 | 6 | 3 | :40 |
| 80 | 60 | 40 | :40 | 55 | | | :45 | 30 | 30 | 15 | :50 | 5 | 5 | | 18:50 |
| 79 | | | :45 | 54 | 47 | 27 | :50 | 29 | 29 | | 15:55 | 4 | 4 | 2 | 19:00 |
| 78 | 59 | 39 | :50 | 53 | | | 13:55 | 28 | 28 | 14 | 16:00 | 3 | 3 | 1 | :30 |
| 77 | | | 11:55 | 52 | 46 | 26 | 14:00 | 27 | 27 | | :05 | 2 | 2 | 1 | 20:00 |
| 76 | 58 | 38 | 12:00 | 51 | | | :05 | 26 | 26 | 13 | :10 | 1 | 1 | | :30 |

Fig 7-4. Performance chart (women).

7-5

## 3. Performance of Events.

a. Pullups (men) (figure 7-5). The bar is grasped with both palms facing either forward or to the rear and the arms are fully extended (dead hang). Feet must be free of the ground. The position of the hands may be changed during the exercise as long as the performer is not assisted or does not dismount from the bar. Pull your body up with the arms until your chin is over the bar, then lower yourself until the arms are fully extended again; this is one repetition. The movement must be fully completed to count. Repeat as many times as possible. Kicking motions such that the feet and/or knees do not rise above waist level are permitted as long as the pullup remains a vertical movement. The body will be kept from swinging by an assistant holding an extended arm in front of the knees of the Marine on the bar. Resting is allowed in the up or down position, but resting with the chin supported by the bar is not allowed.

Starting Position

Fig 7-5. Pullups.

b. Flexed arm hang (women) (figure 7-6). The individual stands on a support or, if necessary, is assisted by others to reach the starting position. Both palms must face in the same direction. The elbows are flexed so that the chin is over or level with the bar. Once the individual is set in the starting position, the support or assistance is removed and she attempts to maintain elbow flexion for as long as possible. The score is the length of time in seconds that some degree of flexion at the elbow is maintained. The chin may not rest on the bar during the exercise.

**Starting Position**          **Final Position**

Fig 7-6. Flexed arm hang.

c. Bent-knee situps (figure 7-7). The time limit for male Marines is 2 minutes; for women Marines it is 1 minute. To assume the correct starting position, the Marine lies on his or her back (supine position) with knees flexed and both feet flat on the ground. One repetition consists of raising the upper body from the supine position until the head breaks an imaginary plane though the knees and returning to the supine position. Repeat as many times as possible during the time limit. During this movement, the hands must remain behind the head and the feet must remain on the ground. Upon return to the supine position, the shoulder blades must touch the ground to complete the repetition; neither the head nor the hands need touch the ground. An assistant will grasp the participant's feet or legs below the knee in whatever manner is most comfortable for the participant. Kneeling or sitting on the feet is permitted. Resting during the exercise is permitted in either the up or the down position.

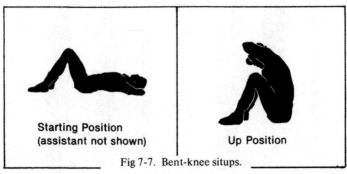

**Starting Position**
**(assistant not shown)**                 **Up Position**

Fig 7-7. Bent-knee situps.

d. Run. The object of this event is to complete the measured course as rapidly as possible. Walking is allowed. Male Marines will run a 3-mile course; women Marines run a 1 1/2 course.

For more information in this area, refer to:

1.  MCO 6100.3H                    Physical Fitness

# Chapter 8.   NBC Defense
# (Nuclear, Biological, Chemical)

## Section I.   Chemical and Biological Defense

Objectives:

1.   On command without reference, identify the types of signals used to give the NBC alarm.

2.   When given examples or color pictures, identify the NATO NBC markers.

3.   Given a field protective mask and collateral equipment, inspect and maintain the field protective mask and collateral equipment.

4.   On command without reference, state the difference between training and combat filters for the field protective mask.

5.   Given a field protective mask and filters, replace the filters in a field protective mask.

6.   Given a field protective mask with hood, on command, or when faced with the appropriate situation, don and clear the field protective mask within 9 seconds (15 seconds is allowed for a field protective mask with a hood).

7.   On command without reference, demonstrate procedures to remove and stow the field protective mask with a hood.

8.   Given MOPP Gear 4, on command, don individual protective clothing within 8 minutes.

9.   While in MOPP 4, remove protective clothing in proper sequence.

10.   Given a field protective mask, M 1 canteen cap, and a canteen with water, drink while masked.

11.   After warning, with mask and individual protective clothing, react to an aerial spray using appropriate items of equipment.

12.   Given simulated chemical or biological attack conditions, react to chemical or biological attack using appropriate items of equipment.

13.   Given simulated nerve, blood, blister, tear, choking, vomiting, and incapacitating agent casualties, demonstrate identification and treatment of the casualties.

14.   Given a simulated biological/toxin agent casualty, demonstrate the identification and treatment of the casualty.

You must be able to protect yourself from the effects of chemical and biological agents to perform your mission. The use of correct individual defensive measures can protect you from many of the hazards. Therefore, you must learn these measures so that you will not become a casualty and so that you may assist your unit in accomplishing its mission. You must be able to take the correct protective action and correctly use your protective equipment.

## A. BIOLOGICAL AND CHEMICAL EFFECTS

Detection of a chemical or biological attack may be difficult. For a chemical attack, you will usually have to rely on your senses to give you indication of the presence of an agent. Biological agents, however, are hard to detect. You will have to watch for certain clues that give indications of their presence. There are some obvious items or events that should make you suspicious of a chemical or biological attack.

1.  General Indicators of Biological or Chemical Attack

    a. Suspicious liquids or solids on the ground or on vegetation

    b. Unexplained smoke or mist

    c. Dead or sick animals, or birds

    d. Suspicious odors

2.  Chemical Agent Detection

    a. Irritation of eyes, nose, throat, skin

    b. Headache, dizziness, nausea

    c. Difficulty with or increased rate of breathing

    d. A feeling of choking or tightness in the throat or chest

    e. Strange or out-of-the-ordinary odors

    f. Strange flavors in food or water

8-2

3. **Biological Agent Detection.** Be aware of clues that may identify the presence of biological agents.

a. Enemy aircraft dropping unidentified material or spraying unidentified substances

b. New and unusual types of shells and bombs, particularly those which burst with little or no blast

c. Smoke from an unknown source or of an unknown nature

d. An increase in sick or dead animals

e. Unusual or unexplained increase in the number of insects

f. Weapons that do not seem to have an immediate casualty effect

## B. ALARM SYSTEMS

Two types of alarm systems may be used to alert you in the event of a chemical or biological attack (figure 8-1). Your unit SOP sets forth how and when local alarms will be given, but they are normally some form of percussion sound. In an emergency, it may be necessary to give visual signals or to sound a vocal alarm. Because of the danger of breathing in the agent if you give a vocal alarm, you should mask first and then shout "GAS" or "SPRAY" (if you see an aircraft spraying a cloud) giving the visual alarm simultaneously.

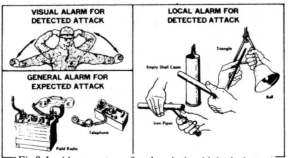

Fig 8-1. Alarm systems for chemical or biological attack.

## C. STANDARD NATO MARKERS

Known or suspected contaminated areas are marked with standard triangular markers. They are color coded and labeled to indicate the contaminated agent. All Marines should be able to recognize the markers shown in figure 8-2.

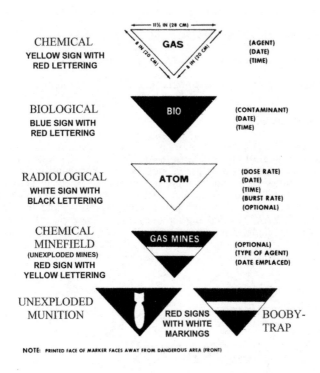

NOTE: PRINTED FACE OF MARKER FACES AWAY FROM DANGEROUS AREA (FRONT)

Fig 8-2. Markers for contaminated or dangerous land areas.

8-4

## D. M17 SERIES FIELD PROTECTIVE MASK

The field protective mask is the most important single item of individual protective equipment in NBC warfare! As such, it must be properly stored and maintained. It is the individual Marine's responsibility to make sure the mask is put together correctly and that the filters are in good shape.

1. **Inspection.** You must ensure that your mask is serviceable prior to needing it in a contaminated environment. Inspection of the mask will help to identify all deficiencies and shortcomings. Some tips on inspecting your mask are listed below:

  a. Check filters. REMEMBER, wet filters DO NOT work!

  b. Check the nosecup to make sure it's in the right position and not loose from the crimping ring (seals the voicemitter and nosecup together).

  c. Make sure the nosecup and cheek pouches are buttoned.

  d. Check the rubber faceblank for any dry rot or rips.

  e. Check the eyelens for scratches that would impair your vision and also for cracks.

  f. Check your head harness for elasticity and make sure that the straps are not torn or frayed.

  g. Check inlet and outlet disks to ensure that they are soft, flexible, and properly installed.

  h. Check for damaged or missing voicemitter and drinking tube.

  i. Make sure the hood is not torn or rotted and that all straps function properly.

2. **Operator Maintenance.** Once you have determined that your mask is serviceable, it is a good idea to make sure that it remains that way. To perform operator maintenance, you will need warm soapy water, clear water, clean rags, a small soft cleaning brush, and a stiff bristle brush. To begin, remove the mask from the carrier, then perform the following steps:

a. Wash the mask

(1) Remove the voicemitter-outlet valve cover and disk, inlet valve assemblies, and eyelens outserts.

(2) Do not remove the filters. Be sure that the pouch flaps are securely buttoned. Keep water away from the inlet valve connectors.

(3) Dip a clean, soft rag into soapy water, then wring it out well. Wipe the hood and mask carefully, inside and out.

(4) Do the same for the voicemitter-outlet valve cover and inlet valve assemblies.

(5) Rinse the cloth in clear, warm water and wring it out. Wipe all of the parts that you washed to remove dirt and soap film.

(6) Dry all parts with a clean, dry, soft cloth.

(7) Use a dry, soft brush to clean around corners, joints, frames, crimped edges, and other hard to reach places.

(8) Replace the voicemitter-outlet valve cover, eyelens outserts, and inlet valve assemblies. Check the rubber disks in the inlet and outlet valve assemblies to ensure they are snug and flat. Press the inlet valves hard to snap them in place, making sure that the louvers point down.

b. Clean the lenses. Use plastic polish according to directions, if available; otherwise, use warm soapy water, rinse, and dry.

c. Clean the carrier. Shake out any debris from the carrier, then use a stiff, dry brush to remove surface dirt and mildew.

**3. Donning and Clearing the Field Protective Mask.** Upon hearing or seeing the alarm for gas, properly don and clear the field protective mask within nine seconds as shown in figure 8-3.

a. Stop breathing.

b. Remove your headgear with your right hand and open the carrier with your left hand. Place head gear as directed.

c. Hold the carrier open with your left hand; grasp the facepiece just below the eyepieces and remove the mask with your right hand.

Fig 8-3. Donning the mask.

d. Grasp the facepiece with both hands, sliding your thumbs up inside the facepiece under the lower head harness straps. Lift your chin slightly.

e. Seat the chin pocket of the facepiece firmly on the chin. Bring head harness smoothly over head, ensuring that the head harness straps are straight and the head pad is centered.

f. Smooth edges of facepiece on your face with upward and backward motion of hands, pressing out all bulges to secure an airtight seal.

Fig 8-3. Continued.

8-8

g. Close outlet valve by cupping the heel of your right hand firmly over the opening; blow hard to clear agent from the facepiece.

h. Block air inlet holes of filter elements, shutting off the air supply. When you inhale, the facepiece should collapse.

i. Resume breathing (give the alarm).

Fig 8-3. Continued.

## E. DRINKING WHILE WEARING THE M17A1/A2 PROTECTIVE MASK

**NOTE:** To use the M17A1/M17A2 mask drinking system, your canteen must be equipped with an M1 canteen cap.

1. Fill your plastic water canteen before entering a contaminated area and cover it with the M1 canteen cap.

2. Steady your mask and withdraw the quick disconnect coupling half (1) from its pocket (2) (figure 8-4).

3. Remove a canteen (3) from its cover, flip open the protective cover (4) of the M1 cap (5), and hold the canteen near your mask.

4. Push the quick disconnect coupling half (1) in and turn to connect it to the cap (5). Check that the connection is tight.

**NOTE:** If the pin in the cap is off center, insert the quick disconnect coupling half at an angle to pick up pin.

5. Turn and hold the lever (6) all the way toward the voicemitter (7). Open your mouth and hold the drinking tube mouthpiece (8) between your teeth. Blow to create positive pressure. You should feel some resistance.

**WARNING:** If resistance is not felt, your drinking system leaks. Do not drink. Replace your mask as soon as possible.

6. If the drinking system does not leak, raise and invert the canteen (3), keeping the lever (6) turned, and drink water from the canteen. Do not tilt your head back while drinking.

7. After several swallows, allow air in your mask to enter the canteen (3). Repeat this as often as required.

8. When finished, turn the canteen (3) upright and blow into drinking mouthpiece. Return the lever (6) to its vertical position.

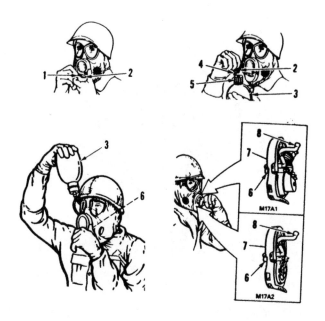

Fig 8-4.  Drinking while masked.

## F. DISCONNECTING THE M17A1/A2 DRINKING SYSTEM

1.   Pull the quick disconnect coupling half (1) from the M1 cap (2) and close its protective cover (3) (figure 8-5).

2.   Stow the canteen (4) in its cover.

3.   Return the quick disconnect coupling half (1) to its pocket (5) and press the quick disconnect coupling half into the channel (6) at the side of the voicemitter-outlet valve assembly cover (7).

Fig 8-5. Disconnecting the drinking system.

## G. DONNING MOPP GEAR

A Marine's Mission Oriented Protective Posture (MOPP) gear protects him against NBC contamination. It consists of the overgarment, mask, hood, overboots, and protective gloves (figure 8-6). Before Marines can protect themselves from NBC hazards, they must first know what individual protective equipment is available and what its capabilities are.

1. **Overgarment.** The overgarment protects the Marine against contact with chemical agent vapors, aerosols, and droplets of liquids; live biological agents; toxins; and radioactive alpha and beta particles. The overgarment comes sealed in a vapor-barrier bag that protects against rain, moisture, and sunlight. Printed instructions for using the overgarment are on the bag label. Do not remove the overgarment from the bag until it is required. When the overgarment is removed from the package and donned, its protective qualities last for 14 days, as long as it remains serviceable and uncontaminated.

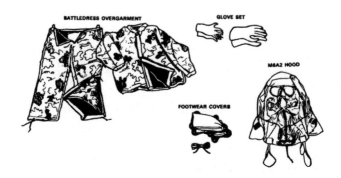

Fig 8-6. MOPP gear.

2. **Chemical Protective Glove Set.** The gloves protect against liquid chemical agents and vapor hazards. They also keep biting insect vectors and radioactive fallout, a dustlike material, away from the hands. Each glove consists of an outer glove for protection and an inner glove for perspiration absorption. The outer gloves are made of an impermeable (black) butyl rubber. The inner gloves are made of thin, white cotton. These inner gloves can be worn on either hand. If either outer glove is punctured or torn, replace the glove. When engaged in heavy work or during cold weather, Marines may wear standard work gloves or black shells over the butyl rubber gloves to protect them from damage.

3. **Chemical Protective Footwear Covers.** Marines wear the chemical protective footwear covers (overboots) over their combat boots. Overboots protect feet from contamination by all known chemical agents, vectors, and radiological dust particles.

a. The overboots are impermeable and have unsupported butyl rubber soles and butyl sheet-rubber uppers. Two variations are in field use. One has a single heel flap. The other, newer version, has a fishtail double heel flap.

b. When wearing the overboots, avoid tearing or puncturing them. Tears and punctures can happen when Marines traverse rough terrain. The laces may catch on protrusions, such as are found on tanks, causing the boots to rip. If an overboot is punctured or torn, replace it.

4. **Protective Mask.** An M17-series chemical-biological mask, when properly fitted and worn with the hood, protects against field concentrations of all known chemical and biological agents in vapor or aerosol form. Filter elements, in the cheeks of the facepiece, remove the agents from air entering the mask.

5. **Donning Sequence.** The proper sequence for donning MOPP gear is listed below:

a. Overgarment. Don the trousers and adjust the waist band for a firm fit. Don the coat, zipping and fastening the closures. Attach the three snaps across the back of the coat to the snaps on the trousers.

b. Chemical protective footwear covers. Put the footwear covers over your combat boots and fasten them according to the instructions on the package. Once tied, blouse the trouser legs over the footwear covers by closing the fasteners and tying them firmly.

c. Protective mask. Don and clear the mask, zipping the hood and fastening its straps.

d. Chemical protective gloves. Don the glove liners and then the rubber gloves. Pull the elastic cuffs of the coat over the cuffs of the gloves.

By donning in this sequence, the Marine will cover the largest exposed area in the least amount of time.

> **NOTE:** This sequence is applicable only in a contamination-free environment. In the event of a chemical or biological attack, the mask will be donned first.

## H. REMOVAL AND STORAGE OF THE M17A1/A2 PROTECTIVE MASK WITH HOOD

1.  Remove your headgear, loosen the cord (1) and unfasten the underarm straps (2) (figure 8-7).

> **CAUTION:** Be very careful in removing hood. The hood can snag on the buckles of the head harness and tear.

2.  Unzip the front, gently pull the back of the hood completely over the front of the mask, and remove the mask with hood attached.

Fig 8-7. Unmasking.

If the head harness is stowed inside of the facepiece assembly, do not force it into the faceblank. Forcing could distort the tabs or the facepiece.

3.  Make sure that your mask is dry and free of oil or solvents before stowing.

4.  Keep the interior of the carrier free of dirt and trash.

5.  When not in use, stow your mask in the carrier with the eyelens outserts installed to protect the eyelenses. The head harness may be stowed inside or outside the facepiece assembly.

> **CAUTION:** Put only authorized items in the carrier. Do not store other items on top of your mask.

6.  Hold the front of the mask in a horizontal position and smooth the hood over it.

7.  Fold the two edges of the hood over the inlet valve to create a "V" in the front of the hood. Store the underarm straps and cord inside the "V."

8. Fold the "V" upward to the left side of the mask if you are right-handed, and to the right side if you are left-handed. Do not let the hood cover the chin opening (3).

9. Hold the mask upright and put it in the carrier (4) facing out the carrier opening.

10. Let the head harness (5) swing free when you store the mask in the carrier.

 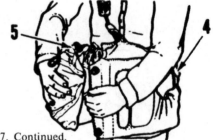

Fig 8-7. Continued.

**WARNING:** Any solid matter (even grass) under valve disks will cause fogged eyelenses, discomfort, and leakage.

**CAUTION:** Abrasives such as sand and grit will scratch eyelenses.

## I. REMOVAL OF MOPP GEAR

Marines will remove their MOPP gear only on command and in accordance with unit SOP. Marines should ensure that they do not touch the outer layer of any contaminated clothing with their exposed hands. Using the "buddy system" will help ensure that contamination is not spread while removing the protective clothing. Once the overgarment has been removed, it will be disposed of in accordance with unit SOP; normally by burial. The overboots and gloves may be decontaminated and reissued.

## J. ACTION UPON HEARING OR SEEING THE ALARM "SPRAY"

At the alarm "SPRAY" or upon being told that an aircraft is spraying a cloud, mask; sound the alarm; kneel, crouch or sit; and cover your body with a poncho within 20 seconds, as shown in figure 8-8.

On the alarm.

Mask (don, clear and check) and give the alarm.

Kneel, crouch, or sit on the ground.

Place your weapon across your lap.

Open your poncho and cover yourself and your equipment.

Check to ensure that the poncho is fully draped around you.

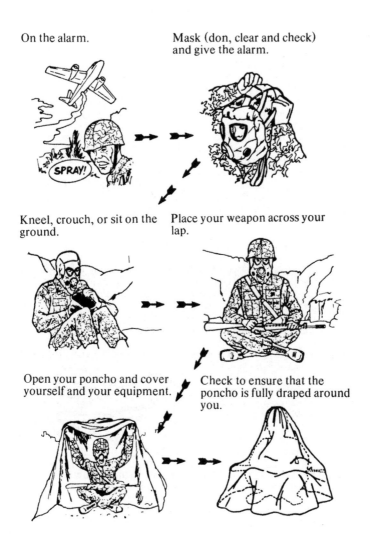

Fig 8-8. Action at the command "SPRAY."

## K. MOVEMENT THROUGH A CONTAMINATED AREA

Avoid contaminated areas if your mission permits, or pass through these areas as rapidly as possible. If you must remain in or pass through contaminated areas, you should:

o   Use all the protective equipment you have to prevent chemical agents from entering your body.

o   When possible, use vehicles and travel upwind of the contaminated area.

o   Select routes or bivouac areas on high ground since chemical agents tend to be heavier than air and settle in low places. Avoid cellars, trenches, gullies, valleys and other low places where agents may collect.

o   Avoid unnecessary contact with contaminated surfaces (such as buildings, debris, woods, shrubbery, tall grass, and puddles) which tend to hold the agent.

o   Do not stir up dust unnecessarily.

## L. FILTER REPLACEMENT PROCEDURE

The M17 series mask has two M13 series filter elements installed in the left and right cheek pouches. These filter elements provide protection to the wearer from all known toxic chemical agents. However, when exposed to agents for long periods of time or if immersed in water or if damaged, the filters break down and must be replaced. In any future conflict, the individual Marine must be able to change the filter elements himself.

1.   To remove the filter elements in the M17 series mask, follow the steps outlined in figure 8-9.

a.   Remove inlet valves by pushing up on bottom edge of valve flange with thumbs.

b.   Work collar from under filter element connector flange.

**NOTE:** To avoid rips, don't stretch rubber any more than necessary to remove or install mask components.

Fig 8-9.   Removing filter elements.

c. Reverse head harness by lengthening all straps and looping harness over front of mask. To avoid distortion, don't pull pad below lenses.

**FLAP BUTTON**

d. Unbutton nose cup from flap button.

**FILTER ELEMENT**

e. Unbutton top pouch flap from both flap buttons. Unbutton both sides of mask before proceeding.

**FLAP BUTTON**

f. Grasp upper part of one filter element between fingers and thumb. Grasp outside of facepiece between voicemitter-outlet valve assembly and connector with other hand. Pull filter element from mask. Remove second filter in same manner.

Fig 8-9. Continued.

2. To replace the filter elements, follow the steps outlined in figure 8-10.

a. Filter elements are marked either right or left. Align filter elements with outside contours of cheek pouches to be sure you're installing them correctly.

b. Hold filter element by square corner with your fingers on connector side. Pull lower pouch flap outward just enough to open cheek pouch. Insert curved edge of element into pouch with a slight turning motion. Push element up into pouch.

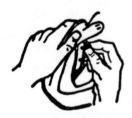

c. Grasp corner of element first inserted into mask and work element into place.

Fig 8-10. Installing filter elements.

d. Allow nosecup and pouch flaps to fall into normal position. Ensure that bottom of nosecup lies on top of chin stop so moist, exhaled air doesn't enter pouches and damage filter elements.

**NOSE CUP**

**CHIN STOP**

e. Work collar under connector flange and recheck filter element position. Adjust if necessary.

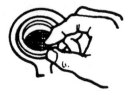

f. After both elements are installed, button pouch flaps and nosecup. Place one finger under short (outer) button and slip corresponding hole in flap over that button. Repeat with long (inner) button.

g. Slip hole in nosecup over inner button.

Fig 8-10. Continued.

h. Button both sides in like manner.

i. Return head harness to normal position and adjust straps as required.

j. Install inlet valves.

Fig 8-10. Continued.

**NOTE:** The M13A2 combat filter should be installed in all masks. This filter differs from the training filter and is identified by a green connector ring. If you have filters with a gold or black connector ring (training filters), you are only protected against riot control agents.

## M. SYMPTOMS AND TREATMENT OF CHEMICAL AGENTS

To master the proper protective measures to protect yourself against a chemical attack, you need to know the effects on your body of those chemical agents that may be used against you, your means of protection against those agents, and the treatment applied to casualties of those agents. Your M17 series Field Protective Mask is the most important single item of protective equipment you have against chemical and biological agents!

Some of the more common agents which you are likely to encounter and their treatment are contained in Table 8-1.

Table 8-1. Chemical agent characteristics

| CHEMICAL | SYMPTOMS | TREATMENT |
|---|---|---|
| Nerve Gas | Breathing difficulties, tightness in chest, nausea, excessive sweating, vomiting, cramps, headache, coma, convulsions, drooling. | Administer nerve agent antidote. |
| Blister Agents (Mustard and arsenical gases) | Eyes inflamed, burning; blisters and tissue destruction. | Decontaminate and protect with a bandage or field dressing. |
| Choking Agents | Coughing, headache, tightness of chest, nausea and vomiting. | Loosen clothing, avoid unnecessary exertion, keep warm. |
| Blood Agents (cyanide, arsine gases) | Increased breathing rate, tightness in chest, reddening of the skin, headache. | Provide supportive first aid. |
| Tear Agents | Eyes water, intense eye pain, irritation of upper respiratory tract. | Air skin, flush irritated surfaces with water. |
| Vomiting Agents (DM, DA, DC) | Sneezing, nausea, salivation, vomiting, tightness in chest. | Vigorous activity helps reduce nausea and its duration. |
| Incapacitating Agents | Abnormal behavior, muscle weakness, central nervous system disorders. | Supportive first aid and physical restraint in some situations. |
| Biological/ Toxin Agents | Varies with the type of agent used. | Provide supportive first aid and treat whatever symptoms occur. |

8-23

For more information in this area, refer to:

1.  FM 3-4                 NBC Protection

2.  FM 21-11               First Aid for Soldiers

3.  FM 21-48               NBC Defense Training

4.  FMFM 11-1              NBC Defensive Operations in FMF

5.  FMFM 11-5              Operational Aspects of Radiological
                           Defense

6.  TM 3-4240-279-10       OM Chem-Bio Field NBC Mask
                           M17/M17A1

7.  TM 8-825               Treatment of Chemical Agent
                           Casualties and Conventional
                           Military Chemical Injuries

8.  TM 10-277              Chemical Toxological and Missile
                           Fuel Handlers Protective Clothing

## Section II.   Nuclear Defense

Objectives:

   1.   *Given a simulated nuclear attack without warning, take immediate action for nuclear attack.*
   2.   *On command, with warning of an imminent nuclear attack, take appropriate action for imminent nuclear attack.*

### A. REACTION TO A NUCLEAR EXPLOSION WITHOUT WARNING

Upon a nuclear explosion without warning, you should drop flat on your stomach with your head toward the explosion. Close your eyes, place your hands under your body, and put your head down (figure 8-11).

Fig 8-11.  No-warning reaction position.

**NOTE:** Remain in position for at least 90 seconds after the blast or until the shock wave has passed and debris has stopped falling.

## B. REACTION TO A NUCLEAR EXPLOSION WITH WARNING

While in defensive positions, you are notified that a nuclear attack is imminent. Your actions should be those as illustrated in figure 8-12. However, if time does not permit, take the best shelter available.

1. Move into the nearest fighting hole or shelter. Stay as low as possible.

2. Cover the fighting hole if material is available.

Fig 8-12. With-warning reaction position.

3.  Lay on your back in the fetal
    position at the bottom of the
    fighting hole or shelter.

4.  Remain in this position for
    90 seconds following the
    blast (until the wave has
    passed and debris has stopped
    falling).

Fig 8-12. Continued.

## C. TYPES OF SHELTERS

Shelters are classified as excellent, very good, good, and fair. Figures 8-13 through 8-16 give examples of these shelters.

### 1. Excellent Protection

Tanks and armored personnel carriers are excellent protection.

Deep covered fighting holes are excellent protection.

Culverts are excellent protection.

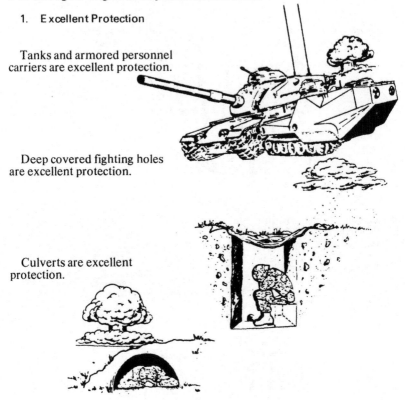

Fig 8-13. Excellent protection shelters.

## 2. Very Good Protection

Deep fighting holes are very good protection.

Fig 8-14.  Very good protection shelter.

## 3. Good Protection

Ditches are good protection.

Hills are good protection.

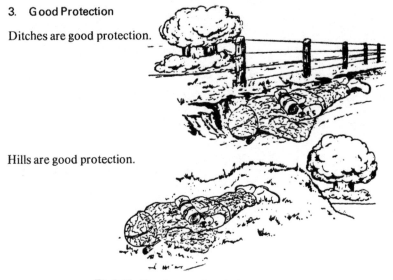

Fig 8-15.  Good protection shelters.

## 4. Fair Protection

Walls are fair protection.

Fig 8-16. Fair protection shelter.

For more information in this area, refer to:

1. FM 3-4            NBC Protection

2. FM 21-11          First Aid for Soldiers

3. FM 21-48          NBC Defense Training

4. FMFM 11-5         Operational Aspects of Radiological Defense

# Chapter 9. Marksmanship

## Section I. Service Rifle Characteristics

Objectives:

*1. On command without reference, list the characteristics of the service rifle.*
*2. On command without reference, state the maximum effective range of the service rifle.*
*3. On command without reference, within a specific time set by the command, field strip and reassemble the service rifle.*
*4. At all times, demonstrate safety procedures when handling and cleaning the service rifle.*

## A. CHARACTERISTICS

The M16A2 rifle is a lightweight, magazine-fed, gas-operated, air-cooled, shoulder-fired weapon. It is designed for either semiautomatic or three-round burst control fire through the use of a selector lever. Figure 9-1 identifies the nomenclature of the major components of the service rifle. Table 9-1 lists general data related to the rifle.

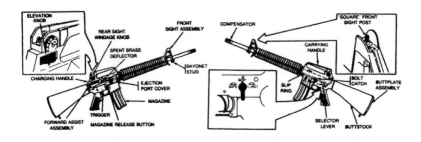

Fig 9-1. Nomenclature.

Table 9-1.  General data
1.  Caliber:  5.56 mm.
2.  Weight:  with 30-round magazine approximately 8.79 lbs.
3.  Length:  rifle with compensator, 39 5/8 inches.
4.  Cyclic rate of fire:  800 rounds per minute (approx).
5.  Maximum effective rate of fire (semi):  45 rounds per min.
6.  Maximum effective rate of fire (burst):  90 rounds per min.
7.  Sustained rate of fire:  12-15 rounds per minute.
8.  Maximum effective range:  550 meters (individual/point targets), 800 meters (area targets).
9.  Maximum range:  3,534 meters.
10.  Muzzle velocity:  3,100 feet per second (approximate).
11.  Chamber Pressure:  52,000 pounds per square inch.
12.  Rifling:  right-hand twist, 6 grooves, 1 turn in 7 inches.
13.  Sight Radius:  19.75 inches.
14.  Trigger pull:  8.5 pounds maximum; 5.0 pounds minimum.
15.  Sights:

    a. Rear: flip type, adjustable for windage and elevation.

    b. Front: adjustable for elevation.

    c. Sight adjustment: Each click of elevation (front sight) will move the strike of the round approximately 1-1/4 inch for each 100 meters; each click of elevation (rear sight) will move the strike of the round approximately 1 inch for each 100 meters; each click of windage will move the strike of the round approximately 1/2 inch for each 100 meters.

## B. MAXIMUM EFFECTIVE RANGE

The maximum effective range of a weapon is the distance to which it may be expected to fire accurately to inflict casualties or damage. The maximum effective range for the M16A2 service rifle is 550 meters for individual or point targets, and 800 meters for area targets.

## C. CLEARING

The first step in handling any weapon should be to render it *completely safe* by clearing it. Follow the steps below to clear the M16A2 service rifle:

1. Point the rifle in a SAFE DIRECTION! Place the selector lever on SAFE. If the weapon is not cocked, the selector lever cannot be placed on SAFE.

2. Remove the magazine if one is in the weapon.

3. Pull the charging handle rearward and lock the bolt to the rear. Return the charging handle forward. If you haven't already done so, place the selector lever on SAFE.

4. Check the receiver and chamber to ensure that no ammunition is present.

5. With the selector lever pointing toward SAFE, ride the bolt forward.

   **NOTE:** The weapon is now considered completely safe.

## D. DISASSEMBLY (FIELD STRIPPING)

Field stripping is the term used to describe the extent to which a Marine may disassemble his service rifle. Field strip your rifle by performing the following steps:

1. The first steps in the disassembly of the service rifle is to clear it.

2. Remove the Sling.

3. Place the service rifle firmly on the ground or on a table. Press down on the slip ring and pull the handguards free (figure 9-2). The "BUDDY SYSTEM" may be used by using both hands to press the slip ring down while having a fellow Marine pull the handguards free.

Fig 9-2. Removal of the handguards.

4. Separate the service rifle into two main groups.

a. Use the nose of a cartridge or other pointed object to press the takedown pin (figure 9-3) toward the right side of the receiver until the upper receiver swings free of the lower receiver. The takedown pin does NOT come out of the receiver.

b. Use the cartridge to press the receiver pivot pin to the right.

Fig 9-3. Pressing of the takedown pin.

    c. Separate the lower receiver group (figure 9-4) from the upper receiver group.

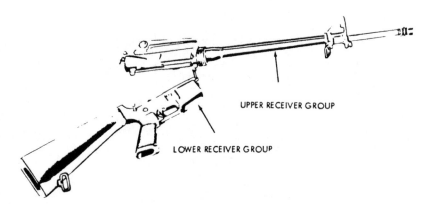

UPPER RECEIVER GROUP

LOWER RECEIVER GROUP

Fig 9-4. Main groups.

5.  Remove the bolt carrier group from the upper receiver group by pulling the charging handle and the bolt carrier out as far as they will go. Then remove the bolt carrier by itself.

6.  Remove the charging handle by lowering it into the receiver, then pulling it rearward.

7.  Disassemble the bolt carrier group (figure 9-5):

　　　　a. Use the point of a cartridge or other pointed object to press out the firing pin retaining pin.

　　　　b. Raise the front end of the carrier and allow the firing pin to drop from its well in the bolt.

　　　　c. Rotate the bolt until the cam pin is clear of the bolt carrier key.

　　　　d. Remove the cam pin by rotating it one-quarter turn and lifting it out of the well in the bolt and bolt carrier.

　　　　e. Slide the bolt out of the recess in the bolt carrier.

　　　　f. Remove the extractor by depressing it with your finger and using the firing pin to push the extractor pin free.

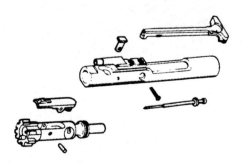

Fig 9-5.  Bolt carrier group.

8.   Remove the buffer and buffer spring by pushing the buffer rearward slightly; then depressing the detent enough to allow the buffer and buffer spring to slide over it.

**STOP! AT THIS POINT NO FURTHER DISASSEMBLY IS ALLOWED.**

**NOTE:** Disassemble the extractor and buffer assembly only when it is necessary to clean them.

Fig 9-6.  Field stripped M16A2 rifle.

## D. REASSEMBLY

Reassembly of the M16A2 is accomplished by reversing the order of the procedures described in paragraph E above; however, several points must be remembered when reassembling the rifle.

1.   The extractor assembly has a rubber insert within the spring. Be sure not to lose it. If the spring comes loose, put the large end of the spring in the extractor and seat it.

2. Don't switch bolts between rifles.

3. Stagger ring gaps on the bolt to stop gas loss.

4. Be sure the cam pin is installed in the bolt group. If it isn't, your rifle can still fire and will explode. Give the cam pin a one-quarter turn after reassembly.

5. The firing pin should not fall out when the bolt carrier group is turned upside down.

6. Be sure the bolt is unlocked (bolt face pulled out from the bolt carrier) before placing it in the upper receiver.

7. The selector lever must be on SAFE or SEMI before closing the upper receiver.

8. The round handguards are identical (top or bottom).

# Section II. Service Rifle Maintenance

Objectives:

*1. On command without reference, state the steps necessary to maintain the service rifle.*
*2. On command without reference, demonstrate immediate action to clear a stoppage in the service rifle.*
*3. Given a description of a malfunction, state the steps necessary to clear the service rifle.*
*4. At all times, demonstrate safety procedures when handling and cleaning the service rifle.*

## A. CLEANING MATERIALS

Normal care and cleaning will result in proper functioning of all parts of the weapon. Improper maintenance causes stoppages and malfunctions. Only authorized cleaning materials should be used. These materials are carried in the compartment provided in the stock of the weapon. Do not use any abrasive material to clean the rifle. Cleaner, Lubricant, and Preservative (CLP) does three things at once: dissolves firing residue and carbon, provides lubrication, and prevents rust from forming. Use CLP as follows:

1. Always shake the bottle vigorously before use.

2. Place a few drops on a patch or rag and clean your rifle with these items until they no longer pick up dirt.

3. Take a clean patch or rag and apply a fresh, light coat of CLP.

> **NOTE**: Don't "dryclean" your rifle. DO NOT use hot water or other solvents or you will wash away the Teflon lubricant that has been building up as a result of your using CLP.

## B. CLEANING

Before you field strip your rifle to clean it, make sure that you have made the weapon completely safe by clearing it.

### 1. Upper Receiver

a. **Bore.** The bore of your M16A2 has lands and grooves called rifling. Rifling makes the round spin very fast as it moves down the bore and downrange. Because it twists so quickly, it is difficult to *PUSH* a new, stiff bore brush through the bore. You will find it much easier to *PULL* your bore brush through the bore. Also, because the brush will clean better if the bristles follow the grooves (called tracking), you want the bore brush to be allowed to turn as you pull it through. This is how you do it:

(1) Attach three rod sections together, but leave each one about two turns short of being tight.

(2) Swab out the bore with the rod tip (patch holder) and a patch moistened with CLP. Holding the upper receiver in one hand, muzzle down, insert the end of the rod *without rod tip* into the chamber. Let the rod fall straight through the bore. About two to three inches will be sticking out of the muzzle at this point. Grab a hold of the rod section sticking out the muzzle and pull it through the bore.

(3) Remove the rod tip and attach the bore brush, but leave it two turns short of being tight.

(4) Holding the upper receiver in one hand, muzzle down (figure 9-7a), insert the end of the rod *without brush* into the chamber. Let the rod fall straight through the bore.

(5) Attach the handle section of the cleaning rod to the end of the rod sticking out of the muzzle (figure 9-7b).

(6) Pull the brush through the bore and out the muzzle. If you watch closely, you can see the rod twisting as you pull it through (figure 9-7c).

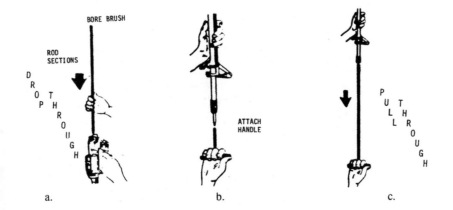

Fig 9-7. Proper steps for cleaning the bore.

(7) After one pull, take off the handle section and repeat the process. After three or four pulls, you will see that the three rod sections and the bore brush are screwing together. Loosen them up and repeat the process.

(8) Run a patch through the bore once in awhile to help clean out the crud that the brush is getting loose. You can use the same technique as described above to save time. Just replace the bore brush with the swab holder and a wet patch. Drop it through. You won't need to attach the handle to pull a patch through. If you leave the rods loose again, the patch will "track" in the rifling as before. But remember, always have the bore wet with cleaner before trying to pull a brush through.

b. Chamber. It is very important that the chamber of your rifle be kept clean. To clean the chamber follow the steps below:

(1) Attach the chamber brush lightly coated with CLP to a section of the cleaning rod and insert it into the chamber (figure 9-8). Use five or six plunging strokes and three or four rotations ($360^o$) of the brush to breakup tough carbon in the chamber.

9-11

(2) Remove the brush and dry the chamber thoroughly with clean patches.

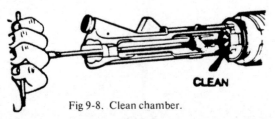

Fig 9-8. Clean chamber.

c. Gas tube. Clean the protruding extension of the gas tube in the receiver with the bore brush attached to a section of the cleaning rod. The top of the gas tube can be cleaned by inserting the rod and brush through the back of the receiver (figure 9-9).

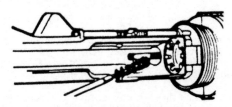

Fig 9-9. Clean gas extension.

d. Locking lugs. Clean the locking lugs in the barrel extension using a small bristle brush dipped in CLP to remove all carbon deposits. The all-purpose brush is good for this operation.

e. Using a clean rag or all-purpose brush dipped in CLP, clean all outer and inner surfaces to remove powder fouling, corrosion, dirt, and rust.

2. Lower Receiver Group

a. With the all-purpose brush or a clean rag, wipe any particles of dirt, corrosion, or powder fouling from the outer surface of the lower receiver.

b. Wipe any particles of dirt from the trigger mechanism with a clean patch or brush.

c. Components of the lower receiver group (buffer, action spring, and buffer tube) can be cleaned with CLP and the all-purpose brush. Use a scrubbing action to remove all carbon. Use the opposite end of the brush with a piece of cloth to clean the hard to reach places. A rag attached to the swab holder may be used to wipe inside the buffer tube. Clean the drain hole with the small end of the brush or with a pipe cleaner.

3. Bolt Carrier Group. Disassemble the bolt carrier group and thoroughly clean all parts with a patch or all-purpose brush dampened with CLP.

a. Clean the locking lugs of the bolt using the all-purpose brush and CLP. Ensure that all carbon deposits and metal filings are removed; then wipe clean with dry patches. Ensure that all carbon deposits are removed from the area behind the bolt rings.

b. Use the all-purpose brush coated with CLP and scrub the extractor and extractor well to remove carbon and metal filings. Also clean the firing pin recess and the firing pin. Use a worn bore brush (figure 9-10 coated with CLP to clean the interior of the carrier key. Wipe the interior dry with a pipe cleaner.

**NOTE:** Do not use a Q-Tip to clean the carrier key because it may break off and become lodged in the gas tube.

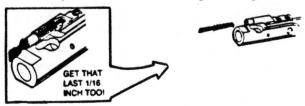

GET THAT LAST 1/16 INCH TOO!

Fig 9-10. Clean carrier key.

4. Magazines. Disassemble the magazines, being careful not to stretch or bend the magazine springs. Scrub all parts of the magazines with the all-purpose brush coated with CLP to remove any foreign material. Once they are clean, wipe them dry. Lightly lubricate the spring. The magazines are made of aluminum. They do need need any lubrication.

## C. INSPECTION

Once you have cleaned your rifle, and prior to lubricating and reassembling it, check to ensure that all parts are serviceable. If parts are missing or defective, see your armorer. When inspecting the bolt carrier group, pay particular attention to the following:

- o  Bolt—Cracks or fractures, especially in the cam pin hole area; bolts that contain pits extending into the firing pin hole need replacing.
- o  Firing pin—Bent, cracked, blunted, or sharp end.
- o  Firing pin retaining pin—Bent or badly worn.
- o  Cam pin—Cracked, chipped, or missing.
- o  Extractor and extractor spring—Check extractor for chipped or broken edges in the area of the lip that engages the cartridge rim. Check to ensure that the rubber insert is inside the extractor spring.

## D. LUBRICATION

Under all but the coldest conditions, CLP is the lubricant to use on your rifle. Remember to remove excessive CLP from the bore and chamber before firing. In this paragraph, the term "lightly lubed" refers to a film of CLP barely visible to the eye. "Generously lubed" means a film heavy enough so that it can be spread with a finger.

1. Upper Receiver. Lightly lube inside the upper receiver, the bore and chamber, outer surfaces of the barrel and front sight, and all of the surfaces under the handguards. Be sure that you lube the locking lugs. When lubricating the sights, perform the following steps:

a. Front sight. Depress the front sight detent and apply several drops of CLP. Depress the detent several more times to work the lubricant into the spring.

b. Adjustable rear sight

(1) Moving parts. Using one or two drops of CLP, rotate all moving parts to ensure that the lubricant is spread evenly above and below them (figure 9-11).

9-14

(2) Elevation screw shaft. Lubricate the shaft from the inside of the upper receiver by putting two or three drops of CLP on the bottom of the elevation screw shaft and in the elevation detent spring hole. Rotate the elevation dial back and forth a few times while keeping the upper receiver upside down.

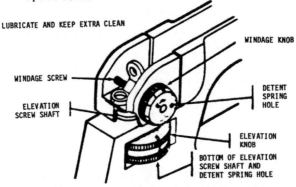

LUBRICATE AND KEEP EXTRA CLEAN

WINDAGE KNOB

WINDAGE SCREW

DETENT SPRING HOLE

ELEVATION SCREW SHAFT

ELEVATION KNOB

BOTTOM OF ELEVATION SCREW SHAFT AND DETENT SPRING HOLE

Fig 9-11. Lubricating the rear sight.

2. Lower Receiver. Lightly lube the inside of the lower receiver extension. Generously lube the takedown and pivot pins and detents, as well as all moving parts inside the lower receiver and their pins.

3. Bolt Carrier Group. Dry the carrier key with a pipe cleaner, then place one drop of CLP in its opening. Lightly lube the charging handle and inner and outer surfaces of the bolt carrier. Generously lube the slide and cam pin area of the bolt carrier. Generously lube the outside of the bolt body, the bolt rings, cam pin area, and firing pin retaining pin. Use only a light coat of CLP on the firing pin and firing pin recess in the bolt. Put a light coat on the extractor and extractor pin.

## E. CORRECTIVE ACTION

A stoppage is an unintentional interruption in the cycle of operation. Proper care of the rifle will prevent most stoppages. When one does occur, the Marine rifleman promptly reduces it and continues his mission.

1. **Immediate Action.** The first step in reducing a stoppage is to apply immediate action in the sequence of the steps listed below:

a. **SLAP** upward on the base of the magazine to ensure that it is fully seated.

b. **PULL** the charging handle to the rear.

c. **OBSERVE** the ejection port to see if a cartridge or cartridge case is ejected. Check the chamber for obstructions.

d. **RELEASE** the charging handle to chamber a new round (do not ride the charging handle forward).

e. **TAP** the forward assist to ensure that the bolt is fully forward and locked.

f. **SHOOT** (attempt to fire). If the rifle won't fire, look for trouble and apply remedial action.

> **NOTE:** SPORTS is an acronym that may help you to remember the six steps of immediate action: *Slap, Pull, Observe, Release, Tap, and Shoot.*

2. **Remedial Action.** If your rifle still fails to fire after performing immediate action, check again for a jammed cartridge case. If a cartridge case is in the chamber, tap it out with a cleaning rod. If the chamber is empty, change magazines and attempt to fire. If your rifle still fails, you will have to troubleshoot the cause of the malfunction. Several common problems are caused by mechanical failure of the weapon, magazine, or ammunition. These problems, their usual causes, and corrective actions to be taken are shown in table 9-2.

3. If an audible "POP" or reduced recoil is experienced during firing, immediately CEASE FIRE. *DO NOT APPLY IMMEDIATE ACTION.* Remove the magazine, lock the bolt to the rear, place the selector on SAFE, and visually inspect and/or insert a cleaning rod into the bore to ensure there is not a bullet stuck in the bore. If a bullet is stuck in the barrel of the weapon, DO NOT attempt to remove it. Turn the weapon in to the armorer.

## Table 9-2. Troubleshooting

| PROBLEM | CHECK FOR | WHAT TO DO |
|---|---|---|
| WON'T FIRE | Selector lever on SAFE. | Put it on SEMI or BURST |
| | Improper assembly of firing pin. | Assemble correctly. Retaining pin goes in back of large shoulder of firing pin. |
| | Too much oil in firing pin recess. | Wipe out with pipe cleaner. |
| | Defective ammo. | Remove and discard. |
| | Too much carbon on firing pin or in firing pin recess. | Clean. |
| BOLT WON'T UNLOCK | Dirty or burred bolt. | See your NCO or unit armorer. |
| WON'T EXTRACT | Broken extractor spring. | See your armorer. |
| | Dirty or corroded ammo | Remove. Push out stuck round with cleaning rod. |
| | Carbon in chamber. | Clean chamber. |
| | Fouling or carbon in extractor recess or lip. | Clean. |
| WON'T FEED | Dirty or corroded ammo. | Clean. |
| | Dirty magazine. | Clean. |
| | Defective magazine. | Replace. |
| | Too many rounds in the magazine. | Take out excess. |
| | Action of buffer assembly is restricted. | Take out buffer and spring and clean. |

Table 9-2. Continued

| PROBLEM | CHECK FOR | WHAT TO DO |
|---|---|---|
| WON'T FEED (continued) | Magazine not fully seated. | Adjust magazine catch. Press button on right side, turn catch on left side clockwise to tighten and counterclockwise to loosen. |
| DOUBLE FEED | Defective magazine. | Replace. |
| WON'T CHAMBER | Dirty or corroded ammo. | Clean. |
| | Damaged ammo. | Replace. |
| | Carbon in chamber or on gas tube | Clean |
| WON'T LOCK | Dirt, corrosion, or carbon buildup in barrel locking lugs. | Clean lugs. |
| WON'T EXTRACT | Frozen extractor. | Remove and clean. |
| | Restricted buffer assembly. | Remove and clean. |
| | Restricted movement of bolt carrier group. | Remove, clean, and lube. Before putting bolt back in, ensure gas tube fits into carrier key and that the carrier moves freely |
| SHORT RECOIL | Gaps in bolt rings (not staggered). | Stagger ring gaps. |
| | Carbon or dirt in carrier key or on outside of gas tube. | Clean. |
| | Q-Tip stuck inside carrier key (check with pipe cleaner). | See your armorer. |

9-18

Table 9-2. Continued

| PROBLEM | CHECK FOR | WHAT TO DO |
|---|---|---|
| BOLT FAILS TO LOCK AFTER LAST ROUND | Dirty or corroded bolt latch. | Clean. |
| | Faulty magazine. | Replace. |
| SELECTOR | Needs oil. | Lubricate with CLP. |
| LEVER BINDS | | |
| | Dirt or sand under trigger. | Clean. |
| BOLT CARRIER "HUNG UP" | Round jammed between bolt and charging handle and/or double feed. | Remove magazine. Push in on the bottom of the bolt latch. |

**WARNING:** KEEP CLEAR OF THE MUZZLE.

Bang rifle butt on the ground. Bolt should lock to the rear.

**CAUTION:** AFTER ROUND IS REMOVED, BOLT IS UNDER TENSION.

While bolt is held to the rear, round should fall through magazine well.

**NOTE:** IF THIS PROCEDURE FAILS, USE A SECTION OF CLEANING ROD TO PUSH BOLT FULLY TO THE REAR THROUGH EJECTION PORT.

# Section III. Firing The Service Rifle

Objectives:

*1. Annually, qualify on the known distance course.*
*2. Given a service rifle, demonstrate procedures to battlesight zero the service rifle.*
*3. From 200 yards, wearing field protective mask and given 10 rounds of ammunition, engage a target with the service rifle.*
*4. At all times, demonstrate safety procedures when handling and cleaning the service rifle.*

## A. FUNCTION CHECKS

Prior to firing your weapon, you should conduct a series of preventive maintenance checks and services. Clear the weapon, then remove excessive oil from the bore and chamber. Retract the bolt to ensure that there is free movement between the bolt carrier and the gas tube. Perform the following functional checks to ensure that the selector lever works properly on:

1. **Safe.** Pull the charging handle to the rear and release. Place the selector on SAFE. Pull the trigger. The hammer should not fall.

2. **Semi.** Place the selector on SEMI. Pull the trigger and hold it to the rear. The hammer should fall. Pull the charging handle to the rear and release it. Release the trigger and then pull it again. The hammer should fall.

3. **Burst.** Place the selector on BURST. Pull the charging handle to the rear and release it. Pull the trigger and hold it to the rear. The hammer should fall. Pull the charging handle to the rear and release it three more times. Release the trigger and then pull it again. The hammer should fall.

> **NOTE:** If your rifle fails to complete any of the function checks in the manner described, take it to your armorer.

9-20

## B. SAFETY PROCEDURES

1. General Rifle Safety

a. Consider every weapon to be loaded until you examine it and find it to be unloaded. Never trust your memory in this respect. There is an old saying among hunters: "the empty gun shoots the loudest."

b. Never point a weapon at anyone you do not intend to shoot, or in a direction where an accidental discharge may do harm.

c. Never fire a weapon until it has been inspected to see that nothing is in the bore. Firing a weapon with an obstruction in the bore may burst the barrel, resulting in serious injury to you or your fellow Marines.

d. Never grease or oil ammunition. Some foreign weapons are designed to use greased or oiled ammunition, but the use of such ammunition in your weapon will result in dangerously high pressure in the chamber and barrel.

e. Never place a cartridge in a hot chamber unless you intend to fire it immediately. Excessive heat may cause the cartridge to cook off.

f. Do not allow your ammunition to be exposed to the direct rays of the sun for any length of time.

2. Range Firing Safety. Range safety rules may vary from command to command, due to a number of different factors. Some of the more common range firing safety rules are shown below:

a. Before dry firing, ensure that your weapon is completely safe. If dummy ammunition is to be used while dry firing, check each round to ensure that no live ammunition is present.

b. Upon completion of firing, each rifle will be inspected to ensure that all live ammunition has been removed from the weapon.

c. Except while being used to conduct live or dry fire exercise, all rifles will have magazines removed, bolts opened and locked to the rear, and safeties on.

d. When carrying a rifle on the range, keep the muzzle pointed upward and downrange.

e. Prior to firing, all individuals including range personnel will be informed of the safety limits of the range and safety procedures to be used while firing or waiting to fire.

f. When not being used, rifles will be placed in such a position as to be easily inspected to ensure that bolts are open and safeties engaged.

g. Dry firing will not be conducted in the rear of the firing line on any range where live firing is in progress. Dry firing may be conducted on any designated and approved dry firing range. Dry firing on the firing line during the conduct of live firing, when firing points are available, may be authorized by the range officer.

h. When on a live firing range, personnel will not move forward of the firing line until given clearance by the officer-in- charge or the line NCO.

i. Anyone observing an unsafe condition during firing exercises is authorized to give the command, CEASE FIRING. When this command is given, it will be relayed immediately to the line NCO who will command CEASE FIRING AND LOCK or CLEAR AND LOCK, as appropriate. The range officer is then responsible for investigation of the unsafe condition and taking necessary corrective action.

## C. BATTLESIGHT ZERO (BZO)

The sights of the M16A2 service rifle give a Marine a capability he never enjoyed with the M16A1. This is the capability to rapidly change ranges on his sights without losing his original battlesight zero. Battlesight zero is a sight setting that will allow you to engage most targets *without* having to adjust your sights. It is normally set for point of aim, point of impact at 300 meters. This is the sight setting that should be routinely carried on your rifle. BZO allows you to engage most targets without having to make a sight setting or aiming point adjustment if you aim at center mass.

1. Known Distance Range. The preferred method of establishing a battlesight zero for your rifle is to use the sight settings you last used on the 300-yard line rapid fire on the known distance qualification course. However, it must be remembered that these sight settings are only good for you on the same rifle that you used that time. If the sights have been worked on by armory personnel, or you now have a different rifle. You must again establish a new battlesight zero.

**2. 25-Meter Range.** Often it is not possible for a Marine to go to the qualification range to establish a battlesight zero for his rifle. In these cases he must use an alternate method. The best alternate method is to use the 25-meter battlesight zero range. To set the sights of the M16A2 service rifle to battlesight zero using the 25-meter range, you must first set the sights to mechanical zero as follows:

      a. On the front sight, depress the detent with an appropriate object, such as the point of a round. Rotate the sight post either up or down until its base is flush with the surrounding housing. This is front sight mechanical zero (figure 9-12). Mark the front sight by placing a straight line across the front sight post and the front sight aperture with paint or fingernail polish.

Fig 9-12. Front sight mechanical zero.

      b. Set the rear sight aperture 0-2 in the down position with the unmarked aperture up.

      c. Rotate the windage knob either right or left until the windage index line is aligned with the center of the windage index scale. This is windage mechanical zero (figure 9-13). Mark the windage knob by placing a straight line across the windage knob and the rear sight aperture with paint or fingernail polish.

9-23

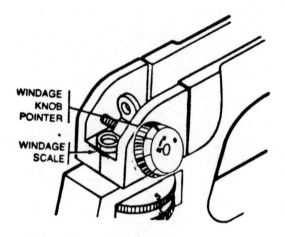

Fig 9-13. Windage mechanical zero.

d. Rotate the rear sight elevation knob in the down direction (counterclockwise) until it will go down no farther. The elevation scale should be on the 8/3 setting minus three clicks. The rear sight should be all the way down and on the last whole "click" before it bottoms out. This is rear sight elevation mechanical zero. This also completes mechanical zero for the M16A2 service rifle. If your range scale will not line up in the above manner, an armorer will be required to adjust the range scale for you.

NOTE: Mark the sights while in mechanical zero to ensure that a positive reference is always available. Particularly on the windage knob where the adjustment of only one or two clicks is difficult, if not impossible, to observe with the eye.

e. To set battlesight zero on the 25-meter range with the M16A2 service rifle, follow the steps listed below:

(1) With the sights set at mechanical zero, add four clicks of elevation. This is done by rotating the rear sight elevation knob in the direction indicated by the up arrow. The rear elevation should now be $3+1$.

(2) Using a good prone firing position, aim in on center mass of a target similar to the one shown in figure 9-14.

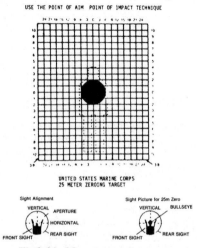

Fig 9-14. 25-meter zeroing target.

(3) Fire a three-round group.

(4) Adjust your sights as follows:

   o  For elevation: Rotate the front sight post as indicated by the arrow to move the center of the shot group onto center mass. Each click will move the impacts approximately 3/8 inch or one line on the target.

   o  For windage: Rotate the windage knob either right or left as indicated by the arrow to move the center of the shot group onto center mass. Each click will move the impacts approximately 1/8 inch, or 3 clicks will move the impacts one line on the target.

(5) Repeat steps (2), (3), and (4) until a shot group is recorded at the point of aim.

(6) Once a shot group is recorded at the point of aim, firing has been completed but not the setting of the sights. Once all weapons have been cleared and all shooters are off the firing line, the rear sight elevation must be set on 8/3 for 300 meters. The initial one click of rear elevation was only needed to adjust for the trajectory characteristics at 25 meters.

(7) Record the sight settings.

## D. RIFLE REQUALIFICATION

Every Marine except for those who are exempt, must requalify annually with the service rifle. Rifle requalification standards and procedures have been established in separate directives, and requalification will be conducted in accordance with them. When requalifying, you will be required to fire from four firing positions. These positions are briefly explained in the following paragraphs.

1. **Prone.** Stand at the ready with a loop sling high on your arm. Holding the rifle securely, drop to your knees. Place the butt of the rifle on the ground, under the center of your body. Place the left elbow right and forward so that it will be directly under the rifle (figure 9-15a). Force the butt of the rifle into your right shoulder, then relax into the sling and obtain your stock weld (figure 9-15b). Spread your feet shoulder width apart. Your shoulders should be level with the ground.

a.                                              b.

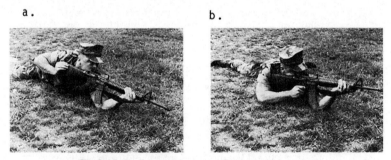

Fig 9-15. Assuming the prone firing position.

2. **Sitting.** Stand at the ready with a loop sling high on your arm. Drop to the ground, breaking your fall with the right hand. Place your upper left arm inside the left knee, then force the butt of the rifle into the right shoulder. Lower your right arm until it rests inside the right knee. Relax forward into the sling and obtain a stock weld (figure 9-16).

Crossed ankle

Crossed leg

Open Leg

Fig 9-16. Sitting position.

3. **Kneeling.** With a loop sling high on your arm, drop to your right knee, keeping your right leg parallel to the target. Your left foot is toward the target and the lower left leg is approximately vertical. Lower your right buttock to your right foot. Place the flat surface of your upper left arm on the flat surface of the left knee. Force the butt of the rifle into your right shoulder. Relax forward into the sling and obtain a stock weld. There are several options in positioning the legs in the kneeling position (figure 9-17).

High kneeling

Medium kneeling

Low kneeling

Fig 9-17. Kneeling position.

**4. Standing.** Spread your feet a comfortable distance apart. Using a modified parade sling (sling cannot be used for support), place the left hand in a place to best support the rifle (figure 9-18a). Grasp the pistol grip and place the rifle into your right shoulder. Obtain a stock weld and hold your right elbow high to form a pocket for the rifle butt (figure 9-18b).

a.

b.

Fig 9-18. Assuming a standing position.

## E. ENGAGE A TARGET UNDER NBC CONDITIONS

With the possibility of being employed on the chemical or nuclear battlefield, being able to effectively engage targets while wearing the protective mask is a task that all Marines must master. When you fire with the field protective mask on, you may find it difficult to align the sights of your weapon. The thickness of the eyelens, and also the bulk of the filter, make it hard to obtain a good stock weld. By placing the butt of the stock slightly down and outward in your shoulder, you may overcome this difficulty.

# "MY RIFLE"

### The creed of a United States Marine
### by
### Major General W. H. Rupertus, USMC

This is my rifle. There are many like it, but this one is mine.

My rifle is my best friend. It is my life. I must master it as I must master my life.

My rifle without me is useless. Without my rifle, I am useless. I must fire my rifle true. I must shoot straighter than my enemy who is trying to kill me. I must shoot him before he shoots me. I will ...

My rifle and myself know that what counts in this war is not the rounds we fire, the noise of our burst, nor the smoke we make. We know that it is the hits that count. We will hit ...

My rifle is human, even as I, because it is my life. Thus, I will learn it as a brother. I will learn its weaknesses, its strengths, its parts, its accessories, its sights, and its barrel. I will ever guard it against the ravages of weather and damage. I will keep my rifle clean and ready, even as I am clean and ready. We will become part of each other. We will ...

Before God I swear this creed. My rifle and myself are the defenders of my country. We are the masters of our enemy. We are the saviors of my life.

So be it, until victory is America's and there is no enemy, but Peace!

---

For more information in this area, refer to:

1. FMFM 1-3                         Basic Marksmanship

2. MCO 3574.2F                     Marksmanship and Familiarization Firing

3. TM 05538C-10/1 w/Ch 1-4    U.S. Marine Corps Operator's Manual w/Components List

# Chapter 10. Individual Tactical Measures

## Section I.    Defense

Objectives:

*1. On command without reference, state the mission of the Marine rifle squad.*
*2. On command without reference, state the procedures used to construct a fighting hole.*
*3. Given appropriate resources, camouflage self and individual equipment.*

### A. MISSION OF THE MARINE RIFLE SQUAD

1.    The mission of the Marine rifle squad is TO LOCATE, CLOSE WITH, AND DESTROY THE ENEMY BY FIRE AND MANEUVER, OR REPEL THE ENEMY'S ASSAULT BY FIRE AND CLOSE COMBAT.

2.    While the offensive portion of the rifle squad's mission is not performed by all Marine units, each unit is responsible for its own defense. Because of this, there are certain defensive tasks that all Marines must master.

### B. THE DEFENSE

The defensive mission of the Marine rifle squad is to repel the enemy's assault by fire and close combat. This requires that the squad be assigned a definite position and sector of fire prior to the expected attack so as to take maximum advantage of the terrain and fields of fire. Certain tasks must be accomplished to prepare the assigned position for the actual conduct of the defense.

1. **Digging Fighting Holes.** Fighting holes provide excellent protection against small-arms fire, shell fragments, airplane strafing or bombing, effects of nuclear detonations, and the crushing action of tanks. The one-man and two-man fighting holes are basic types. The choice of type rests with the squad leader if not prescribed by higher authority. The type of fighting hole used is based on squad strength, fields of fire, and size of the squad sector.

a. Construction of a one-man fighting hole. In most types of soil, the fighting hole gives protection against the crushing action of tanks, provided the occupant crouches at least two feet below the ground surface. In sandy or soft soils, it may be necessary to revet the sides with sandbags to prevent them from caving in. The soil is piled around the hole as a parapet, approximately three feet thick and six inches high, leaving a shelf wide enough to be used as an elbow rest by a Marine firing his weapon. Other characteristics of the one-man fighting hole are depicted in figure 10-1.

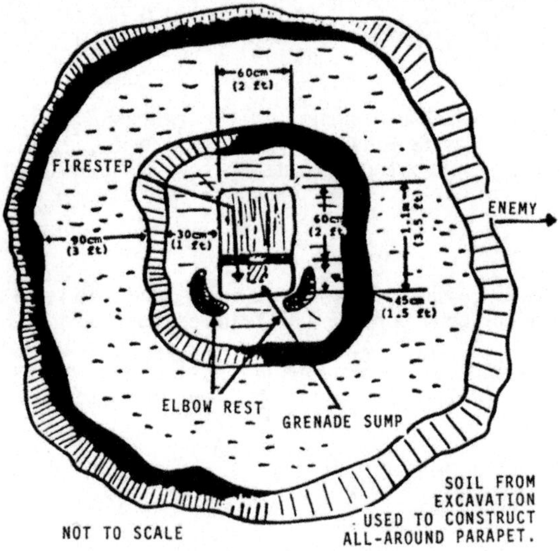

Fig 10-1. One-man fighting hole without overhead protection.

b. **Comparison of the one-man and two-man fighting holes.** Since it is longer than the one-man type, the two-man fighting hole offers somewhat less protection against tanks crossing along the long axis, as well as less protection against strafing, bombing, and shell fragments. Some advantages of the two-man fighting hole (figure 10-2) are continuous observation (one man rests while the other man maintains security), assistance and reassurance for each other, and redistribution of ammunition between the two Marines.

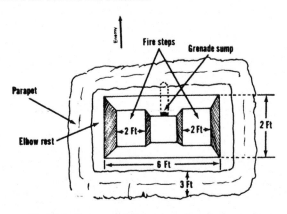

Fig 10-2. Two-man fighting hole (overhead view).

2. **Camouflage and Concealment.** Camouflage is the use of concealment and disguise to minimize the possibility of detection and/or identification of troops, equipment and positions. It includes taking advantage of the natural environment, as well as the application of natural and artificial materials. Concealment is protection from enemy observation or surveillance. Camouflage measures are strictly carried out from the moment the position is occupied.

a. **Position.** Camouflage of individual positions includes the use of all available natural materials. The following techniques are recommended:

    o    Do not disclose the position by excessive or careless clearing of fields of fire.

    o    Use the same turf or topsoil that has been removed from the area of the fighting hole to camouflage the parapet.

10-3

o   Dispose of all soil from the fighting hole not used on the parapet. Carry the soil away in sandbags or shelter halves. Dispose of it under low bushes, on dirt roads or paths, in streams or ponds, or camouflage it.

o   Avoid digging-in next to an isolated bush, tree, or clump of vegetation.

o   Conceal the fighting hole from observation, both overhead and ground level, by the use of a camouflaged cover. Construct the cover from natural materials.

o   Replace natural material used in camouflage before it wilts or changes color.

o   Avoid creating fresh paths near the position. Use old paths or vary the route followed to and from the position.

o   Avoid littering the area near the position with paper, tin cans, and other debris.

**b. Equipment.** The outline of the helmet is one of the striking characteristics of a Marine's equipment. Take steps to change the form of the helmet (figure 10-3), as well as the shape of your other equipment. If your pack or other 782 gear has faded, darken it with mud or burnt cork. You can change the shape of your weapon by wrapping it with strips of burlap, but be sure not to interfere with its sighting and firing. Be especially careful with shiny objects such as belt buckles, mess gear, goggles, binoculars, and personal items such as rings and watches.

Fig 10-3. Techniques of camouflaging the helmet.

10-4

c. Body and clothing. Your face, neck, and hands should be toned down by painting them with a disrupted pattern (figure 10-4). Pay particular attention to areas that will reflect light, such as nose, cheekbones, chin, and eye sockets. Use camouflage sticks, charcoal, mud, or burnt cork to camouflage all exposed skin. Table 10-1 provides information on color combinations to be used when camouflaging the skin.

Fig 10-4. Camouflaging the face.

Table 10-1. Colors used in camouflage.

| CAMOUFLAGE MATERIAL | SKIN COLOR<br>LIGHT OR DARK | SHINE AREAS<br>FOREHEAD, CHEEKBONES, EARS, NOSE AND CHIN | SHADOW AREAS<br>AROUND EYES, UNDER NOSE, AND UNDER CHIN |
|---|---|---|---|
| LOAM AND LIGHT GREEN STICK | ALL TROOPS USE IN AREAS WITH GREEN VEGETATION | USE LOAM | USE LIGHT GREEN |
| SAND AND LIGHT GREEN STICK | ALL TROOPS USE IN AREAS LACKING GREEN VEGETATION | USE LIGHT GREEN | USE SAND |
| LOAM AND WHITE | ALL TROOPS USE ONLY IN SNOW-COVERED TERRAIN | USE LOAM | USE WHITE |
| BURNT CORK, BARK CHARCOAL, OR LAMP BLACK | ALL TROOPS, IF CAMOUFLAGE STICKS NOT AVAILABLE | USE | DO NOT USE |
| LIGHT-COLOR MUD | ALL TROOPS, IF CAMOUFLAGE STICKS NOT AVAILABLE | DO NOT USE | USE |

For more information in this area, refer to:

1. FM 5-15            Field Fortifications

2. FM 5-20            Camouflage

3. FM 5-34            Engineer Field Data

4. FM 21-75           Combat Skills of the Soldier

5. FMFM 6-5           Marine Rifle Squad

6. TEC Lsn            Camouflage, Cover, and Concealment I
   937-061-0130-F

7. TEC Lsn            Camouflage, Cover, and Concealment II
   937-061-0131-F

8. TEC Lsn            Camouflage, Cover, and Concealment III
   937-061-0132-F

9. TEC Lsn            Hasty Fighting Positions
   010-071-1044-F

10. TEC Lsn           Supervise the Preparation of a Squad
    010-071-1072-F    Defensive Position

# Section II. Grenades

Objective: *Given a simulated defensive position, demonstrate the procedures to be used in the employment of grenades.*

## A. PURPOSE

Handgrenades are designed to be thrown at a target. They assist the individual Marine in the accomplishment of the following missions:

o   Producing casualties
o   Signaling
o   Screening
o   Illuminating
o   Producing incendiary effects
o   Riot control (gas only)

## B. IDENTIFICATION

You should be able to identify, by sight and touch (for night employment), the type of grenade required for the particular mission. Most grenades are different in size and shape from each other. Examples of these are the baseball-shaped M67 fragmentation grenade and the egg-shaped MK 1 illumination grenade (figure 10-5).

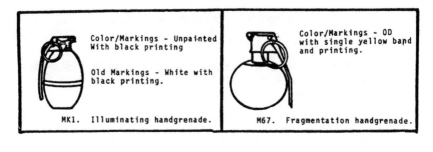

Color/Markings - Unpainted With black printing

Old Markings - White with black printing.

MK1.   Illuminating handgrenade.

Color/Markings - OD with single yellow band and printing.

M67.   Fragmentation handgrenade.

Fig 10-5. Handgrenades.

## C. INSPECTION

Any time you draw grenades, you should inspect them for any obvious defects. If you cannot correct any defect found, turn the grenade in. Figure 10-6 labels the nomenclature of grenades and highlights areas to be inspected.

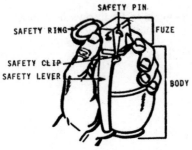

Fig 10-6. Grenade nomenclature.

1. Make sure the fuze is not unscrewed from the body of the grenade.

2. Ensure that the safety clip is in the correct position. If no clip is present, attach a clip to the grenade.

    a. Slide the clip onto the handle.

    b. Attach the loop portion of the clip around the fuze.

    c. Snap the clip end around the safety lever.

3. Check the safety pin. If it is partially removed, carefully push it into place while holding the lever securely down. If the pin is bent, carefully bend it back into position.

4. Check the safety ring. If it is cracked, turn the grenade in.

5. Check the lever. Return the grenade if it is broken.

6. Check for dirt. If the grenade is dirty or grimy, clean it with a damp cloth.

## D. THROWING

1. **Removal of the Safety Clip.** The safety clip must be removed before you attempt to throw the M67 fragmentation grenade (figure 10-7).

  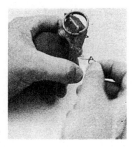

Fig 10-7. Removing the safety clip.

2. **Holding the Grenade.** Safety is the primary factor to be considered when determining the proper method of holding the grenade (figure 10-8).

Right-handed thrower            Left-handed thrower

Fig 10-8. Holding the grenade.

3. Technique

a. Observe the target to fix the throwing distance in your mind.

b. From a covered position, hold the grenade near the chest at shoulder level and grasp the safety ring with the index finger of your opposite hand. Pull the pin with a twisting motion.

c. Look at the target again. Align yourself with the target so you can throw comfortably.

d. Throw the grenade with an overhand motion that is most natural to you and that will allow the grenade to spin in flight.

e. Follow through as you release the grenade. Take cover.

4. Positions. The positions illustrated are used primarily for training purposes to ensure uniformity and control. In combat, your position will be dictated by the amount of cover and distance to the target.

a. Standing (figure 10-9)
Balance your weight. Hold the grenade near the chest shoulder high. Pull pin with twisting motion.

Look at the target.

Fig 10-9. Standing position.

10-10

Throw with natural motion.
Follow through.

Take cover. If none available,
drop to prone position with helmet
facing the target.

b. Kneeling (figure 10-10)

Kneel comfortably and look at
the target.

Throw naturally.
Push off with foot.

Take cover.

Fig 10-10. Kneeling position.

10-11

c. Prone to kneeling (figure 10-11)

Hold grenade forward so that you can see the safety pin.

Assume kneeling position. Throw and take cover as above.

Fig 10-11. Prone to kneeling.

d. Alternate prone (figure 10-12)

Body perpendicular to intended flight.

Brace right foot firmly on ground. Pull pin and hold grenade away from your body, arm cocked for throwing.

Fig 10-12. Alternate prone.

Throw grenade by pushing off with foot and pulling downward with outstretched left arm.

Follow through. Take cover.

Fig 10-12. Continued.

For more information in this area, refer to:

1.  FM 23-30                     Grenades and Pyrotechnic Signals

2.  TEC Lsn                      Identification of Handgrenades and Grenade
    645-093-7315-F               Ammunition

## Section III.    Employment of Flares and Boobytraps

Objective:

*Given a simulated defensive position, demonstrate procedures to be used in the employment of flares and boobytraps.*

### A. EMPLOYMENT

Effective employment of flares and boobytraps can significantly enhance the security of your defensive position. In employing these devices, you are limited only by the quantity and types of materials available, preparation time, and your imagination. You may use these devices to perform functions, such as providing early warning or illumination, confusing or delaying the enemy, covering gaps between positions, and producing casualties.

1.    When using boobytraps, always consider the following:

a. All boobytraps should be indicated on tactical maps, fireplan overlays, and minefield records. This ensures that friendly troops are alerted to their location.

b. Boobytraps should be recovered or neutralized before advancing. All should be approached and handled with extreme caution, as they may have been tampered with by the enemy.

2. When employing tripflares and other devices to provide early warning, consider extending the devices across any avenue of approach into your position. The positioning of tripflares should allow for maximum observation of the illuminated area from your position.

### B. M49A1 TRIPFLARE

1.    Purpose. The M49A1 surface tripflare is used to give early warning of infiltrating troops by illuminating the field of the advancing enemy.

2. Emplacement

   a. The location chosen for installation of the flare and tripwire should be in the logical path of infiltrating troops and so positioned that the field toward the enemy will be illuminated and friendly defense positions will not be disclosed.

   b. In most instances, it is easier to install the flare using the pullpin method because the amount of slack in the tripwire is less critical. Also, the tripwire may be installed to the left or the right of the flare.

   c. To mount the bracket by nailing, use two of the nails provided. The bracket must be as near vertical as possible and 15 to 18 inches above the ground.

   d. To mount the flare, align the lever with the trigger pivot.

   e. Carefully slide the flare downward into its bracket until the bottom edge of the lever is no more than 1/16 inch above—but not past—the bracket. In this position, note that the flare base is about 1/2 inch below the upper carriage bolt. The bottom end of the lever is about 3/8 inch below the bracket prongs and is centered between those prongs (figure 10-13).

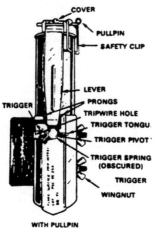

Fig 10-13. M49A1 tripflare.

10-15

**NOTE:** If the flare is positioned below the slot in the bracket, or if the lever is not aligned with the trigger pivot and centered between the prongs, the lever will not be free to move for proper arming.

f. Clamp the flare in its bracket by tightening the wingnut on the upper carriage bolt with enough force to grip the flare firmly.

3. Arming (Pullpin Method)

a. Fasten one end of the tripwire to a post, stake, or other rigid object, at the desired distance (usually 40 feet) from the flare and to the right or left of the flare when facing the flare trigger.

b. Press the lever down and hold it with one hand. Remove the safety clip assembly.

**WARNING:** DO NOT RELEASE LEVER WHEN PRESSING IT DOWN BECAUSE RELEASE OF THE LEVER WILL CAUSE THE FLARE TO FUNCTION.

c. While still holding the lever, insert the pullpin, which is attached to the safety clip, through two safety clip holes of the cover loading assembly.

**WARNING:** BEFORE RELEASING LEVER, ENSURE PULLPIN WILL HOLD IN THE SAFETY CLIP HOLES.

d. Carefully release your hold on the lever. Ensure that the pullpin is retained in the safety clip holes by the lever.

e. Pull the loose end of the tripwire taut and fasten it to the loop in the pullpin.

f. Check to see that the tripwire is taut and tightened at both ends.

g. The flare is now prepared for firing. Enough pressure applied to the tripwire will pull the pullpin from the flare and release the lever.

10-16

4. **Misfire.** In case of a failure to fire, the flare should not be approached for 5 minutes. After the waiting period, the flare should be removed carefully and forwarded to authorized personnel for disposal.

5. Disarming

    a. Carefully depress the lever against the flare body.

    b. Remove the pullpin.

    c. Secure the lever by inserting one end of the safety clip through one of the safety clip holes of the cover loading assembly. Snap the other end of the safety clip into the other safety clip hole.

> **WARNING:** USE ONLY THE SAFETY CLIP HOLES IN THE COVER LOADING ASSEMBLY WHEN REASSEMBLING THE SAFETY CLIP. DO NOT USE ANY OTHER HOLES.

    d. Detach the tripwire from the pullpin.

    e. Return the flare to its original packing container.

    f. Inspect the flare prior to storage.

> **WARNING:** MAKE NO ATTEMPT TO REASSEMBLE OR TIGHTEN A LOOSE COVER LOADING ASSEMBLY ON THE FLARE. FORWARD TO AUTHORIZED PERSONNEL FOR DISPOSAL.

> **NOTE:** THE M49A1 TRIP FLARE MAY ALSO BE INSTALLED USING THE BRACKET TRIGGER ASSEMBLY METHOD. TM 9-1370-203-12 DESCRIBES THE PROCEDURES TO FOLLOW.

## Section IV.  Mines and Boobytraps

Objectives:

*1.  On command without reference, demonstrate procedures for moving through a minefield containing surface or buried mines.*
*2.  On command without reference, demonstrate precautionary measures needed to move through a booby-trapped area.*

### A. GENERAL PRECAUTIONARY MEASURES

To reduce the effectiveness of enemy mines and boobytraps, the individual Marine can take several precautionary measures.

1.  Wear body armor and helmet.

2.  Sandbag vehicle flooring.

3.  Keep arms and legs inside vehicle.

4.  Maintain dispersion of personnel.

5.  Do not travel alone.

6.  Do not pick up souvenirs.

7.  Approach mine/boobytrap casualties with caution.

8.  Keep U.S. material and equipment from falling into enemy hands.

### B. DETECTION AND SEARCH TECHNIQUES

Once emplaced, an enemy mine or boobytrap must be found before it causes multiple casualties to Marines. The following techniques are recommended to detect these devices:

10-18

1.  Do not wear sunglasses. You are less able to detect tripwires and camouflaged mines or boobytraps.

2.  Be alert for tripwires in these places:

    o  Across trails
    o  On the shoulders of roads at likely ambush sites.
    o  Near known or suspected antitank or antivehicle mines.
    o  Across the best route through dense plant growth.
    o  In villages and on roads or paths into them.
    o  In or around likely helicopter landing sites.
    o  In approaches to enemy positions.
    o  At bridges, fords, and ditches.
    o  Across rice paddy dikes.

3.  Look for indications of mine/boobytrap placement such as:

    o  Mud smear, mudballs, dung, boards, or other materials on a road.
    o  Signs of road repair.
    o  Disturbed tire marks, ruts, or skid marks.
    o  Wires leading away from the side of the road.
    o  Unusual terrain features.
    o  Suspicious items in trees or bushes.
    o  Enemy markings (the enemy will mark most mine/boobytrap locations in some way).
    o  Civilians. They may know where mines or boobytraps are located. Observe where they don't go.
    o  Nonexplosive traps below, at or above the ground level.
    o  Enemy flags, banners, equipment or supplies. They may be boobytrapped.

4.  Probing. Probing is a way of detecting mines by piercing the earth with a sharp object (preferably nonmetallic). It is the best way to find buried mines, but it is slow, careful work. Suspicious spots must be probed with a pointed stick (figure 10-14).

    a. Preparation

    (1)  Remove any items that might interfere with your ability to probe, for example, ALICE pack or web gear. Depending upon the circumstances under which you find yourself, these items may either be staged or be placed behind you and pulled along as you go.

10-19

(2) Retain your weapon (slung across your back) and your protective mask. Your helmet should be securely fastened or removed. Rolling up your sleeves will help you detect tripwires at night or in thick vegetation. Lower your body as you look and feel downward. Inspect the ground for a spot to place your knees. You will probe from the prone or kneeling position.

b. Conduct

(1) Hold the probe in your hand, palm up, and probe every 2 inches across a 1-meter front. Push the probe gently into the ground at an angle less than 45 degrees, putting just enough pressure on the probe to sink it slowly into the ground.

(2) If the probe does not go into the ground, chip or pick away the soil with the tip of the probe. Remove loose dirt by hand.

(3) When a solid object is touched, stop probing and remove the earth to find out what the object is. If a mine is found, remove enough earth to show what type of mine it is, then mark and report its location.

(4) After probing across the 1-meter front, move the probe forward 2 inches and probe across the 1-meter front again. Continue this procedure until the minefield has been breached.

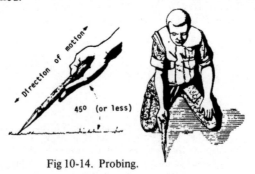

Fig 10-14. Probing.

## C. MARKING THE MINE/BOOBYTRAP

Clearly mark detected mines or boobytraps with whatever is available: rocks, sticks, pieces of clothing, etc. This allows friendly troops to safely bypass them without taking the time to remove them.

## D. REPORTING THE MINE/BOOBYTRAP

Report information about the mine or boobytrap to your unit leader.

## E. MOVEMENT THROUGH A MINEFIELD OR BOOBYTRAPPED AREA

When Marines come to a mined or boobytrapped area, they may follow one of two courses of action: bypassing the area or crossing it. Bypassing is usually the best course of action; however, there are times when the tactical situation will not permit this. When a minefield must be crossed, the objective is to make a mine-free lane that friendly troops may use to pass through the area. Several methods are available to accomplish this task.

1. Probing. In addition to detecting mines and boobytraps, probing can be used to clear a footpath through an area. You may not discover that an area is mined until you are well within its perimeter. In such a case, your primary objective is to move safely and rapidly out of the area. Consider the following points:

a. Don't panic!

b. Establish security. The principle of covering obstacles by fire is universal.

c. Designate one Marine to lead in clearing a lane. All other members of the unit should probe directly toward that man, then proceed along the cleared path to exit the minefield.

2. Mine Removal Techniques. After mines have been located, they may be detonated in place, pulled out by rope or wire, or neutralized and removed by hand. The decision as to which of these methods to use depends on the location of the mine, its type and fuse, and the tactical situation.

a. Detonation in place. Several methods are available to accomplish in-place detonation of mines.

10-21

o       Use of grapnels. Tripwire and tilt rod fuzed mines can be detonated by throwing a grapnel with rope attached into the minefield and pulling it back to explode the mines.

o       Hand-placed charges. A standard 1-pound block of TNT or C-4, placed on top of the mine, is sufficient to detonate it. Other explosive devices such as bangalore torpedos or line charges may also be used to clear lanes.

o       Vegetation fires. Where conditions permit and the vegetation cover is thick and dry, mined areas can be set on fire to expose individual mines. Some types of mines may actually be detonated in this manner.

o       Use of weapons fire or grenades. Aimed small-arms fire, as well as the throwing of grenades, may cause detonation of most types of mines. This method is useful in destroying scatterable surface mines.

b. Removal by rope or wire. Pulling mines out of their installed positions with a rope eliminates the potential hazard to mine-clearing personnel of mines fitted with antihandling devices. This method requires uncovering as much of the mine as possible to expose a point where a rope or grapnel may be attached. After pulling, wait 5 minutes before leaving cover and approaching the mine to guard against the possibility of a delay firing mechanism.

c. Hand neutralization. Under normal circumstances, foreign mines and boobytraps should only be neutralized by trained specialists. Mines are neutralized by hand under the following circumstances when:

o       A silent breach of the mined area is a tactical necessity.

o       The mine is located in a facility required for use by friendly forces.

o       It is of an unknown type and is required for intelligence purposes.

o       Chemical mines are located in an area where contamination would restrict use by friendly forces.

**F. AVOIDANCE COUNTERMEASURES.** There are several countermeasures that an individual can take to avoid and reduce the effectiveness of enemy mines and boobytraps.

1.  Stay off trails, footpaths, etc., as much as possible.

2.  Move where local inhabitants move.

3.  Avoid patterns.

4.  Maintain appropriate intervals.

5.  Move slowly if possible.

6.  Be alert when pursuing the enemy.

7.  Use artillery and mortar fire to help neutralize boobytraps.

8.  Mark detected mines and boobytraps.

9.  If on roads, stay in well-used portions.

10.  Follow in the tracks of the vehicle ahead of you.

11.  Avoid holes, depressions, and objects lying on the road.

12.  On command, or upon tripping a mine or boobytrap device, take immediate action:

   a. Warn others.

   b. Drop to ground immediately.

   c. If possible, present the smallest target to the force of the explosion by pointing the feet in the direction of the charge.

---

For more information in this area, refer to:

1.  FM 20-32          Mine/Counter Mine Operations at the Company Level

# Chapter 11.  Security of Military Information

Objectives:

*1. On command without reference, name and define three levels of security classification.*
*2. On command without reference, describe procedures to safeguard classified information.*
*3. On command without reference, describe methods of information collection used by foreign agents.*

Security is a protective condition that prevents unauthorized persons from obtaining information of military value. Such information is afforded a greater degree of protection than other material, and is given a special designation or classification.

## A. SECURITY CLASSIFICATION

Classified matter which requires protection in the interest of national defense shall be limited to three categories of classification and will carry one of the following designations: **TOP SECRET, SECRET, CONFIDENTIAL.**

1. Top Secret.  A "Top Secret" classification is limited to information or material which requires the highest degree of protection. Defense of this material is vital and unauthorized disclosure could result in exceptionally grave damage to the Nation. Examples of "exceptionally grave damage" include war against the United States or its allies, the breaking down of foreign relations vitally affecting the national security, and the compromise of vital national defense plans or complex cryptologic and communications intelligence systems. Also included are the revealing of sensitive intelligence operations and the disclosure of scientific or technological developments vital to national security.

**2.  Secret.** The "Secret" classification is limited to information or material that unauthorized disclosure of which could result in serious damage to the Nation. An example of "serious damage" is the breaking down of foreign relations significantly affecting national security.

**3.  Confidential.** The "Confidential" classification is limited to information or material that unathorized disclosure of which could cause identifiable damage to the Nation. Examples of "identifiable damage" include the compromise of information which indicates the strength of ground, air, and naval forces in the United States and overseas areas; the disclosure of technical information used for training, maintenance, and inspection of classified munitions of war; and the revealing of performance characteristics, test data, design, and production  data on munitions of war.

## B. PROTECTING CLASSIFIED INFORMATION

Classified information is any official information which has been determined to require, in the interest of national security, protection against unauthorized disclosure. To be considered classified, it also must have been so designated.

1.  Custodians of classified material shall be responsible for safeguarding classified material at all times, particularly for locking classified material in appropriate security containers whenever it is not in use or under direct supervision of authorized persons. When classified information is removed from storage during working hours for use by authorized persons in officially designated offices or working areas, the material shall be kept under constant surveillance. It should be placed face down when not in use. Classified information or material shall not be removed from officially designated office or working areas for the purpose of working on such material during off duty hours. It can be removed if specifically approved by the commanding officer or his representative who must be designated in writing. At the end of the working day, commanding officers will require a security check of all work spaces to ensure that all classified material is properly secured.

2. Each Marine is responsible for ensuring that classified information which he prepares, receives, or handles is properly accounted for and that it is made available only to those who have the appropriate clearance and the need to know. The individual having knowledge and/or custody of

classified matter is responsible for any failure, on his part, which may contribute to its loss, compromise, or unauthorized disclosure.

3. Effective physical security is attained only when all established methods and procedures are carefully carried out. These include: the proper storage of material when not in use; the proper handling when in use, to include constant surveillance and accountability; and ensuring that classified information is not discussed over the telephone or in an area where unauthorized persons may overhear the discussion.

## C. STORAGE, DISPOSAL, AND DESTRUCTION OF CLASSIFIED INFORMATION

Whenever classified information is not under the personal control and observation of an authorized person, it will be protected or stored in a locked security container. Those Marines who serve in billets in which classified information is used receive detailed instruction on their responsibilities regarding the storage, disposal, and destruction of that information. Most Marines rarely come in contact with classified information, but should know that all classified information, regardless of its classification, should be safeguarded, properly stored, and disposed of or destroyed in accordance with OPNAVINST 5510 Series. All Marines should be aware that it is their responsibility to report any apparent violation of the safeguarding of military information.

## D. ACCESS TO CLASSIFIED DOCUMENTS

Access is the ability and opportunity to obtain knowledge or possession of classified information.

1. The Department of Defense employs a security system based on the simple principle of circulation control, i.e., control of access to classified information. Knowledge or possession of classified information shall be permitted only to individuals whose official duties require access in the interest of promoting national security and only if they have been determined to be trustworthy.

2. To have access to classified information, one must possess the proper level of clearance and *also* have a "need to know" the information.

3. These principles are equally applicable if the prospective recipient is an organizational unit, including commands, other Federal agencies, defense contractors, foreign governments, and others.

4. Commanding officers should ensure that personnel under their jurisdiction are briefed in accordance with Chapter 3, OPNAVINST 5510 Series before granting access to classified information.

## E. TYPES OF UNCLASSIFIED AND CLASSIFIED INFORMATION

1. Valuable Unclassified Information. Unclassified information most likely sought by intelligence officers or agents includes:

o   Names, duties, personal data, and characteristics of military personnel
o   Technical orders, manuals, or regulations
o   Base directives
o   Personnel rosters
o   Unit manning tables
o   Information about the designation, strength, mission, or combat posture of a unit
o   Development of ship, aircraft, and weapons systems

2. Classified Information. Classified information most likely to be sought by intelligence officers or agents includes:

o Military plans, weapons, or operations
o Foreign government information
o Intelligence activities, sources, or methods
o Foreign relations or foreign activities of the United States
o Scientific, technological, or economic matters relating to national security
o United States Government programs for safeguarding nuclear materials or facilities
o Communications security material to include: cryptographic systems, their codes, cipher devices, and machines

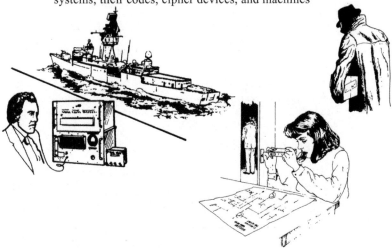

## F. METHODS BY WHICH FOREIGN NATIONS COLLECT INFORMATION

1. Methods by which foreign nations obtain information are as follows:

o Air, sea and ground reconnaissance and surveillance
o Communications intelligence through intercepting unsecure telephone, radio, and microwave telecommunications
o Electronic surveillance using devices which monitor conversations

o   Eavesdropping or wiretapping
o   Prisoners of war and refugees
o   Documents, newspapers, and magazines
o   Press and radio/television releases, photographs and editorials
o   Careless talk

2.   Foreign agents, both male and female, will use several of the above methods and sources to obtain intelligence. They will also resort to other subversive actions:

o   Cultivating friendships with U.S. citizens to the extent of placing personnel under an obligation which may prove embarrassing, or by offering money to obtain information
o   Coercion of personnel by blackmail, threats, or promises of harm to relatives living in foreign countries
o   Exploitation of personnel who may be dissatisfied or in personal difficulaties
o   Intimidation, harassment, entrapment, discrediting, searching, spying on, or recruiting personnel traveling in unfriendly countries
o   Persuading personnel to defect
o   Obtaining information from personnel by correspondence (including "pen pals"), questionnaires, amateur radio activities, and other forms of communications

## G.  USE OF SEEMINGLY INSIGNIFICANT MILITARY FACTS

Foreign agents use many single, seemingly insignificant facts to piece together a total picture of an operation or plan. As the following illustrations show, each single fact, by itself, means little; but once put together, these seemingly insignificant facts could prove to be very damaging.

11-6

Bill's unit is leaving for Norway for a five-week operation

Well, Business should be slow for you all next week with 2/6 leaving Monday.

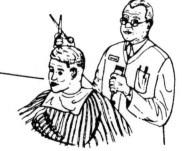

Man, what a day, we had to issue 900 sets of cold weather gear to 2nd BN 6th Marines

**KGB INTELLIGENCE REPORT:**

UNIT                    2d Bn 6th Marine
STRENGTH                900
DESTINATION             Norway
DATE OF DEPARTURE       Monday 17 Jan 1986
LENGTH OF OPERATION     5 weeks

The agent of a foreign intelligence service need not be a foreigner. The individual you meet at a disco could be a foreign diplomat or a fellow American who has been recruited as an agent. Do not expect the agent to expose his role. Usually there is a long period of cultivation during which your conversations could be completely normal. However, at any time someone may begin to inquire into activities which are classified. Then you should stop to consider whether the inquiry is innocent or the beginning of an attempt to secure intelligence information.

You should report the circumstances to a responsible official, for example, your OIC, security manager, or commanding officer.

---

For more information in this area, refer to:

1. FM 30-17                 Counterintelligence Operations

2. FMFM 2-4                 Counterintelligence

3. OPNAVINST 5510.1         Department of the Navy
                            Information Security
                            Program Regulations Sep 78

4. DOD 5200.1-R             Information Security Program
                            Regulations Dec 78

5. OPNAVINST 5510 Series    Department of the Navy Information
                            Security Program Regulations Sep 78

6.                          Security Manager's Handbook

# Chapter 12.  Substance Abuse

## Section I.  Illegal Drug Use

Objectives:

*1.  On command without reference, state the Marine Corps policy on the use of illegal drugs.*
*2.  On command without reference, state the legal and/or administrative actions which may result from the use, distribution, or possession of illegal drugs.*
*3.  On command without reference, state the purpose of the Marine Corps Urinalysis Testing Program.*
*4.  On command without reference, state the purpose of the Voluntary Drug Disclosure Program.*

## A. DEFINITION OF ILLEGAL DRUG USE

A drug is a substance that when taken changes the functions of the body or mind. Many drugs are legal and can be bought "off-the-shelf." Others are controlled by law. Of these controlled substances, some have no proven medical use and are illegal. Examples of these are heroin, LSD, and hashish. Other controlled substances are available with a doctor's prescription. Using prescription drugs when you have no prescription or taking more than the prescribed amount is also illegal.

## B. MARINE CORPS POLICY ON ILLEGAL DRUG USE

The distribution, possession, or use of illegal drugs is not tolerated in the United States Marine Corps. Distribution means selling or giving drugs to another person in any given quantity. It is also illegal to own drug paraphernalia such as roach clips, coke spoons, syringes, wrapping papers, and any other items intended for the illegal use of drugs.

## C. LEGAL ACTIONS

The use of illegal drugs may result in nonjudicial punishment or a court martial under the Uniform Code of Military Justice (UCMJ). The results can be restriction, loss of rank or pay, confinement at hard labor, and even a bad conduct discharge. More importantly, as a Marine, you are responsible for your actions whether you use drugs or not. Even if you are not charged with illegal drug use, your actions while under the drug's influence may cause you to find yourself charged with assault, destruction of government property, or any other misconduct that occurred while you were "high."

## D. ADMINISTRATIVE ACTIONS

1. Commanding officers have been instructed by the Commandant of the Marine Corps to use every lawful means at their disposal to identify those who illegally use drugs. One way that commanders do this is by conducting urinalysis tests on a regular basis. Other means include random vehicle searches, health and welfare inspections, marijuana dogs, undercover agents, and review of logbook entries and incident reports.

2. Commanding officers have a wide variety of administrative actions available to discourage illegal drug use and to prevent illegal drug use from harming others. Some of these actions are:

- o  Unmarried Marines may be denied the privilege of living off base
- o  Married Marines may be evicted from government quarters.
- o  On base driving privileges may be revoked.
- o  Confirmed incidents of illegal drug use may be recorded in the Service Record Book (or be reported on an As Directed by CMC (DC) fitness report for Sergeants and above).
- o  Marines trafficking in illegal drugs will be discharged.
- o  Marines found illegally using drugs are not eligible for promotion for a period of six months.
- o  Marines found illegally using drugs the first time may be discharged if the commander decides that a pattern of misconduct has been established.
- o  Marines found illegally using drugs a second time will usually be discharged
- o  Marines found illegally using drugs a third time will be discharged.

## E. MARINE CORPS URINALYSIS TESTING PROGRAM

1. The purpose of the Urinalysis Program is to provide the unit commander with a means of deterring any Marine from using illegal drugs, identifying those who illegally use drugs, and confirming drug presence necessary for administrative and/or disciplinary action.

2. Drug abuse reduces readiness and is not tolerated in the Marine Corps. Every legal means is used to provide the drug-free environment expected for every Marine. As a major means of drug abuse detection and deterrence, the Marine Corps Urinalysis Program has contributed significantly towards control of illegal drug use.

## F. VOLUNTARY DRUG DISCLOSURE PROGRAM

The Marine Corps has a program that permits Marines who have used illegal drugs and who sincerely intend to discontinue that use to obtain assistance. The purpose of the Marine Corps Voluntary Drug Disclosure Program is to provide a method through which Marines can stop using illegal drugs. Any Marine with a drug use problem may obtain treatment or rehabilitation by means of voluntary disclosure. A Marine can obtain assistance under this program only once during his career.

1. Marines who seek assistance for drug use may initiate the evaluation and treatment process by voluntarily disclosing the nature and extent of their personal drug use to the unit Substance Abuse Control Office (SACO). Voluntary disclosure made to the SACO relating to the Marine's past or present drug use is a privileged communication and may not be used in any disciplinary action under the Uniform Code of Military Justice. Information disclosed to persons other than drug screening, counseling, treatment, or rehabilitation personnel is not privileged.

2. For a Marine to receive assistance under this program, specific eligibility criteria must be met:

   a. The Marine must clearly demonstrate a sincere desire to seek help to eliminate personal drug use.

   b. Traffickers in illegal drugs are not eligible.

   c. The Marine must not have previously been identified as a drug user, regardless of the means of identification, including a preservice illegal drug use waiver.

d. A Marine identified as a drug user during the disclosure process of another Marine is not eligible.

## G. DRUGS AND THE INDIVIDUAL

1. Most drugs that are used illegally affect the body's central nervous system. The central nervous system controls our senses of sight, hearing, taste, smell, and touch; our movements and thoughts; and our heart and lungs. The effects of drugs depend on the type of drug and the amount taken, and can range from mild changes in sensation or mood to death.

2. The human body has the capacity to develop tolerance to many drugs. When this happens, larger and larger doses of drugs are required to achieve the same effect. This results in physical dependence. The body requires the drug to function normally. If the drug is not taken, withdrawal symptoms (which can be very dangerous) occur. After withdrawal, the body returns to normal if no damage has been done.

3. Another kind of dependence is psychological. The mind needs the drug. This is caused by the desire to repeat the artificial sensations of illegal drug use, and results in more and more frequent use. Nearly all illegal drug use can result in psychological dependence.

## H. DRUGS AND THE UNIT

1. A Marine under the influence of drugs cannot do his job effectively. Other Marines will have to carry the weight of the illegal drug user, thus impairing unit efficiency. In combat, one Marine illegally using drugs endangers the survival of the entire unit.

2. Illegal drug use itself is a breach of unit discipline. Since drugs are fairly expensive, their use often leads to theft and other offenses to raise the money needed to buy them. The result is a breakdown in discipline and morale that can leave a unit ineffective.

3. Trafficking means distributing, either by selling or giving drugs to someone else. By providing the drugs that are used illegally, the trafficker contributes to problems of the illegal drug user and the unit. The trafficker wants to increase his business and profits. He takes advantage of the weaknesses of individuals and causes the problem of illegal drug use to grow.

## I. YOUR RESPONSIBILITY AS A MARINE

Most people who are well-informed about the effects of drugs rarely abuse them. You owe it to yourself to learn what the effects of drugs really are and to avoid them. Do not be satisfied, though, with avoiding drugs yourself. Marines take care of their own. If you cannot convince your fellow Marines that they should not use drugs, report them. Do not let friendship or negative peer pressure stop you from doing what you know is right. In the long run, it is best for all concerned.

*The Commandant of the Marine Corps has said, "There should be no question in anyone's mind that those who do not meet these standards will be separated from the Marine Corps. I expect the full support of every Marine in combatting the illegal use of drugs."*

---

For more information in this area, consult the unit Substance Abuse Control Officer (SACO) or refer to:

1. MCO 5255.1            Marine Corps Drug Abuse Administration and Management Program

2. MCO 5355.2            Marine Corps Urinalysis Testing Program

3. MCO P5300.12          Marine Corps Substance Abuse Program

4. SECNAVINST 5300.28    Alcohol and Drug Abuse Control

5. ALMAR 246/81          Marine Corps Policy Concerning Illegal Drugs

6. NAVMC 2750            Marine's War on Drugs

# Section II. Alcohol Abuse

Objectives:

*1.  On command without reference, state the Marine Corps policy on alcohol abuse.*
*2.  On command without reference, define alcohol abuse.*
*3.  On command without reference, list the indicators of alcohol abuse.*
*4.  On command without reference, list the administrative and/or disciplinary actions which may result from alcohol abuse.*
*5.  On command without reference, list the assistance Marines may receive to control alcohol abuse.*

## A.  MARINE CORPS POLICY ON ALCOHOL ABUSE

Alcohol abuse is not tolerated in the United States Marine Corps.

## B.  DEFINITION OF ALCOHOL ABUSE

Alcohol abuse, as defined in MCO 5370 6A, is any irresponsible use of alcohol which leads to misconduct, unacceptable social behavior, or impairment of an individual's performance of duty, physical or mental health, financial responsibility, or personal relationships.

## C.  ALCOHOL AND ITS SYMPTOMS

1.  Alcohol is the most frequently abused drug in our society. It is a depressant. Like other depressants, alcohol abuse dangerously affects one's reasoning ability, coordination, social behavior, and performance. It is dangerously addictive both physically and mentally. Over a period of time, alcohol abuse usually leads to serious illness involving the heart, liver, and other organs. Alcohol abuse can lead to alcoholism, which is a progressive, treatable disease; however, if left untreated, it will result in death or permanent brain damage.

2. Alcohol is legal, but all too often, resulting actions while intoxicated are not. This is the other side of the effects of alcohol. Misconduct, accidental injuries, motor vehicle accidents, and arrest are some of the results of alcohol abuse.

## D. INDICATORS OF ALCOHOL ABUSE

A few of the many recognizable indicators of alcohol abuse are listed below:
1. Hangover. The nausea, headache, and dry mouth following heavy drinking are signs of the irritation of the body that alcohol abuse has caused. A Marine in this condition does not perform well on the job.
2. Blackout. Blackout is a loss of memory while drinking. If a Marine cannot remember how he arrived home after a drinking session, then that Marine has had a blackout.
3. Fatigue. The depressant effect of alcohol plus the late night on the town can leave a Marine tired. This might cause the Marine to be late for work or to be absent entirely, jeopardizing the Marine's effectiveness and reliability.
4. Frequent Sick Calls. The frequent alcohol abuser may be severely "hungover" and require medical assistance. Additionally, that trip to sick bay might be used to cover up the problem of constantly being late for work.
5. Social Problems. Sometimes the alcohol abuser is the "life of the party," but the frequent abuser becomes embarrassing to himself and to others. Ultimately, this can lead to the loss of family and friends.

## E. ADMINISTRATIVE ACTIONS

To protect Marines from the effects of alcohol abuse, the commanding officer may take several administrative actions. Some of these are listed below:

o   If a Marine is an alcohol abuser, it is quite possible that this abuse will have a negative effect on his proficiency and conduct marks. This can delay promotions.

o        Authorization to operate a government vehicle can be denied.
o        Base driving privileges for private vehicles will be suspended for one year for any Marine convicted of driving under the influence of alcohol on or off base.
o        Unmarried Marines may be denied the privilege of living off base.
o        Married Marines may be evicted from government quarters if that Marine's alcohol abuse affects quarters residents.
o        Confirmed incidents of alcohol abuse will be entered in the Service Record Book. The Marine involved will be formally counseled by the Commanding Officer.
o        Continued alcohol abuse will result in separation from the Marine Corps for reasons of unsuitability.

## F. ASSISTANCE

1. A Marine may obtain help for himself, his family, or another Marine by contacting the unit Substance Abuse Control Officer, medical personnel, or the Chaplain. These persons have access to a large number of agencies and publications designed to assist those who abuse alcohol.

2. The Marine Corps recognizes that alcohol abuse and alcoholism are conditions which can be positively affected through education, counseling, treatment, and rehabilitation programs. Because of this, the Marine Corps Substance Abuse Program has established three levels of treatment services that a Marine may receive to control alcohol abuse.

Level I, Unit Programs. Conducted at regiment, group, battalion, squadron, separate battalion, or barracks level to provide command counseling, basic alcohol abuse/alcoholism preventive education, discipline, and rudimentary screening for a nondependent first-time alcohol abuser.

Level II, Major Command Programs. Conducted at division, wing, FSSG, base, station, or depot level to provide in-depth screening and evaluation for possible alcohol dependency and outpatient and/or short term (not to exceed 30 days) residential treatment for the nondependent alcohol abuser who failed to benefit from a Level I program, or whose degree of alcohol abuse exceeds the capabilities of the unit's Level I program.

Level III, Navy Residential Treatment Programs. Located at Navy Alcohol Rehabilitation Services (ARES) and Navy Alcohol Rehabilitation Centers (ARC) to provide residential treatment for those Marines diagnosed as alcohol dependent.

## G. ALCOHOL AND THE UNIT

A Marine under the influence of alcohol is just as dangerous to the unit as a Marine under the influence of any other drug. Incidents of violent crime, motor vehicle accidents, spouse and child abuse are frequently alcohol related. Drunk drivers are an especially dangerous menace who take the lives of many innocent victims each year. Substandard performance, financial irresponsibility, and unacceptable behavior all adversely impact upon organizational efficiency.

## H. YOUR RESPONSIBILITY AS A MARINE

1. Alcohol is legal; however, misconduct as a result of alcohol abuse is illegal. Every Marine is responsible for his own actions whether under the influence of alcohol or not and will be held strictly accountable for those actions under the Uniform Code of Military Justice. If you don't drink, don't start. If you do drink, learn not to drink too much. If you think that you need to prove something to your friends, prove that you are responsible for taking care of yourself and avoid the problems of alcohol abuse.

2. Marines take care of their own. Alcohol abuse by any Marine, on liberty or in garrison, is the responsibility of every other Marine. Alcohol abuse must be avoided or corrected. Stopping alcohol abuse by Marines is a responsibility of all Marines.

*The Commandant of the Marine Corps has said, "Those who do not meet these standards will be separated from the Marine Corps. The privilege of being a Marine includes the responsibility for maintaining the highest standards of discipline, conduct, and performance. Alcohol abuse is a form of indiscipline that can seriously reduce the overall value and effectiveness of the individual Marine and degrade the operational effectiveness of the Marine's organization. Those who choose to abuse alcohol will be identified and assisted to the degree possible, but in all cases, held accountable for their actions."*

12-9

For more information in this area, consult the unit Substance Abuse Control Officer (SACO), or refer to:

1. SECNAVINST 5300.28    Alcohol and Drug Abuse Control

2. MCO 5370.6A           Marine Corps Alcohol Abuse Administrative and Management Program

3. NAVMC 2662A           Marine Corps Policy on Alcohol Abuse

4. ALMAR 125/82          A Seminar on Alcohol and Alcoholism

# Chapter 13.   Land Navigation


## Section I.   Manmade and Natural Terrain Features

Objective:   *Given a standard 1:50,000 scale map with legend, identify three manmade and four natural terrain features without error.*


## A. MARGINAL INFORMATION

A map is defined as a scale drawing of a portion of the earth's surface, showing various features by symbols or drawings. The purpose of a map is to permit you to visualize an area of the earth's surface with the important features properly positioned. Mapmakers use symbols to represent man-made and natural terrain features. Information and illustrations placed around the border of a map are called marginal information.

In the marginal information, each map sheet has a sheet name, a series number, a sheet number, an identification number (used for ordering map sheets), an index to adjoining sheets, an elevation guide, a declination diagram, graphical scales, and a legend. Two common uses of the marginal information by Marines are described in the following paragraphs.

1.  Map Legend. Since it would be difficult for each manmade or natural terrain feature to be shown on a map, the mapmakers use symbols and colors to represent these features. The map legend, located in the lower left margin of the map, illustrates and identifies the topographic symbols used to depict some of the more prominent features on the map. The symbols are not always the same on every map; therefore, to avoid error in interpretation you should refer to the legend when reading the map. Figure 13-1 provides an example of a map legend.

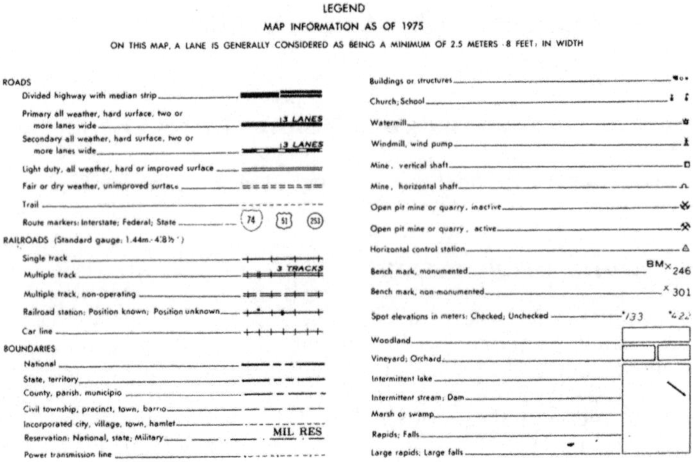
LEGEND
MAP INFORMATION AS OF 1975
ON THIS MAP, A LANE IS GENERALLY CONSIDERED AS BEING A MINIMUM OF 2.5 METERS (8 FEET) IN WIDTH
ROADS
Divided highway with median strip
Primary all weather, hard surface, two or more lanes wide
3 LANES
Secondary all weather, hard surface, two or more lanes wide
3 LANES
Light duty, all weather, hard or improved surface
Fair or dry weather, unimproved surface
Trail
Route markers: Interstate; Federal; State
74
51
253
RAILROADS (Standard gauge: 1.44m.-4'8½")
Single track
Multiple track
3 TRACKS
Multiple track, non-operating
Railroad station: Position known; Position unknown
Car line
BOUNDARIES
National
State, territory
County, parish, municipio
Civil township, precinct, town, barrio
Incorporated city, village, town, hamlet
Reservation: National, state; Military
MIL RES
Power transmission line
Buildings or structures
Church; School
Watermill
Windmill, wind pump
Mine, vertical shaft
Mine, horizontal shaft
Open pit mine or quarry, inactive
Open pit mine or quarry, active
Horizontal control station
Bench mark, monumented
BM×246
Bench mark, non-monumented
×301
Spot elevations in meters: Checked; Unchecked
133
Woodland
Vineyard; Orchard
Intermittent lake
Intermittent stream; Dam
Marsh or swamp
Rapids; Falls
Large rapids; Large falls

Fig 13-1. Map legend.

2. **Map Scale.** On a map, everything has been reduced in size at a uniform rate. The scale of the map, which can be found in the top-left corner of the map sheet, indicates the amount that objects and distances have been reduced. For example: one inch between two points on a map with a 1:50,000 scale is equal to 50,000 inches between them on the ground. Maps are classified into three categories according to scales: large, medium, and small. Large-scale maps meet the tactical needs of field units. A large-scale map covers a very small ground area, so the mapmaker has enough space to show a considerable amount of detail such as individual buildings, bridges, water towers, and other important information. The standard large-scale map is 1:50,000.

## B. MAP COLORS

To aid in identifying features on the map by providing a more natural appearance and contrast, the topographic symbols are usually printed in different colors, with each color identifying a different class of feature. On large-scale maps, five colors are used: black, red, blue, green, and brown.

1. **Black.** The color black is used to indicate most manmade features, such as buildings, bridges, railroads, trails, and roads not shown in red. Figure 13-2 shows some common manmade features.

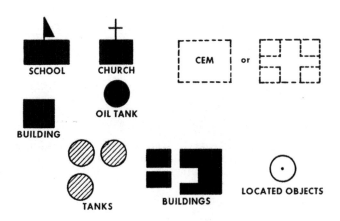

Fig 13-2. Manmade features.

2. **Red.** The color red on military maps is used to indicate road classification, built-up areas, and special features such as military reservation boundaries. Since 1982, the color red has been slightly tinted with brown to make the map readable under red light conditions.

3. **Blue.** The color blue is used to indicate water features such as streams, rivers, lakes, oceans, and swamps. Figure 13-3 shows some water features that would appear in blue on the military map.

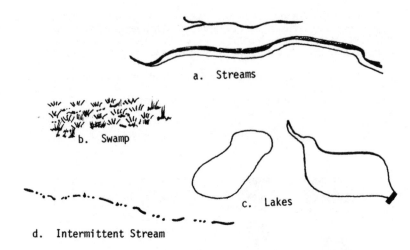

a. Streams

b. Swamp

c. Lakes

d. Intermittent Stream

Fig 13-3. Water features.

**4. Green.** The color green is used on a military map to depict vegetation features such as forests, orchards, and jungles. Figure 13-4 illustrates some of these features. Remember that they are colored GREEN on the military map.

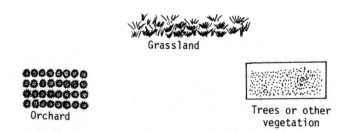

Grassland

Orchard

Trees or other vegetation

Fig 13-4. Trees and vegetation.

**5. Brown.** The color brown is used to represent terrain features, such as contours, cuts and fills. The brown lines on your map indicate the elevation and shape of the ground and are called contour lines (figure 13-5).

## C. CONTOUR LINES AND TERRAIN FEATURES

Contour lines are used to show both elevation and relief. Basically, elevation is the height of an object and relief is the represenation of the shape and height of landforms. The distance between contour lines is called contour interval (figure 13-5), and it is found in the marginal information in the center of the lower margin of the map.

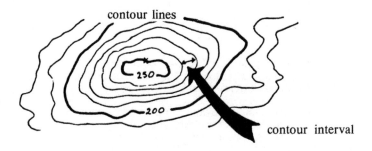

Fig 13-5. Contour lines.

**1. Elevation.** Starting at zero elevation, every fifth contour line is drawn with a heavier "index" contour line. Someplace along each index contour the line is broken and its elevation is given. In addition to contour lines, bench marks and spot elevations are used to indicate points of known elevation on the map. Bench marks are the more accurate of the two and are symbolized by a black X, for example, X BM 124. Spot elevations, shown in brown, are generally located at road junctions, hilltops, and other prominent landforms. Using the contour lines on the map, you can determine the elevation of any point by doing the following:

a. Find the contour interval of the map from the marginal information and note its amount and unit of measure (e.g., 40 meters, 20 feet, etc.).

b. Find the numbered contour line nearest the point for which you are trying to determine elevation.

c. Determine the direction of slope (uphill or downhill) from the numbered contour line to the desired point.

d. Count the number of contour lines that must be crossed to go from the numbered line to the desired point and note the direction—up or down. The number of lines crossed multiplied by the contour interval is the distance above or below the starting value (index contour found in b. above).

    o   If the desired point is on a contour line, its elevation is that of the contour.

    o   For a point in between contour lines, most military needs are satisfied by estimating the elevation to an accuracy of one half the contour interval.

    o   To estimate elevation to the top of an unmarked hill, add one half the contour interval to the elevation of the highest contour line around the hill.

2. Relief. The elevation and relief of an area affect the units' movement and deployment by limiting its route, speed, and ability to attack or defend an area. Observation, fields of fire, cover, concealment, and the selection of key terrain features are also affected. By evaluating the pattern formed by the contour lines on your map, you can get a very accurate mental picture of the elevation and relief of the area. The major terrain features found on a map are described in the following paragraphs. A sketch of the feature is provided, along with its characteristic contour pattern.

a. Hill. A point or small area of high ground (figure 13-6). When you are on a hilltop, the ground slopes down in all directions.

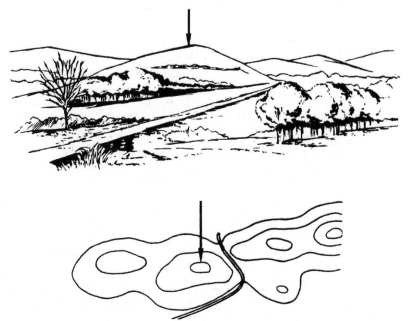

Fig 13-6. Hill.

b. Ridge. A line of high ground with height variations along its crest (figure 13-7a). The ridge is not simply a line of hills; all points of the ridge crest are higher than the ground on both sides of the ridge.

c. Spur. A usually short, continuously sloping line of higher ground normally jutting out from the side of a ridge (figure 13-7b). A spur is often formed by two roughly parallel streams cutting draws (defined on page 13-9) down the side of the ridge.

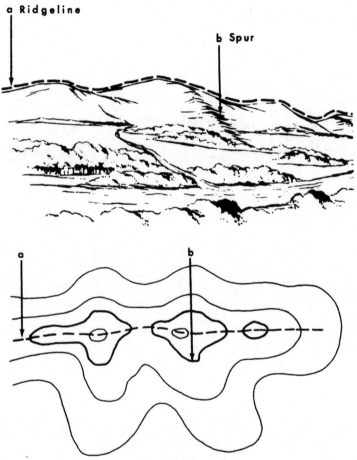

Fig 13-7. a. Ridge. b. Spur.

    d. **Valley**. A stream course which has at least some reasonably level ground bordered on the sides by higher ground (figure 13-8a). A valley generally has maneuver room within its confines. Contour lines indicating a valley are U-shaped and tend to parallel a stream before crossing it. The more gradual the fall of the stream, the farther each contour parallels it. The curve of the contour line crossing the stream will always point upstream.

13-8

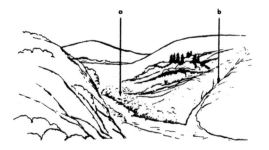

e. Draw. A stream course in which there is essentially no level ground and therefore little or no maneuver room within its confines (figure 13-8b). The ground slopes upward on each side and toward the head of the draw. Draws occur frequently along the sides of ridges at right angles to the valleys between them. Contours indicating a draw are V-shaped, with the point of the "V" toward the head of the draw.

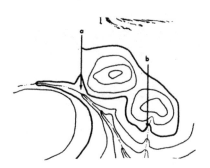

Fig 13-8. a. Valley. b. Draw.

13-9

f. Saddle. A dip or low point along the crest of a ridge (figure 13-9). A saddle is not necessarily the lower ground between two hilltops; it may be simply a dip or break along an otherwise level ridge crest.

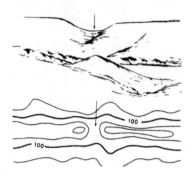

Fig 13-9. Saddle.

g. Depression. A low point or hole in the ground surrounded on all sides by higher ground (figure 13-10).

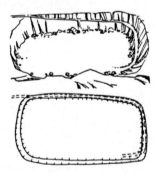

Fig 13-10. Depression.

h. Cuts and fills.  Manmade features by which the bed of a road or railroad is graded or leveled off by cutting through high areas (figure 13-11a) and filling in low areas (figure 13-11b) along a right-of-way.

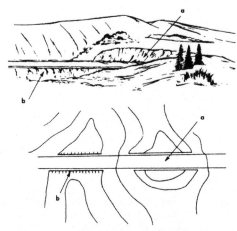

Fig 13-11.  a. Cut.   b. Fill.

i. Cliff.  A vertical or near vertical slope (figure 13-12). When a slope is so steep that it cannot be shown at the contour interval without the contours overlapping, it is shown by a "carrying" contour or contours marked with ticks. The ticks always point toward lower ground.

Fig 13-12.  Cliff.

# Section II.  Location and Distance

Objectives:

*1.  Given a standard 1:50,000 scale map with legend, determine the six-digit coordinate of a designated point within 100 meters.*
*2.  Given a standard 1:50,000 scale map with legend, measure a curved and a straight line distance within 50 meters.*

## A. LOCATION

1. Military Grid Reference System. The military grid reference system consists of a network of equally spaced vertical and horizontal lines superimposed on the map. On a large-scale map, grid lines form squares 1000 meters on each side. The "grid squares" are used to locate areas and points quickly, easily, and accurately. The vertical (north-south) grid lines are numbered consecutively with numbers increasing to the right. The horizontal (east-west) grid lines are also numbered consecutively with numbers increasing up the map. To designate the location of a grid square, combine the numbers of the grid lines that form its lower left corner (figure 13-13). You will only read the two-digit number printed in large type in the margin of the map. The combination of the two numbers, in the order RIGHT and then UP, is the coordinate reading of the grid square. Coordinate readings will always contain an even number of digits.

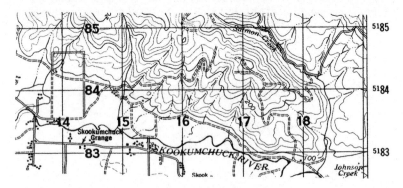

Fig 13-13.  Grid squares.

2. Six-Digit Coordinate. The accuracy of a point location is shown by the number of digits in the coordinates: the more digits, the more accurate the location. A four-digit coordinate indentifies a grid square and provides an accuracy of a point location to within 1000 meters. You will normally be required to determine accuracy to the nearest 100 meters. This accuracy is provided by a six-digit grid coordinate.

a. To locate a point to the nearest 100 meters, you will again follow the rule of reading RIGHT and then UP. Always estimate from the center of mass of the object you are locating. First, read right across the map to the last vertical grid line crossed before reaching the point, then estimate the tenths of the grid square from the grid line to the point. Repeat this procedure reading up the map to the last horizontal grid line crossed before reaching the point and then estimating the tenths of the grid square from the grid line to the point. Combine the complete coordinate RIGHT with the complete coordinate UP to get the six-digit coordinate. With practice, you can learn to estimate the tenths in a grid fairly accurately.

b. Refer to figure 13-14. To determine the location of point A to the nearest 100 meters, read right until you reach the 30 vertical grid line. You estimate that point "A" lies seven-tenths of a grid square to the right of that line. The complete coordinate RIGHT is 307. Reading up the map, you cross the 48 horizontal grid line, and estimate that point "A" lies four-tenths of a grid square above that line. The complete coordinate UP is 484. Combining these estimates in the order RIGHT and then UP, the coordinates of point "A" to the nearest 100 meters are 307484.

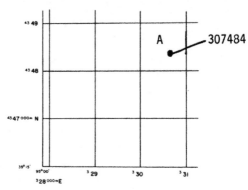

Fig 13-14. Six-digit coordinate.

13-13

3.  Coordinate Scale. The most accurate way to determine the location of a point on a map is to use a coordinate scale (figure 13-15), following the military principle "Read RIGHT and then UP." You do not have to estimate because you can read the exact coordinates from the scale.

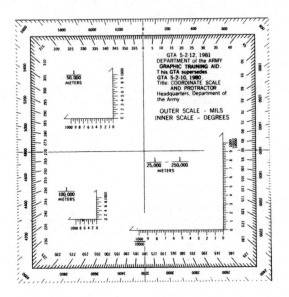

Fig 13-15. Coordinate scale.

**CAUTION:**  When using a coordinate scale, make sure that the scale corresponds to the scale on your map.

Follow these steps when using the coordinate scale to determine coordinates:

a. Place the scale with the zeros of the coordinate scale at the lower left (southwest) corner of the grid square.

b. Keeping the bottom of the scale on the lower horizontal grid line, slide it to the right until the point for which coordinates are desired touches the vertical (right-hand) scale.

13-14

c. When reading coordinates, examine both sides of the coordinate scale to ensure that the horizontal scale is aligned with the east-west grid line and the vertical scale is parallel to the north-south grid line (figure 13-16).

d. The number at the bottom of the coordinate scale on or closer to the vertical grid line is the third digit of the six-digit coordinate, and the number at the right of the coordinate scale on or closer to the point is the sixth digit of the coordinate.

e. The six-digit coordinate of point "X" in figure 13-16 is 142841.

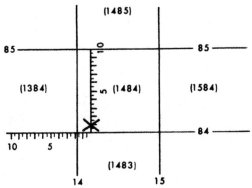

Fig 13-16.   Using the coordinate scale.

## B. DISTANCE

1. Graphic (Bar) Scales.  Graphic scales, which resemble rulers, are printed on military maps. Measured map distance can be converted to ground distance by using the graphic scales. Distance can be converted to meters, yards, statute miles, or nautical miles on the graphic scales of most military maps.

a. Each graphic scale consists of a primary scale and an extension scale (figure 13-17). The primary scale is used to convert distance in whole units. The extension scale divides whole units into ten equal parts.

13-15

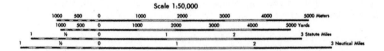

Fig 13-17.   Graphic scales.

b. The graphic scale most commonly used by Marines is the meter scale. Measurements on the extension scale are read from 0 to the left (toward 1000). Measurements from the extension scale are added to measurements obtained from the primary scale. Distance to a point between 100-meter graduation on the extension scale is estimated to the nearest 10 meters.

2. Straight Line Distance.  You can measure straight line distances on your map between two points by laying a straightedge piece of paper on the map so that the edge of the paper touches both points (figure 13-18). The map distance is recorded on the straightedge piece of paper by using tick marks. This distance can be converted to ground distance by aligning the tick marks on the straightedge with the desired graphic bar scale.

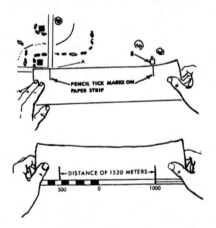

Fig 13-18.   Measuring straight line distance.

13-16

**NOTE:** A map distance that exceeds the length of the primary scale and the extension scale requires you to place the paper straightedge on the graphic scale several times to determine the remaining distance. The total distance is determined by adding the separate measurements.

3. Curved Line Distance. Sometimes you may be required to measure distance along a winding road, stream, or any other curved line. The straightedge of a piece of paper is again used. Make a tick mark at or near one end of the paper and place it at the point from which the curved line is to be measured (figure 13-19, point A). Align the edge of the paper along a straight portion of the curved line and make a tick mark on both the paper and the map at the end of the aligned portion (figure 13-19, point B). Keeping both the tick marks together, place the point of the pencil on the paper's tick mark to hold it in place. Pivot the paper until another approximately straight portion is aligned, and again make a tick mark on both the map and the paper (figure 13-19, point C). Continue in this manner until your measurement is complete, then use the graphic scale to determine ground distance.

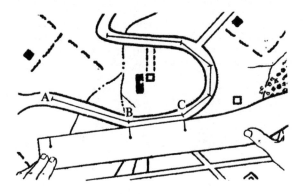

Fig 13-19. Measuring curved line distance.

# Section III.   Direction

Objectives:

1.   *In the field, with a standard 1:50,000 scale map and compass, orient a map within 30 degrees using natural terrain features and/or a compass.*
2.   *Given a standard 1:50,000 scale map, compass, pencil, and two known points, perform intersection to find an unknown point within 100 meters.*
3.   *Given a standard 1:50,000 scale map, compass, and pencil, perform resection to determine own location within 100 meters.*

## A. AZIMUTHS

1.   **Azimuth Definition.**  An azimuth is an "angle" measure within a circle clockwise from the base direction, north. When used with land navigation, the directional circle is divided into 360 possible asimuths or degrees (figure 13-20).

2.   **Azimuths and Land Navigation.**  When we speak of following an azimuth in land navigation, think of yourself in the center of a circle at the origin. A line drawn from you to the objective would be on a certain angle or azimuth, in this case 60 degrees, when measured within a circle from a base direction, north (figure 13-21). This system of finding and following an azimuth to an objective is universal within the U.S. military and ensures that the objective is found with accuracy each time.

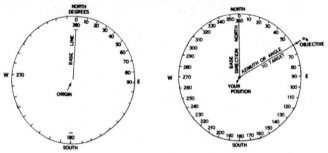

Fig 13-20.   Directional circle.   Fig 13-21.   Locating an azimuth.

3. Base Direction (North). There are two base directions or norths used when navigating over land with the aid of the map and compass. These base directions are known as GRID NORTH and MAGNETIC NORTH. The difference between these two points is known as the Grid-Magnetic or G-M angle and is shown in the margin of all military maps by what is called a declination diagram (figure 13-22). When navigating over land with the aid of the map and compass, TRUE NORTH, the actual direction of the North Pole, is seldom used so it will not be discussed.

a. Magnetic north. Magnetic north is measured with a lensatic compass. The north-seeking arrow on the compass points to an area in the Hudson Bay area of Canada where the magnetic attractions from the earth's core are the strongest in the northern hemisphere. This is known as magnetic north and is shown by a half arrow on the declination diagram (figure 13-22). Whenever you use an azimuth from a compass to plan or follow a route in the field, keep in mind that it is a magnetic azimuth.

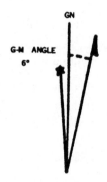

Fig 13-22.   Declination diagram.

b. Grid north. The vertical grid lines on the map run from south at the bottom of the map to north (called GRID NORTH) at the top of the map. Because the grid lines are placed on each map sheet in the same way, the base directions, grid and magnetic north, will seldom be on the same angle. The grid north angle is shown in the declination diagram as GN (figure 13-22). Whenever you plot an azimuth with a protractor on a map, keep in mind that it is a grid azimuth.

13-19

**4. G-M Angle Conversion.** Before you begin to navigate, it is very important that you determine whether the initial direction you are given to follow is expressed as a magnetic azimuth or a grid azimuth. The angle between the two may vary as much as $20^o$ in some parts of the United States. If an azimuth is determined with the map and protractor, it is called a grid azimuth and cannot be followed on the ground with a compass until it is converted to a magnetic azimuth. By the same token, an azimuth determined with the lensatic compass is a magnetic azimuth and cannot be correctly plotted on the map until it has been converted to a grid azimuth. When converting from one type of azimuth to another, a convenient "tool" provided by the mapmaker is the declination diagram (figure 13-22). Your first concern in converting an azimuth when using the declination diagram is to determine how much difference there is between grid north and magnetic north, the G-M angle (figure 13-22). If a newer map is in use, it will have instructions with the declination diagram as shown in figure 13-23. If an older map which does not have instructions for converting azimuths is used, follow this procedure:

a. Determine the amount of the G-M angle for your map. This is the number of degrees difference between grid and magnetic north.

b. Place your finger on the symbol for the base direction you are converting from (grid north or magnetic north).

c. Move your finger to the symbol for the base direction to which you wish to convert.

d. Apply the LEFT ADD, RIGHT SUBTRACT (LARS) rule. This means that if your finger moves to the Left, add the amount of the G-M angle to the given azimuth. If it moves to the Right, subtract the amount of the G-M angle from the given azimuth.

e. Using the declination diagram (figure 13-23), a grid azimuth of $36^o$ when converted to a magnetic azimuth would be $30^o$ (RIGHT SUBTRACT, $6^o$ from $36^o = 30^o$).

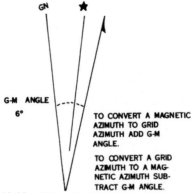

GN ★

G-M ANGLE
6°

TO CONVERT A MAGNETIC
AZIMUTH TO GRID
AZIMUTH ADD G-M
ANGLE.

TO CONVERT A GRID
AZIMUTH TO A MAG-
NETIC AZIMUTH SUB-
TRACT G-M ANGLE.

Fig 13-23.  Using the declination diagram.

5.  The Protractor

a.  Description.  A protractor is an instrument for measuring or constructing angles. It may be circular, semicircular, square, or rectangular. Regardless of its shape, the protractor will consist of an index point, a base line, and a scaled outer edge (figure 13-24). The scaled edge has two sets of numbers: 0 to 180, representing the right side of a circle, and 180 to 360 representing the left side of a circle. As a result, by rotating a semicircular or rectangular protractor it can be made to represent a complete circle. It is important to remember that if the outer edge of such a protractor is to the right, the azimuth is read or plotted using readings between 0° to 180°. If the outer edge is to the left, the values of the readings will be between 180° to 360°.

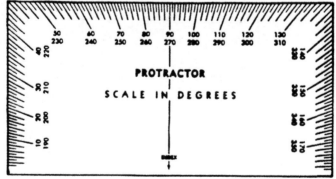

Fig 13-24.  Protractor.

13-21

b. Measuring a grid azimuth (map direction). To determine the direction from one point to another on the map, you first draw a straight line through the two points, making sure that the line is long enough (3 to 4 inches) to extend beyond the outer edge of the protractor. Then you position your protractor on the map so that the index point is on the starting point and the protractor base line ($0^O$ line) is exactly parallel to the nearest vertical grid line on the map. Then you read the grid azimuth at the point where the line you drew between the two points crosses the protractor scale. For example, in figure 13-25 the line between points A and B crosses the protractor scale at the $130^O$ mark; therefore, the grid azimuth from point A to point B is $130^O$.

c. Plotting an azimuth with the protractor. To plot a grid azimuth from a certain point on a map, place the protractor index at the point and rotate the protractor until the base line exactly parallels the nearest north-south grid line. Make a tick mark on the map at the point indicated by the desired azimuth on the protractor. Remove the protractor and use some form of straightedge to draw a line from the starting point to the tick mark. Figure 13-25 shows a grid azimuth of $225^O$ plotted from point C to point D.

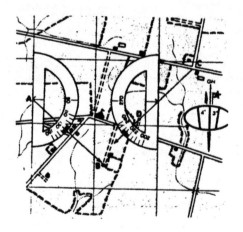

Fig 13-25.   Measuring and locating a
grid azimuth with protractor.

13-22

d. It is essential that the protractor straightedge be exactly parallel to a vertical grid line. Even a slight variation from parallel will result in a measurement error of several degrees. It is often difficult to achieve this parallel alignment by visual inspection. Therefore, the following expedient method is suggested for greater accuracy; extend the line between the two points (such as C and D in figure 13-25), until it intersects the nearest vertical grid line. Then place the index arrow exactly at the point of intersection and align the protractor straightedge exactly on the grid line.

6. Setting Magnetic Azimuths

a. Setting magnetic azimuths on the lensatic compass can be accomplished by two methods. The first method is commonly referred to as the "day" method but can be accomplished any time as long as there is sufficient light. With the day method, first rotate the compass until the desired azimuth is under the black index line, then turn the bezel ring until the luminous line is directly over the north arrow. Once this is done, follow a line formed by the black index line and the sighting wire in the compass cover, ensuring that the luminous line remains directly over the north arrow (use figure 13-26 to clarify the names of the compass components).

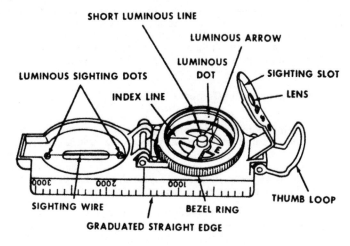

Fig 13-26.  Lensatic compass.

13-23

b. The second method of setting a magnetic azimuth on the lensatic compass is commonly referred to as the "night" method, as no light is required. Around the base of the bezel ring is a series of 120 notches. On the forward edge of the body of the compass is a bezel detent spring with its tip seated in one of the notches (figure 13-26). As the bezel ring is turned, the spring moves notch to notch producing a click. Each click of the bezel ring is equal to $3^0$ of change in direction. To set an azimuth of $51^0$ onto the lensatic compass at night:

(1) Rotate the bezel ring until the luminous line is over the black index line.

(2) Rotate the bezel ring counterclockwise 17 clicks (51 divided by 3 = 17, remember each click equals $3^0$).

(3) Turn the compass until the north arrow is directly under the luminous line. The azimuth is directly under the black index line, and you would go in the direction indicated by a line formed on the two luminous dots in the compass cover.

## B. MAP ORIENTATION

Using the skills you have learned, you can now orient a map using natural terrain features and/or a compass. Before a map can be used, it must be oriented. A map is oriented when it is in a horizontal position with its north and south corresponding to north and south on the ground. There are two simple ways to orient a map: with a compass and by using natural terrain features.

### 1. Map Orientation With a Compass

a. With the map in a horizontal position, place the compass parallel to a north-south grid line with the cover side of the compass pointing toward the top of the map. This will place the black index line on the dial of the compass parallel to grid north. Because the needle on the compass points to magnetic north, we have a declination diagram on the face of the compass formed by the index line and the compass needle.

b. Rotate map and compass until the directions of the declination diagram formed by the black index line and the compass needle match the directions shown on the declination diagram printed on the margin of the map. The map is then oriented.

c. If the magnetic north arrow on the map is to the left of grid north, the compass reading will equal the G-M angle (given in the declination diagram). If the magnetic north is to the right of grid north, the compass reading will equal $360^o$ minus the G-M angle. Remember to point the compass north arrow in the same direction as the magnetic north arrow (2 above), and the compass reading (equal to the G-M angle) will be quite apparent.

**NOTE:** If G-M angle is less than $3^o$, do not line up north arrow.

2. Map Orientation Using Natural Terrain and Manmade Features. When a compass is not available, map orientation involves a careful examination of the map and the ground. Sometimes referred to as "orientation by inspection," this method requires you to identify linear or prominent terrain features on the ground that also appear on your map. Holding your map in a horizontal position, rotate it until the features on the map are aligned with the same features on the ground (figure 13-27). The map is then oriented.

a. Linear features such as roads, railroads, or power lines are best to use with this method; however, care must be taken to prevent the reversal of directions when only one linear feature is used. This reversal may be prevented by aligning two or more of these features.

b. If no second linear feature is visible, but your position is known, a prominent object may be used. With the prominent object and your position connected with a straight line on the map, rotate the map until the line points toward the feature.

c. If prominent terrain features are used to orient the map, selecting at least three widely separated features will improve your accuracy.

d. If two prominent objects are visible and plotted on your map, and your position is not known, move to one of the known positions. Place a straightedge on the line between the plotted positions and turn the straightedge and the map until you can sight along the edge to the other known point. The map is then oriented.

Fig 13-27.   Orientation by inspection.

## C. INTERSECTION

A method of locating unknown points on a map is called intersection. This method requires the occupation of at least two known points and the determination of an azimuth from each of these points to the unknown point (figure 13-28). Intersection may be performed by using a map and compass, or by using a map alone.

1.   Map and Compass Method

a.  Orient the map using the compass.

b.  Locate and mark your position on the map.

c.  Measure the magnetic azimuth to the unknown position, then convert it to a grid azimuth.

d.  Draw a line on the map from your position on this grid azimuth.

13-26

e. Move to a second known position from which the unknown point is visible. Locate this position on the map and again orient your map using the compass.

f. Repeat c and d above.

g. As a check on accuracy, move to a third known position if possible and repeat a through d above.

h. Where the lines cross is the location of the unknown point.

**NOTE:** Using three lines, a triangle is sometimes formed instead of an intersection. This is called the "triangle of error." If the triangle is large, recheck your work to find the error. Do not assume that the position is at the center of the triangle.

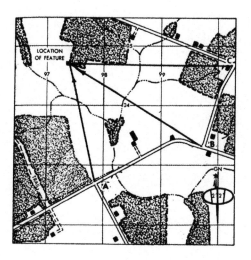

Fig 13-28.    Intersection using the map and compass.

2. **Straightedge Method** (When no compass is available)

    a. Orient the map on a flat surface by the inspection method.

    b. Locate and mark your position on the map.

    c. Lay a straightedge on the map with one end at your position. Using this end as a pivot point, rotate the straightedge until the unknown point is sighted along the edge.

    d. Draw a line along the straightedge.

    e. Repeat the above procedures at a second position, and as a check for accuracy at a third known position.

    f. The intersection of the lines is the location of the unknown point.

## D. RESECTION

Should you become disoriented in the field, you can use azimuths to determine your location. This method is called resection and it involves finding an unknown location by sighting on two or three known terrain features (figure 13-29). As with intersection, resection can be done with or without a compass.

1. **Map and Compass Method**

    a. Orient the map using the compass.

    b. Locate two positions or terrain features on the ground and mark them on the map.

    c. Measure the magnetic azimuth to a known position, then convert it to a grid azimuth.

    d. Change the grid azimuth to a back azimuth and draw a line on the map from the known position back toward your unknown position.

**NOTE:** A back azimuth is the reverse direction of an azimuth. It is comparable to executing an "about face." To obtain a back azimuth, add 180° if the original azimuth is 180° or less. Subtract 180° if the original azimuth is 180° or more. The back azimuth of 180° may be stated as either 0° or 360°.

e. Repeat c and d above from a second known position.

f. For a check on accuracy, repeat c and d above from a third known position, if possible.

g. The intersection of the lines is your location. Using three lines, a triangle of error may form. If the triangle is large, recheck your work.

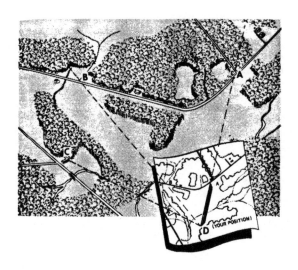

Fig 13-29.   Resection.

13-29

2. **Straightedge Method** (When no compass is available)

    a. Orient the map on a flat surface by the inspection method.

    b. Locate two or three known positions on the ground and mark them on the map.

    c. Lay a straightedge on the map with the center of the straightedge at a known position. Using the known position as a pivot point, rotate the straightedge until it points exactly at the known position on the ground.

    d. Draw a line along the straightedge away from the known position on the ground and toward your location.

    e. Repeat c and d above using a second known position. Check your accuracy by repeating these steps using a third known position, if possible.

    f. The intersection of the lines is your location.

---

For more information in this area, refer to:

1. FM 21-26      Map Reading

2. TEC Lsn 930-071-0016-F      Terrain Features

3. TEC Lsn 930-071-0164-F      Determine Distance While Moving

4. TEC Lsn 930-071-0014-F      Measuring Distances and Azimuths

# INDEX

## Military Security

## First Aid and Field Sanitation

## Uniform Clothing and Equipment

**Physical Fitness**

**Nuclear, Biological, and Chemical Warfare**

**Marksmanship**

## Individual Tactical Measures

## Security of Military Information

## Substance Abuse

## Land Navigation

# ★ WE STRIVE ★

**...To bring you**
**THE BEST**
**HOW-TO BOOKS**
★ **IN THE WORLD** ★

**If you enjoyed this one,**
**please TAKE A MOMENT to**
**LEAVE A REVIEW at:**

★ **AMZN.COM/1795745665** ★

*Thank you!*

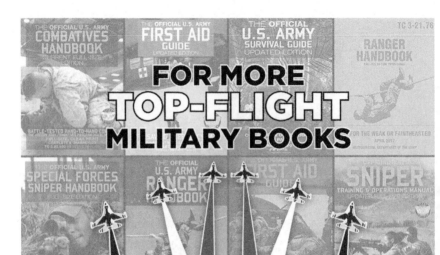

Printed in Great Britain
by Amazon